Addison-Wesley
Nitty Gritty

PROGRAMMING SERIES

Delphi 6

Frank Eller

ADDISON-WESLEY
An imprint of Pearson Education

London • Boston • Indianapolis • New York • Mexico City • Toronto • Sydney • Tokyo • Singapore
Hong Kong • Cape Town • New Delhi • Madrid • Paris • Amsterdam • Munich • Milan • Stockhom

PEARSON EDUCATION LIMITED

Head Office

Edinburgh Gate, Harlow, CM20 2JE
Tel: +44 (0)1279 623623 Fax: +44 (0)1279 431059

London Office

128 Long Acre, London, WC2E 9AN
Tel: +44 (0)20 7447 2000 Fax: +44 (0)20 7447 2170

Websites:

www.it-minds.com
www.aw.com/cseng

First published in Great Britain in 2002
© Pearson Education Limited 2002

First published in 2001 as Delphi 6 Nitty Gritty by Addison-Wesley Verlag, Germany.

The right of Frank Eller to be identified as the author of this work has been
asserted by him in accordance with the Copyright, Designs and Patents Act 1988.

British Library Cataloguing in Publication Data
A CIP catalogue record for this book can be obtained from the British Library.

Library of Congress Cataloging-in-Publication Data
Eller, Frank.
   [Delphi 6 nitty gritty. English]
   Delphi 6 / Frank Eller.
      p. cm. -- (Addison-Wesley nitty gritty programming series)
   Translation of: Delphi 6 nitty gritty.
   Includes index.
   ISBN 0-201-75882-2 (pbk. : alk. paper)
   1. Delphi (Computer file) 2. Computer software--Devlopment. I. Title. II. Series.

QA76.76.D47 E44713 2003
005.265--dc21

                                  2002074571

ISBN 0-201-75882-2

10 9 8 7 6 5 4 3 2 1

Translated by Transcript Alba Ltd, Oban, Scotland.
Typeset by Pantek Arts Ltd, Maidstone, Kent.
Printed and bound in Great Britain by Biddles Ltd of Guildford and King's Lynn.

The publishers' policy is to use paper manufactured from sustainable forests.

Contents

Preface

The idea behind the Nitty Gritty series

When you are programming, you also usually read a great deal. The fact is that the various programming languages have reached performance levels that make it almost impossible to get an overview of all the functions offered by a programming environment. This is why there are so many and varied reference books that attempt to provide a lot of information in an understandable way. Unfortunately, the really good reference books from the reputable publishing houses are usually weighty tomes that will just clutter up your desk. The slimmer books are easier to handle but often do not contain the information you are actually looking for. It is just when you are learning something new that you could really do with a book that has sections that contain reference material about the programming language, and sections that show you how to create functioning programs quickly, and how to make best use of many of the options available in a programming environment.

The Nitty Gritty series of books is based on this idea. These books are interesting not only for people who are learning a programming language, because they contain a lot of basic facts, but also for people who already know how to use other programming languages and want to extend their knowledge.

This is the next chapter of the Delphi story, which began with Borland and Delphi 5 and continued with Delphi 6. Although the software has become more expensive, the Personal Edition (previously the Delphi Standard Edition) still has almost all the same features as Version 5. I am rather disappointed by this. It would have been possible to increase the price slightly and introduce a few of the new features in return. Sadly, this didn't happen.

There isn't much point in writing a book about the Personal Edition (it really can't do a great deal), and there is nowhere near enough space for the features of the Enterprise Edition (I could write 1000 pages in this format and would still only scratch the surface), so I have restricted myself mainly to the options offered by the Professional Edition. In my last book, I mentioned that this version is the very least you should purchase, and I am still convinced of this. It really is a wise investment because Delphi 6 has become even better than I dreamed it could. The critics among you will say that it took long enough to appear. But you will have a product that is well worth the money and lives up to its reputation. It is a professional development tool that gives you all the freedom and possibilities of programming under Windows and (if you also have Kylix) Linux. I wish you every success and hope that this book will be of some use.

Style conventions

I have tried to design this book so that you can easily see what it contains. The following styles and ways of emphasizing text are used in this book:

→ Menu items and directories are shown in SMALL CAPITAL LETTERS.

→ Source code and descriptors associated with the source code are shown in the body of the text in `Courier` font. Reserved words are shown in **bold** text.

→ Keys and shortcuts are shown as if they were keys on your keyboard, e.g. [Ctrl] + [C] means that you must press the [Ctrl] and [C] keys one after the other, then release them at the same time.

Tip This icon is used to indicate tips and typical programming errors.

This is the second Nitty Gritty paperback about Delphi. The first Nitty Gritty book was also the very first book I wrote, and when I handed over the manuscript I still had a few doubts about my abilities as an author. Luckily for me (and all the readers), my worries were groundless. Numerous letters and other communications have reassured myself and my editor, Christina Gibbs, that we had found a successful concept and selected the right authors for all the books, and that the books themselves were also very useful. You could say it was a real success. So, I would like to thank everyone who has purchased and read this book, despite the delay in its appearance.

I must thank the editing department at Addison-Wesley Germany, especially the editors Christina Gibbs and Christiane Auf. Christina started the book and then the support tasks passed on to Christiane. At this point, I would like to give them both my warmest thanks for all their support and hope that we will be able to work together again on the next Nitty Gritty edition.

Another person who deserves my thanks is my former tutor Klaus Kappler, who is now a good friend of mine. He supported my decision to leave my former job and to break into completely new areas in my professional life. I am sure that this was a very good decision. So thank you very much. If you are ever in Munich, I'll buy you a coffee.

My last thank you goes to Anders Ohlsson from Borland who was kind enough to allow me to use his code in this book. You will see his code for a cgi counter in the internet chapter of this book.

The last thing for me to say is that I hope that you enjoy the book.

Frank Eller
June, 2002

Part I

Start up!

Before you get started ...

As with everything, before you can start programming you must first create a base to work from. For Delphi, this means that you must familiarize yourself with the programming environment and get to know its features and options so that you can achieve a result as quickly and effectively as possible.

This chapter is aimed at people who are learning how to program for the first time, and for those who have already used other programming languages. If you have already used a previous version of Delphi, you can ignore most of this introduction. However, you may find section 1.7 interesting because it describes the new features in Delphi 6. Once again, Borland have made great efforts here to improve Delphi's design and make its structure clearer.

1.1 What is Delphi?

Delphi is a rapid application development (RAD) tool. All the components required to develop a program are grouped together into an easy-to-use and clearly structured development environment. A large part of programming consists of putting together the application's interface with the help of components. These are pre-prepared modules with basic functionality. The actual programming just involves adding the main functions of the program.

Delphi is one of the most comprehensive tools for programming under Windows. The programming language on which Delphi is based (Object Pascal) is clearly structured and is ideal for both advanced programmers and beginners. You can use Delphi to create any kind of application. From independent applications to dynamic linked libraries (DLLs), system control modules, screen savers, console applications up to finished web server applications – anything is possible.

Object Pascal itself is a strictly defined programming language whose rules must be followed exactly. Despite this, it is easy to learn because there aren't too many rules. However, one of the greatest advantages of this programming system is that the source code for the components is supplied with it. This means that you can see how the professionals at Borland programmed particular features. Absolutely all the components are programmed in Object Pascal: there are no exceptions to the rule.

Delphi also supports ActiveX control elements, which are used mainly by Visual Basic programmers. Although Delphi can also use ActiveX or OCX modules, you will often find that the solutions created in Object Pascal, or a component, are just as good or even better. In addition, Delphi is fast, as are the programs created in Delphi.

1.2 Delphi is object-oriented

Delphi is a completely object-oriented programming system. All the modules used in Delphi are further developments of objects known as "classes". These classes have their own functionality and their own properties, and can react to events.

The Object Pascal programming language is a further development of Turbo Pascal or Borland Pascal. Under DOS, Turbo Pascal was used for structured programming, which was good enough for DOS. However, when Windows came on the scene, this type of programming was no longer acceptable. Under DOS, the program guided the user in a particular direction; only one task could be performed at a time, and that had to be finished before the next action started. Aditionally, only one program could be executed at a time.

With Windows, all that changed. Windows gave the user the option of canceling actions that had started, such as printing, entering commands in any sequence they liked, or starting several programs at the same time. This meant that the concept of structured programming was no longer relevant.

As a result, Borland developed both objects and an object-oriented programming system. (The programming system was unsuccessful and Borland dropped it after Version 1.5.) An object is a construct in which data, and the functions and procedures necessary to process those data, are grouped. New objects could "descend" (be derived) from existing objects: either their entire functionality and data could be passed on to the new objects, or new data, functions or procedures could be added to them. It was therefore possible to develop an independent object with a particular range of basic functions, and then modify it to suit different circumstances.

Originally, Borland planned to bolt a visual system on to this object-oriented model, but that didn't work because the original object model was not suitable for supporting visual components. So Borland did something very clever; they threw it all out and started again using the experience they had already built up. Having completely redefined the object model and made it suitable for a visual programming environment, in the end Borland actually used Delphi to program the programming environment itself. The essential classes were developed from the objects (with the objects remaining as elements of the Object Pascal programming language, as before). The first version of Delphi was born. It was based on an excellent scalable and extendable concept.

Although classes and objects share the same basic concept, they are very different. The functions and procedures in a class are called methods. A class can also have properties (which correspond roughly to the data in an object) and they can react to events. Within classes there are different visibility levels that can be used to prevent the user from accessing all the variables and methods declared in a class, and restrict them to the ones that are relevant. All the Delphi components that you use to build your interface are classes. The "Adam and Eve" class on which all other components are based is TObject.

There have been no further changes to the basic programming language, so if you have ever programmed something in Pascal, you will very quickly start to feel confident in Delphi.

1.3 Delphi is event-oriented

Everything that happens under Windows is an event. If the user presses a key, that is an event. If the user moves the mouse over a control element, that is an event. Closing a program, clicking on a button, opening or closing a database, and so on, are all events that you can trap and react to in Delphi. Delphi is completely event-oriented, and you can use the individual components to react to particular events affecting those components and develop your own event-handling routines.

Events do not necessarily have to come from Windows; you can also trigger events in your own application or send messages to Windows. This approach to programming makes many things simpler.

You will be familar with the prompts you see at the end of a program, asking you to confirm that you want to do something. For example, if changes have been made to a document, but not been saved yet, the prompt asks you whether you want to save them before you close the program. It is very easy to create a prompt like this in Delphi. When a command is sent to close the program, an event occurs. In this event, you place the query that prompts the user to specify whether the current document is to be saved or whether the program should be closed without saving the changes. You can then use the user's reaction to define what your application is to do next.

1.4 Delphi's development environment

The Delphi integrated development environment (IDE) consists of several windows that are arranged on your desktop. You can dock (fix) many of these windows next to each other, or even overlay them (if you do so, the system displays tabs with which you can switch between each open window). You can see the entire IDE in Figure 1.1.

The IDE consists of the main window, the object list (known as the Object Treeview), the Object Inspector, the editor window, and of course a visual display of your current form. Naturally, development under Windows mainly affects the forms, which are later used to form the windows for your application. Let's take a look at the individual elements of the Delphi development environment.

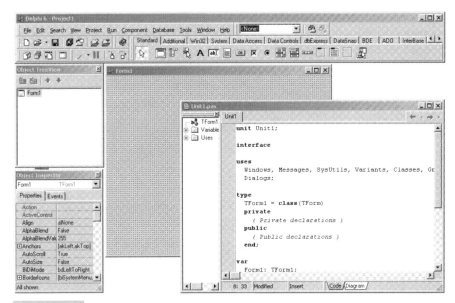

Figure 1.1 *The complete initial Delphi IDE*

1.4.1 Main window

In the main window (Figure 1.2), you will find the basic user interface features that you will be used to from other programs, such as the menu bar and various toolbars. You can customize all toolbars, and move or remove them. You can also customize the individual buttons to suit you enabling you to create your own IDE.

The main window also contains the components list. In this, you will find all the components that are registered in Delphi. These include the standard components, which are always supplied, and the components added later by third-party suppliers. On the internet, you can find a huge number of freely available components, sometimes with their source code, which you can use in your programs.

The number of components supplied by Borland varies according to the version you are using. Even with Delphi 5 there was no point in buying the Standard Version (which corresponds to the Delphi 6 Personal Edition) as you couldn't use it to develop a database application. The Personal Edition in Delphi 6 does not contain the database

Figure 1.2 *The Delphi IDE main window*

or internet functionality you need. The minimum you need for proper programming is the Delphi Professional Edition, which is more than worth the money you spend on it.

1.4.2 Object Inspector

The Object Inspector (Figure 1.3) gives you an overview of a particular component's properties and events. When you are at the design stage (referred to in Delphi as "designtime"), you can use it to change the most frequently used properties and immediately see what the effects are. The Object Inspector has been fine-tuned and is now slightly different from previous versions. You can find out more about this in section 1.7, which describes the new features in Delphi 6.

The Object Inspector provides you with two windows, known as pages: one for the properties of a component, and one for the events that can occur when that component is used. You can change the settings in the Object Inspector's local context menu to display the properties according to their category, or sorted alphabetically, or to hide particular properties. With the mouse pointer on Properties or Events, click the right-hand mouse button and select VIEW or ARRANGE from the menu, as required.

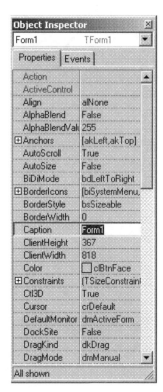

Figure 1.3 *Delphi's Object Inspector*

If you select the view according to categories, some properties will be displayed several times since they are contained in several different categories. If you change the value for one of these properties, the value will be changed in every place at which it occurs.

Some properties contain other subordinate properties, subproperties, which you can recognize by the plus (+) sign to the left of their name. To open a list of subproperties, click on this + sign. To close the list, double-click on the name.

The second Object Inspector view, the Events page, contains the events to which the current component can react. In the current selection list, you can double-click next to the event name to move to the place in the source code where the corresponding event-handling routine is defined. If there is no event-handling routine for this event, Delphi automatically generates the appropriate default action.

1.4.3 Object Treeview

Object Treeview shows the current component and its subcomponents in a hierarchical view. This view is therefore an ideal way to see the hierarchy of components in your application. This part of the IDE is a new feature of Delphi 6, so it is described in more detail in section 1.7.

1.4.4 Code Editor

You use the Code Editor (also extended in Delphi 6) to input the actual program code that defines the functionality of your application. Delphi helps you in two ways here: it provides programming help, and it automatically inserts many parts of the program you are creating, such as the declarations for the components and the event-handling routines, into the program text so that you only have to write the code for the actual functionality. Even there, Delphi's object-oriented component approach helps a great deal. You will see that, with Delphi, it really is very easy to create professional programs that work well in a short period of time.

1.4.5 Code Explorer

To the left of the Code Editor, you will see the Delphi Code Explorer. This is also a hierarchical view, but instead of showing the components it shows the declared methods, variables, and constants within the unit. The Code Explorer is helpful if you want to jump quickly within the program source code to a declaration for a variable or to a procedure or function. However, it displays only the data that relate to the unit currently in the editor.

1.5.1 Environment Options

To display the Environment Options dialog, select the TOOLS | ENVIRONMENT OPTIONS menu option. This is divided into different tab pages.

Preferences

Figure 1.4 shows the dialog's Preferences page. On this tab page, you can define some basic settings that apply globally to all Delphi sessions. The settings are almost the same as in Delphi 5, but the sequence has changed a little. The Designer options now have their own tab page.

On the Preferences tab page, you can also define whether the system displays a progress bar when compiling, or whether it should carry out compiling entirely in the background. In addition, you can specify the files that are to be saved when Delphi closes.

Designer

On the Designer tab page, you can find the settings that relate to the behavior of the development environment and its appearance. You can, among other things, change the grid size and specify the format that is to be used to save form data (binary or ASCII).

Since Delphi 5, it has been possible to save new forms as ASCII (plain text) or as binary data. Up to Delphi 4, it was only possible to save forms in binary format.

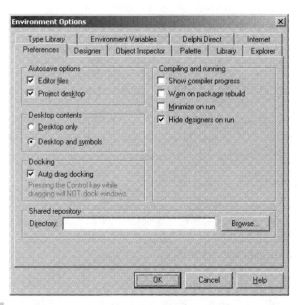

Figure 1.4 *The Environment Options Preferences tab page*

However, if you save forms as ASCII, you will not be able to display them in Delphi 4 or earlier versions.

You can display a grid on forms, and specify the spacing of that grid. The standard grid size is 8 points. Personally, I prefer to change this setting to 4 or 5 points so that I can position components more accurately on the form.

On this tab page, you can specify whether forms and data modules should be generated automatically when the program starts. All forms and data modules are classes from which an instance must be generated before you can use them. If you leave it to Delphi to generate these instances, it will generate all required objects in memory when the program runs, which increases use of system resources. You can switch off this automatic instance generation, but you will then have to remember to generate your own instances of the objects you need.

Object Inspector

On this tab page, you can adjust the appearance of the Object Inspector. You can, for example, change the font colors for the different categories that are displayed. You can also specify which categories are to be displayed, and make small changes to the appearance of the Object Inspector itself.

Palette settings

You can display the Component palette via the Palette tab page in the Environment Options dialog. You can rearrange all the components installed in the Component palette and move, delete and rename its individual sections. For example, if there is no longer enough space on the screen to display all the pages of the Component palette, you can assign shorter names to those pages so that they can all be displayed again. I usually have a large number of additional components installed and have, for that reason, deleted some Component palette pages and renamed the rest.

Library directories

Before Delphi can work with the different libraries, packages and units, it must know where they are located. In the Library tab page in the Environment Options dialog, you will find all the necessary directories. You can change these directories to suit your requirements, or you can add new directories. You should not change the standard directories created by Delphi because Delphi would then be unable to find its own files.

Explorer settings

On the dialog's Explorer tab page, you can modify the Code Explorer, which is docked on to the Code editor window. You can define which elements are to be displayed, what they are to look like, and the sequence in which they are to be displayed. Usually, you can leave the default settings as they are.

Delphi Direct

On the Delphi Direct tab page, you can make the settings for online updates, which Delphi fetches from the internet or fetches automatically if you start it during a running internet session (or if Delphi is running and you connect to the internet). You can specify the time interval at which the page checks for information and whether the Delphi Direct window should be displayed as soon as Delphi is started. Delphi also displays the date on which it last checked for information. The default time interval of seven days is a good value and probably does not need to be changed.

Internet

With Delphi 6, it is easier than ever to develop internet applications. These do not necessarily have to be client applications such as a news reader: you can also develop common gateway interface (cgi) scripts, active server pages (ASP) objects or web services. In addition, Delphi 6 can handle the extensible markup language (XML) data format. On the Internet page, you can specify the file extensions for different types of file used on the internet, and also switch debugging on or off.

1.5.2 Editor Properties

You can use the Editor Properties dialog to change settings that affect the Delphi Code Editor window, including how source code is displayed and how the input window works.

General

On the General tab page, you will find some basic settings for the Code Editor. The settings shown in Figure 1.5 are the ones I normally use.

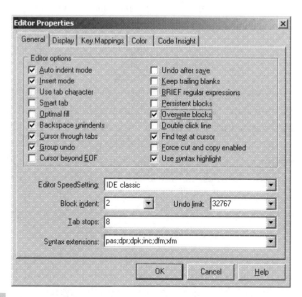

Figure 1.5 *The settings for the Code Editor*

Display

The Display page contains two sets of settings: the font settings for the editor window (in which, for obvious reasons, only fixed-space fonts are permitted) and the display settings for the input window. For example, you can display a line on the right-hand margin so that you can see how many characters you have entered.

Keyboard assignment

On the Key Mappings page, you can specify how the Delphi IDE works with keyboard shortcuts. On my system, I use the standard IDE as provided by Borland Pascal, since I am used to it, but if you are more familiar with Microsoft Visual Basic or Visual C++, then Delphi can also use the key mapping defined in Visual Studio.

Color

On the Color page, you can change all the colors used in the Code editor window to suit your requirements. You can also change the way code syntax is highlighted. A small pre-view window shows you the effect your settings will have.

Code Insight programming help

You can find details of the programming help available in section 1.6. In the Editor Properties dialog page, you can modify Delphi's integrated programming help, called Code Insight, to suit your own requirements.

1.5.3 Project Options

As their name suggests, Project Options are project-specific, i.e. you can specify options for each project. You can also specify standard options that are used as defaults for each new project.

Forms

On the Forms page, you can specify which forms Delphi is to generate automatically when your application starts (known as "Auto-create forms") and which ones are to be available but not generated until needed (to save resources). You will have to generate the available forms later, but that is straightforward. On this page, you must also specify the main form for the application, but you should leave Delphi to create it. Delphi usually assumes that the first draft form is the main form, but you can change this. Delphi creates the main form, and it is the only form that Delphi displays automatically.

Tip In the final product, you should ensure that as many forms as possible are generated dynamically (at runtime). A program should always use resources as efficiently as possible; if a lot of resources are used, a very heavy load is placed on the operating system.

Application

On the Application page, you can specify some basic settings, such as the name of the application, the name of the help file, or the icon that is to be used for the application.

Compiler

On the Compiler page, you can find the compiler options for the project. You can specify how the compiler is to react to syntax errors, how it is to handle the different syntactical elements, and whether the individual units (or the entire project) are to contain information for bugfixing.

When you are developing an application, you should always include the debug information in project compilation. If you don't do this, it will be almost impossible to fix bugs. As soon as the project is finished, you can then regenerate it completely and remove the debug information. You will notice how much this slims down the executable file when you work on larger projects.

Another function that you should not switch off is code optimization in the Optimization checkbox. When it is selected, the compiler removes invalid or unnecessary references during compiling and creates a code that can be executed as quickly as possible. Sometimes, you might prefer to switch off optimization for bugfixing, but you should switch it on again when you do the final compile.

You should also always leave Extended syntax switched on. You can use this to call functions such as procedures and then simply ignore those functions' return values.

You should also always leave Open parameters and Huge strings switched on. Huge strings are standard for 32-bit programs and can become so long that their length is restricted only by the available memory. Short strings, which were still the standard in 16-bit Delphi, have a completely different structure and have a maximum length of 255 characters. The only time it can be of benefit to switch off this option is when you want to convert a 16-bit program to a 32-bit program. In such a situation, the data type string can be handled as a short string (with a length of 255 characters).

If you specifically want to use short strings in your application, you should use the data type ShortString. This has been provided in Object Pascal's language definition to ensure backwards compatibility. In some cases, such as data aggregates, there may be big advantages in using this data type.

Figure 1.6 shows the Compiler page from the Project Options dialog.

Linker

After compiling, the system combines the individual parts of the application into a whole, i.e. they are linked. On this Project Options page, you can specify how the Linker is to function. The default settings are usually good enough for most projects. The only options we need to take a closer look at are the EXE and DLL options.

Using Delphi, you can create a 32-bit console application, which is just about a DOS program. This is useful if you don't actually need a form but, for example, just want to register a program. In this case, select the appropriate option. Delphi will then

Figure 1.6   *The Project Options Compiler page*

generate not a main form but an application for a text VDU instead. However, this is still a 32-bit application.

Version Info

You can store version information in a project. This information includes, among other things, the version number, the date the application was last compiled, and the name of the programmer. Delphi can also insert the build number of the project. You can also store your own information in the project by using the context menu to add new keys to the table in the lower part of the dialog or to remove some keys.

The build number does not record the number of partial compiles that have been carried out (the number of times the program has been started in the Delphi IDE), but shows the number of complete compiles. These are incremented by one each time you recreate the project.

Figure 1.7 shows the Version Info page.

Packages

Delphi can create an application that consists of only one executable file. However, this can cause problems in the case of bigger projects, since the resulting file is then very large. To prevent these problems, you can store parts of the application separately. To do this, the functionality of the components used in Delphi should be saved in packages. There are designtime packages and runtime packages, which are all actually DLL files but use a different file extension. On the Packages page, you can specify the packages that are to be installed in the IDE, and then instruct Delphi to use these runtime packages during compiling (instead of compiling all code in one single file). Of course,

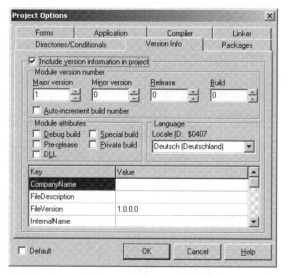

Figure 1.7 *The Project Options Version Info page*

you must then also supply these packages along with your program when you make it available to customers. Do not copy the files into the Windows System folder but into the folder in which your application is located. This is the first place that the system will look for those files, therefore they will be found faster.

1.6 Programming help

Delphi provides a great deal of programming help, which is helpful while you are working and can save you a lot of time. The page containing the settings for this help is called Code Insight (on the Editor Properties dialog) and includes the Automatic features options. Most of the programming help is very well explained, but some of it is not so clear. You can specify the settings for programming help on the Code Insight page (Figure 1.8).

1.6.1 Code completion

As mentioned above, all classes in Delphi have properties and methods that the programmer can use. However, there is so much information that it is impossible to remember all of these properties, methods or variables.

When you enter the name of a component or class, Delphi displays a list of the methods or properties that you can use with it. You see a list that contains all properties and methods. You can now type in the name of the required method/property, or select a method/property from the list. If you only type in the first couple of letters, Delphi

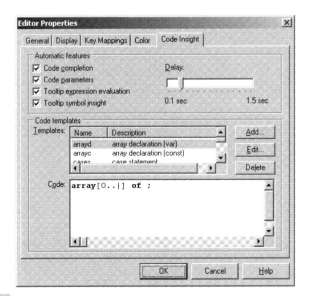

Figure 1.8 *The Editor Properties dialog Code Insight page*

displays the required property in the list, and you simply need to press ⏎ to select the relevant list item. In this way, you can generate large quantities of code very quickly.

Tip You can also use this function if you have switched it off by using the keyboard shortcut [Ctrl] + ⬚.

1.6.2 Code parameters

Delphi contains a large number of functions and procedures, not all of which are declared in components or classes; some are in other collections. These functions and procedures all require different code parameters, but you do not need to remember them all.

When you program a function call or procedure call in Delphi, a small help window called a Tooltip opens, as in other standard applications. In this window, you can see the required parameters for the function/procedure concerned with the parameter you need to enter displayed in bold text. Consequently, you always know which parameters are required, which saves you a lot of time.

Tip You can also use this help function if you have switched it off by using the keyboard shortcut [Ctrl] + [⇧] + ⬚.

1.6.3 Evaluation via tooltips

When you are debugging a program, and busy with bugfixing, Delphi can show you the value that a particular variable takes. When the program stops scrolling, move the mouse over the variable; Delphi displays a tooltip window containing the value. Naturally, this works only if the variable has not been optimized (deleted).

1.6.4 Code templates

If you have a range of source code segments that get repeated over and over again, you can create code templates for them and a shortcut for each of these templates. Press `Ctrl` + `J` to call the templates. If there is only one code template present for the shortcut that you have entered, Delphi inserts this code template directly into the source code. If several templates have been defined, Delphi displays a list window in which you can select the code template you require.

1.6.5 Class completion

Another useful feature that saves lots of time is class completion. Usually, you will declare the procedures and functions that belong to a form in that form's class definition, so that any function/procedure that you want to create becomes one of the form's methods. A form is naturally also a class (diverted from the `TForm` class). When you have declared your procedures, all you need to do is position the cursor over part of the class declaration to use class completion. If you press `Ctrl` + `⇧` + `C`, Delphi automatically inserts all the default actions for the declared methods; you only have to add the actual functionality. This programming help is very useful when you are working with methods that use a lot of parameters, or when you are programming your own components. It also works in the opposite direction.

When programming your own components, you need to declare only the properties. As soon as you call class completion, Delphi automatically inserts the methods for reading and writing, or more specifically, the variables required for that purpose.

1.6.6 Hyperlinks in source code

Often, you will need to jump to a function or procedure that you have declared somewhere in a unit. To do this, you don't have to know exactly where it has been declared, because Delphi keeps an overview. Simply keep pressing the `Ctrl` key and move the mouse over the name of the procedure/function whose declaration you are looking for. The name becomes a hyperlink, and when you click it Delphi opens the unit in which the function is declared, then jumps to the correct place.

1.6.7 To-Do List

The To-Do List was introduced in Delphi 5, and is another very useful programming help. As the application you want to create becomes more and more extensive, you are

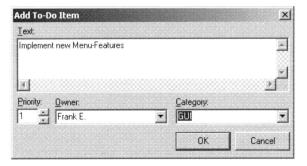

Figure 1.9 *A To-Do item*

likely to forget something occasionally or notice small errors. Usually, you would have to write a reminder note to yourself to fix them later, since it's not possible to deal with several things at once.

If you have already written a program in Delphi, Pascal or one of the other programming languages, you probably already have a few of these notes. Usually, they are too small and they have a tendency to disappear without warning. Delphi's To-Do List provides a solution to this problem; you can use it to save jobs that need to be done in a project-specific list. The entries in this list will be saved either in a file with the file extension *.todo* or directly in the source code. You can call them at any time. The associated menu item is VIEW | TO-DO LIST.

You can also add an entry directly when you are working by pressing Ctrl + ⇧ + T. The list entry will then be inserted directly into the source code.

Figure 1.9 shows a To-Do item in the list.

1.7 New in Delphi 6

Once again, Borland have greatly improved and extended the latest version of Delphi. They have added so many components, and extended so many options, that it impossible to cover them all in the space available in this book. However, I will attempt to shed a little light on the most important and interesting changes.

1.7.1 Object Inspector

The Object Inspector has been completely reworked. The various display modes we are familiar with from Delphi 5 are still there as they have proved themselves in practice. However, there have been some interesting additions:

→ Properties that apply to a particular object are displayed in a different color from the rest of the properties. You can set these colors in the ENVIRONMENT OPTIONS | OBJECT INSPECTOR dialog.

→ You can now process the properties of linked components directly.

→ You can hide the selection list at the top of the Object Inspector.

→ Each component's type is displayed in the selection list.

→ The Object Inspector can now also display properties that are read-only.

Figure 1.10 shows the Object Inspector, using the view mentioned above, and containing the read-only properties, which were previously not visible.

1.7.2 Code Editor

The Delphi Code Editor now has some additional views, called loadable views. All views, apart from the standard view, are provided by packages that you can access via the small tabs on the bottom edge of the Code Editor window. This means that you can, for example, select Component view when working on a form, and then see all the used components in it. You use similar controls to those in MS Windows Explorer to select the type of view you want (large or small icons, list or details).

1.7.3 Object Treeview

Object Treeview is usually located above Object Inspector on the screen. Like most Delphi windows, you can also dock this window, e.g. on to the Object Inspector.

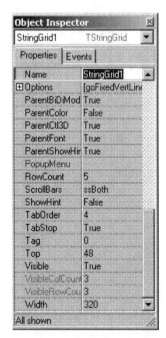

Figure 1.10 *Two read-only properties in the Object Inspector*

Object Treeview always shows the currently selected component or its hierarchically superior component (such as a parent) and is synchronized with the Object Inspector. Both change the view if you select a new component.

Object Treeview has been given the complete functionality of a data module; as a result, the view of the data module has been simplified again. You can now access all components present via Object Treeview. You can also dock Object Treeview on to the Code editor window, providing you with almost the same view as you are used to from Delphi 5 when working with a data module.

1.7.4 Subcomponents

In Delphi 6, each component can also have a subcomponent, making it the owner of an additional component. Previously, it was possible for a component to reference another component, as was the case, for instance, with `TActionList` and `TImageList`. `TActionList` referenced a `TImageList`, which then contained the images for the corresponding actions. However, this `TImageList` was still just one of the elements in the form, the form was the owner of the component and the `TActionList` simply contained a link to it. Referencing of this kind was called external referencing.

In Delphi 6, it is now possible to carry out internal referencing in which the referenced component becomes an element of the referencing component. For the example above, this would mean that the owner of the `TImageList` was now not the form but the `TActionList` itself. An example of this kind of referencing is the new `TLabeledEdit` component, which combines a `TLabel`-type component and a `TEdit`-type component to form one single component.

1.7.5 New components

Delphi 6 has a few new components. For brevity, the overview below does not go into detail.

TValueListEditor

`TValueListEditor` is a grid component for displaying key/value pairs, similar to in Object Inspector.

TActionManager

This new component makes it a lot easier to design your own applications. When you use it along with the `TMainMenuActionBar` and `TToolActionBar` components, you not only have better control over your application's user interface, but you can also give the user a way to modify their user interface to suit their wishes – and there's no additional programming involved.

TColorBox

TColorBox is a combo box in which you can select a color.

TXMLDocument

In Delphi 6, you can use this component to create, load or save documents based on the XML standard.

TIPAddress

TIPAddress is for processing Internet Protocol (IP) addresses.

TLabeledEdit

TLabeledEdit is a standard input field with a label attached to it. It was planned to be a demonstration of how to use subcomponents. The label is an element of the input field and also appears as such in the Object Inspector.

Indy

Indy components (the name is a short form of "Internet Direct") are the further development of the WinShoes components of earlier versions, and are now fully integrated in Delphi 6. There is a large number of these components, with which you can create complete client applications for the internet without writing much code (in fact, you just have to write a little code and define some meaningful links and relationships).

CLX

Kylix has already been released, and there has also been talk that it should now be possible to develop multiplatform applications with Delphi. Indeed, Delphi now contains both standard visual component library (VCL) and CLX (pronounced "clicks") for developing non-system-specific applications. You can therefore develop simultaneously for Windows and Linux if you have the Professional Version or better. Here, Borland have achieved something that others have already attempted.

> **Tip** If you want to develop for both the Windows and the Linux operating systems, you must ensure that you do not program any operating-system-specific calls. For example, if you make calls to the Windows application programming interface (API) they will not work under Linux and will cause an error.

1.8 Choosing a version

At this point, I will briefly discuss again the choice of version, an important issue when working with Delphi. I cannot recommend the Personal Edition (which corresponds to the Standard Version in previous releases) as it is suitable only for people who want to play around with programming. You will need the Professional Edition if you want to carry out proper application development.

The Personal Edition does not provide internet or database functionality, XML support, or many other important features. It is much cheaper for a reason; everything you actually need is missing, unless you want to restrict your development to what you can achieve with a text editor.

I recommend that you buy at least the Professional Edition. Although the price is much higher than that of the Personal Edition, it is justified. You will be glad you spent the money.

Tip The list of new features is fairly long, and not all of them have been covered here. The Enterprise Edition of Delphi now has over 300 components. In this book I will limit myself as far as possible to the components provided in the Professional Edition of Delphi.

Hello world ...?

As in every other programming book, this chapter contains an exemplar program. Normally, the standard program is the "Hello world!" example. However, for two reasons I have decided against using this particular mini-program. First, it gets served up time and again in every programming book; second, developing applications with Delphi is so easy and quick that we can safely work on a more complex example to explain how to program with Delphi.

The program I will use is a calculator that works out gross and net amounts. It will use a gross value and a percentage rate to calculate the net value.

2.1 Creating the interface

Usually, the interface is the last thing you optimize in a program. In visual programming systems such as Delphi, efforts are usually concentrated on the functionality and only then on the interface. In practice, this means that although all the necessary elements are present in your program (otherwise the functionality could not be created), the final version of the interface itself, i.e. its look and feel, is not defined until later.

For our mini-program, we will create the interface at the same time as we create the functionality. We use a form whose size we will reduce a little. Additionally, we will need the following: one component of the type TButton or TBitBtn for closing the program; two components of the type TEdit (one for the user to enter the gross value, and one for the user to enter the percentage rate); and an input field of the type TEdit, which we will use to output our result. For that reason, we assign this TEdit field (in the example, Edit3) a different color. We set that input field's Color property to the value clBtnFace.

We use three components of the type TLabel to assign titles to the input fields so that the user knows where they are to enter particular data. The value set in the Caption property is what will be displayed. In just the same way, we set the value for the form's Caption property.

Our complete program interface, which still has no functionality, is shown in Figure 2.1.

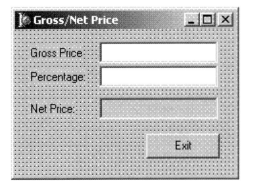

Figure 2.1 *The interface of the example program*

2.2 Adding the base functionality

Let's think about the basic functions we require. In this case, we can say that all functions that a Windows user would consider "normal" are basic functions. The main function of the program is to calculate the result.

2.2.1 Closing the program

First, we must ensure that our `TButton` for closing the program works properly. Delphi automatically provides the functionality for the buttons in the form's title bar. They work just like the same buttons in Windows usually do.

To assign the same functionality to our button, we must now enter program code for the first time. If you double-click on the button, Delphi automatically creates the default action for the button's default event-handling routine. In this case, it is the `OnClick` event that occurs when the user clicks on the button.

The line of code that we must insert is actually only one word, terminated with a semicolon:

```
close;
```

Via this statement, the application's main window is closed, which closes the application itself.

2.2.2 Configuring the result field

A user would normally expect not to be able to enter anything in the result field. After all, it is a field in which the program is supposed to output something. For this reason, we must prevent the input focus from shifting to this field. To do this, we simply set the correct properties in the Object Inspector; there is no need to write a single line of program code.

To prevent the user entering anything in our `Edit3` input field (which is used to display the result), we set its `ReadOnly` property to `true`. Then, even though the focus can still shift to the input field, the user cannot enter anything in it.

2.2.3 Tab sequence

All components on the form are set in a sequence that defines the order in which the cursor jumps from one to the next. Usually, this sequence is the same as the sequence in which you create the components, but you can change it if you like. You can also remove a component from the sequence so that the cursor does not jump to it. To do this, we set the `TabStop` property for that component to `false`. We now do this for our result field, `Edit3`. Now we have removed it from the tab sequence, the user can no longer use the tab key to jump to it. This means that we have also already completed this part of the functionality, and consequently we have actually already created all the base functionality. If you want to, you can run the program now to test it. You will see that you can already enter data, that the tab key and the different buttons work properly, and that the window also works exactly like all other windows in a Windows system. And all it took was one line of program code.

2.2.4 Text in the input fields

Naturally, the user will have to input their text themselves, and it is important for us to stop the input fields' names from being displayed in the input fields. We therefore have to delete this text. You will find it in the Text property for each component. Simply delete the contents of this property to empty the fields.

2.3 Adding the main function

The main function is our calculation. Since we have not provided a button for this function, we must work out another way. A sensible approach would be, for example, if the program carried out the calculation when the focus shifted from one input field to another one.

Delphi works in an event-oriented way. Even a shift of focus causes an event, which we can use to carry out the calculation. All we have to decide is whether we want the calculation to occur when the focus leaves an input field or enters an input field. In this case, I have choosen calculation when the focus leaves the input field. The event concerned is called `OnExit`; in the event-handling routine for this event, we will carry out the actual calculation.

Delphi again creates the default action for the event-handling routine if we double-click on the empty field next to the event name in the Object Inspector. All we need to do now is add the functionality.

Before we can calculate anything, we need some variables. However, all we are interested in is the result of the calculation; we will not need to access these variables again later. For this reason, we declare them as local, and therefore only valid for the function in which we currently find ourselves:

```
procedure TForm1.Edit1Exit(Sender: TObject);
var
  GrossValue  : double;
  Percentage  : integer;
  PercValue,
  NetValue    : double;
```

Now we check if both input fields – the one for the gross value and the one for the net value – really contain input. To do this, we check the input fields' Text property:

```
begin
  if (Edit1.Text='') or (Edit2.Text='') then
    exit;
```

If one of the input fields is empty, no calculation will be carried out and the program will immediately quit the event-handling routine. We use the exit command for that purpose. If both fields contain inputs, we can carry out the calculation. However, the data still consist of values of the data type String, and we need Integer or Double values. To create these, Delphi provides conversion functions, which we can use to assign the inputs in the input fields to our locally declared variables:

```
GrossValue := StrToFloat(Edit1.Text);
Percentage := StrToInt(Edit2.Text);
if (Percentage>99) or (Percentage<1) then
  exit;
```

At this point, we have also inserted a small control that quits the routine without another calculation if the percentage rate does not lie between 1 and 100. A percentage rate of 0% would be just as pointless as a percentage rate that was 100% or higher.

The next step is to calculate the net value. This is a simple percentage calculation for us, and very easy for Delphi too:

```
PercValue := ((GrossValue*Percentage)/100);
NetValue  := GrossValue-PercValue;
```

Finally, we write the result to the appropriate field, Edit3, which we have provided for that purpose. Here we have to arrange conversion once again, because our result has the data type `Real`, and the `Text` property of `Edit3`, to which we want to send the result, has the type `String`:

```
  Edit3.Text := FloatToStr(NetValue);
end;
```

Below is the entire function as it appears in Delphi. I have added comments so that you can identify the different parts of the code:

```
procedure TForm1.Edit1Exit(Sender: TObject);
var
  GrossValue   : double;
  Percentage   : integer;
  PercValue,
  NetValue     : double;
begin
 //Check if edit fields are empty or not
  if (Edit1.Text='') or (Edit2.Text='') then
    exit;

  //Convert values into the correct type
  GrossValue  := StrToFloat(Edit1.Text);
  Percentage := StrToInt(Edit2.Text);
  if (Percentage>99) or (Percentage<1) then
    exit;

  //Calculate
  PercValue := ((GrossValue*Percentage)/100);
  NetValue   := GrossValue-PercValue;

  //Write result
  Edit3.Text := FloatToStr(NetValue);
end;
```

As it stands, the program will carry out the calculation when the user leaves the `Edit1` field. This is not quite what we intended, for we want the calculation to be carried out when they leave `Edit2`, otherwise no calculation would be carried out after they input the percentage rate.

We use the same event-handling routine, but this time apply it to the `Edit2` field. Instead of reprogramming everything again, we can divert this event-handling routine. We therefore tell Delphi that if the `OnExit` event occurs in `Edit2`, then carry out the appropriate event-handling routine defined in `Edit1`.

On the Events page in the Object Inspector, you can see pull-down list fields next to the events. Select EDIT2 in the list, and pull down the list field next to the OnExit event. You will find the entry EDIT1EXIT. Selecting this completes the functionality.

And that completes the program's main function. Still missing, however, is a certain amount of user-friendliness. This primarily involves making sure that the user cannot enter the wrong data.

2.4 Preventing incorrect input

It is very important to prevent the user from entering invalid data. For example, if they entered a letter or a name, our calculation routine would determine that there was something in the field concerned and begin calculation. As soon as it tried to convert the values in the user input from String to Integer, we would have an error and the calculation would not work correctly.

Naturally, we could recognize this error at runtime and trap it, display a suitable message for the user, and prompt them to enter a new value. But this is not an elegant approach, and it does not comply with the way programs work nowadays. It is better to prevent the user from entering the wrong kind of data in the first place.

Again, we can use an event for this. If the user presses a key, two events occur that we could use: OnKeyPress and OnKeyDown, each for the input field in which it is located. We use the first since it gives us the ASCII code of the character whose key has been pressed.

It is very easy to prevent the user from entering an incorrect percentage rate since we are using a whole-number percentage rate for the calculation. We therefore have to trap each character that is not a number. In addition, we have to take into account the ← key. Unlike the Del key, which is a special function key, ← has an ASCII value (decimal 8). We find the numbers in the ASCII codes 48 to 57, each of which is a decimal value. The value 0 tells the program that no key has been pressed. The event-handling routine therefore looks like this:

```
procedure TForm1.Edit2KeyPress(Sender: TObject;
                               var Key: Char);
begin
  if not (Key in [#8,#48..#57]) then
    Key := #0;
end;
```

The Key parameter that contains the ASCII code of our character will be returned again after the routine is processed. Therefore, if we do not wish Windows to react when the user presses a key, we must return the ASCII value 0. This is expressed by the diamond character and the value. We do this if the key that has been pressed is not a number or the ← key. This completes the functionality.

This small example should hopefully have given you an idea of what it is like to program with Delphi and shown you a couple of Delphi functions. Of course, I don't keep all the functions in my head; I also look at the Delphi online help again and again (by pressing F1). With time, you will get to know some of the more important functions because you will use them so often. It's always difficult to begin something new, but you will quickly start achieving attractive and respectable results.

To complete this chapter, Figure 2.2 shows the complete program at runtime.

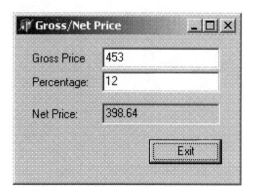

Figure 2.2   *The complete program at runtime*

Part I

Take that!

Object Pascal

The programming language on which Delphi is based is called Object Pascal. This was developed from Turbo Pascal, a procedural programming language that was very popular when DOS was in common use. The language was greatly extended to create Delphi. From the entirely structured language grew an object-oriented, extendible programming system that provided the programmer with an efficient way to develop complex programs in a relatively short period of time.

Although Delphi's functionality has become very powerful in the meantime, the actual programming language has hardly changed. This chapter describes the programming language itself, including its basic functionality and syntactical elements. The whole system is based on this language structure (something that is also a special feature). All Delphi components are native Delphi components, written with the programming language that is the basis of the programming system of which they are elements.

3.1 Basic language components

A Pascal program consists of a series of statements that follow a particular syntax. Some of these language elements are predefined. These include, for example, the operators for calculation functions, the names of the standard data types, or the different keywords of the language, also known as reserved words. These characters and words have a fixed meaning, so you cannot use them for anything else.

3.1.1 Symbols and separators

In Object Pascal, there are some symbols to which a fixed meaning has been assigned. Table 3.1 shows the most important of these and describes what they mean for programming.

3.1.2 Reserved words and directives

Reserved words

Table 3.2 contains a list of all Object Pascal reserved words. The meaning of these words is fixed, so they cannot be used for anything else.

Symbol	Meaning
=	Queries whether two values are equal, and assigns a value to a constant when it is declared.
<>	Queries whether two values are unequal.
<=	Queries whether a value is less than or equal to another.
>=	Queries whether a value is greater than or equal to another.
>	Queries whether a value is greater than another.
<	Queries whether a value is less than another.
:=	Assigns a value to a variable.
:	Assigns a data type to a variable.
;	Separates Pascal statements from each other; however, there are some exceptions: there must be no semicolon after the reserved word `begin`, or in front of the reserved word `end`; nor can there be a semicolon in front of the reserved word `else`.
,	Separates list elements or set elements from each other.
.	Separates variable names and field names during qualification; the period or full stop (also known as the dot) also stands for the end of a unit or of the program, and the compiler ignores any statements that appear after the period.
'	Marks the start and end of character strings.
[ ]	Marks the start and end of set constants.
( )	Marks the start and end of set definitions; when used in mathematical expressions, they represent standard mathematical brackets also used to group expressions for evaluations.
{ }	Indicates a comment in the program text (source code); comments are used to make the program clearer, so you should add them frequently (don't go over the top, or the program will become hard to follow).
(* *)	Alternative to curly brackets (left and right brace); used for comments in the source code.
//	Comes from the programming language C; shows the start of a comment that carries on to the end of the line (no program code to the right of it).
^	Stands for pointer.
@	Stands for address assignments.
$	The number is interpreted as a hexadecimal number.
#	The number is interpreted as a decimal number.

Table 3.1   *Special characters used in Object Pascal*

Directives

Directives are also words that have a special meaning in Object Pascal. However, in contrast to the reserved words, they are only used in environments in which user-

And	Exports	Mod	Shr
Array	File	Nil	String
As	Finalization	Not	Then
Asm	Finally	Object	Threadvar
Begin	For	Of	To
Case	Function	Or	Try
Class	Goto	Out	Type
Const	If	Packed	Unit
Constructor	Implementation	Procedure	Until
Destructor	In	Program	Uses
Dispinterface	Inherited	Property	Var
Div	Initialization	Raise	While
Do	Inline	Record	With
Downto	Interface	Repeat	Xor
Else	Is	Resourcestring	
End	Label	Set	
Except	Library	Shl	

Table 3.2   *Reserved words*

defined names cannot occur. This means that you could, in theory, use these directives to declare your own variables or constants, but you should not do so. You will find a list of the directives in Table 3.3.

Absolute	External	Override	Reintroduce
Abstract	Far	Package	Requires
Assembler	Forward	Pascal	Resident
Automated	Implements	Private	Safecall
Cdecl	Index	Protected	Stdcall
Contains	Message	Public	Stored
Default	Name	Published	Virtual
Dispid	Near	Read	Write
Dynamic	Nodefault	Readonly	Writeonly
Export	Overload	Register	

Table 3.3   *Directives*

3.1.3 Variables and constants

Variables and constants are used to save used values. You can choose almost any name, even if it is longer than the reserved variable names. You should take this opportunity to use names that indicate clearly what they actually do. In Object Pascal, all variables and constants must be declared before you can use them. In the case of a variable, you also specify its data type, which defines what type of data can be stored in that variable. These data types include different numerical types, character strings and self-defined types or objects.

Declaring variables

You use the `var` keyword to declare variables. The exact syntax is:

```
var
   MyNumber: Integer;
```

This statement declares a variable called `MyNumber`, of the type `integer`, a whole-number data type. When you declare a variable, you only assign a data type; a value is assigned later in the program text. You should always ensure that you initialize all declared variables by assigning them an initial value. Immediately after declaration, a variable always has an arbitrary value.

Declaring constants

If you require a value that never changes, it is better to declare a constant instead of a variable. Constants are assigned a fixed value that cannot be changed afterwards. You use the `const` keyword to declare a constant. To assign its value, you use the equals (=) sign. This is an example of a constant declaration:

```
const
   MyNumber = 100;
```

The constant now contains the value 100 and can never be changed.

Typed constants

Typed constants are assigned a data type as well as a value. Unlike a normal constant, the value of a typed constant can be changed later within the same program. In technical programming terms, they are actually variables that are initialized as soon as they are declared. You use the reserved word `const` to declare them:

```
const
   MyNumber: integer = 100;
```

Local and global declarations

Variables, constants and data types can be declared locally or globally. Local variables are valid only in the program section in which they have been declared. A global variable, or constant, applies to the entire program, or rather to all parts of the program in which the unit in which that variable or constant was declared is integrated. Global variables are usually declared in the `interface` section of a unit. All program elements that can access the unit can then also work with these variables.

You find local variable declarations in functions and procedures, for example. Any variable declared within the body of a function or procedure is valid only there. If there is another call to the function or procedure, then the variable no longer has the value that was last assigned to it.

3.1.4 Data types

You must assign a data type to a variable before you can use it in your program. Delphi provides you with a number of predefined data types. However, you can also declare your own data types and use them in your programs.

Predefined data types

Delphi offers several predefined data types. They include, for example, integer types, character-based types, and also complete objects or the components from the toolbar. Table 3.4 shows some of the basic data types that Delphi provides.

Data type	Value
Integer	32-bit integer value with prefix operator (–2 147 483 648 to 2 147 483 647).
Longint	32-bit integer value with prefix operator, retained for reasons of compatibility; use `integer` instead.
Word	16-bit integer value without prefix operator (0 to 65 535).
Cardinal	32-bit integer value without prefix operator (0 to 4 294 967 295).
String	Pascal character string.
Char	A character.
PChar	Null-terminated character string, as found in C; you can use the `PChar(character string)` function to convert a Pascal character string into a null-terminated string.

Table 3.4 *Some standard Object Pascal data types*

Type conversions

In some situations, such as for passing a variable's value to a procedure or function, it is necessary to convert the variable's type to another type. In this case you carry out type conversion:

```
var
   MyValue: integer;
begin;
   MyValue := Integer('A');
end;
```

After conversion, the variable `MyValue` contains the value 65.

Type conversion, as already mentioned, can also be used for passing values to procedures and functions. For example, most Windows API functions require `PChar` character strings. If you have used a `String` variable, you can use type conversion to convert it to the appropriate `PChar` equivalent so that its value can be passed. Nothing happens to the actual variable itself. An example of this kind of conversion is the `MessageBox` function:

```
procedure MyMessage(Msg: String);
begin;
  Application.MessageBox(PChar(Msg),'Message',mb_Ok);
end;
```

3.1.5 Arrays

One-dimensional static arrays

An array is a collection of values that have the same data type. The easiest way to understand them is to imagine an array as a table that contains only one row (which may have many columns). Each column contains a value, and a program can use the number of each column to access the value in it. An array of this kind is called a one-dimensional array, since it has only one row. To define an array, use the `array` keyword:

```
var
   MyArray: Array[0..9] of integer;
```

`MyArray` now consists of ten elements of the type `integer`. To address an individual element in it, write the element's index in square brackets straight after the variable name. You enter this command to obtain the first value in the example array:

```
FirstValue := MyArray[0];
```

and you obtain the last value accordingly by entering

```
LastValue := MyArray[9];
```

You can, of course, change the initial and final value of the array. If, for example, you wanted to create an array whose first value had the index 2 and that also contained ten values, you would simply change the declaration as follows:

```
var
   MyArray : Array[2..11] of integer;
```

Multidimensional static arrays

An array is not restricted to one dimension. For example, if you wanted to save values from a table in an array you could also add a dimension to the array:

```
var
    TwoDimensionArray : Array[1..10,0..5] of string;
```

This array corresponds to a table with ten columns and six rows (or ten rows with six columns). This means that 60 values of the type `String` can be stored in it.

As mentioned already, an array is not restricted to a particular number of dimensions. You could also have a construction like this:

```
var
    ThreeD_Array : Array[1..5,1..5,1..5] of integer;
```

In this case, you would have a table that could, for example, hold values for mathematical functions, which would later be displayed in a coordinates system with axes.

Arrays as self-defined data types

An array can also be declared as a data type. To do this, replace the `var` keyword with the `type` keyword to declare the appropriate type. This is useful if several arrays with the same structure are to be used within the program. Instead of having to type in a huge array declaration for each variable, you can declare the array as a data type and assign the variables:

```
type
    TMyArray = Array[1..10] of string;
```

```
var
    FirstArray : TMyArray;
    SecondArray: TMyArray;
```

The "T" in the name `TMyArray` is used to identify the purpose of the declared type. As a type is involved, I have added "T" to the front of the name. Although you do not have to do this, it is a useful technique.

Constant arrays

The following construction declares an array containing constants. The keyword, as in the case of other constant declarations, is `const`. All the values must also be entered since constants are involved:

```
const
    MyArray = (0,17,23,45,64,13,45,89,45,18,90,45);
```

The values in this array are fixed and cannot be changed. Nevertheless, as for normal constants, you could create a typed array, which is an array of typed constants. In that case, the declaration would be similar to the typed constants declaration:

```
const
    MyArray : array[1..5] of integer = (12,14,16,18,19);
```

This declaration has the same effect as a typed constant declaration; the values are initialized when they are created. What may not seem important when only one constant is involved becomes much more significant in the case of an array. Imagine if you had to initialize an array that contained 100 entries. This would not only cause unnecessary delays when the program was executed but would also mean a lot of typing, and the source code would become harder than ever to follow.

One-dimensional dynamic arrays

In contrast to static arrays, you do not specify the size of dynamic arrays when you declare them. Instead, there is a function, SetLength, with which a size can be defined at runtime. Dynamic arrays can also be released at runtime. As you can release a dynamic array and then assign a new size to it later, you can always change its size whenever you want. To release a dynamic array, assign Nil to a variable that references the array:

```
var
    A: array of integer;
begin;
    SetLength(A,20);
    A[10] := 5;
    A := NIL;
end;
```

The index for a dynamic array always begins at 0, unlike the index for static arrays. In addition, dynamic arrays always explicitly involve pointers. This means that you only have to define the size of a dynamic array once, even if it will be referenced several times. In other words, if A and B are both the same type of variable array, then A references the same array as B. After the following program code has been executed, when A[2] is queried, the result is the value 4:

```
var
    A,
    B: array of integer;
begin
    SetLength(A,5);
    A[4] := 5;
    B[2] := 4;
end;
```

Multidimensional dynamic arrays

Multidimensional dynamic arrays are declared as follows:

```
var
   A : array of array of integer;
```

To assign the array a size, use the SetLength procedure but pass two integer values to it instead:

```
var
   A: array of array of integer;
begin;
   SetLength(A,5,5);
end;
```

You can also define arrays that are not symmetrical. For a table, this would mean that it would have a fixed number of rows, each of which would have a different number of columns. To define this, specify the size of the first dimension and then the size of the second dimension, for each column individually. After the following declaration, the third row of the array would have five columns, and the fourth row would have ten columns:

```
var
   A: array of array of integer;
begin;
   SetLength(A,5);        //Array with 5 rows
   SetLength(A[3],5);     //4th line with 5 cols
   SetLength(A[4],10);    //5th line with 10 cols
end;
```

Accessing the values in dynamic arrays

Since you do not always know the size of a nondynamic array, you can use the High and Low functions to access the first or last field in it:

```
var
   A: array of integer;
   i: integer;
begin;
   SetLength(A,10);
   for I := Low(A) to High(A) do
      A[I] := I*10;
end;
```

3.1.6 Sets

Sets, as the name suggests, are groups of objects of the same kind. Examples of sets are a list of the days of the week and the numbers from one to nine:

```
type
    MyWeekDays = (Monday,Tuesday,Wednesday,Thursday,
                  Friday,Saturday,Sunday);

    MyNumbers  = set of 1..9;

var
    TheDay : MyWeekDays;

begin;
    TheDay := Monday;
end;
```

To define a set, either use the reserved word Set or define a list of the expressions contained in the set. This is the best way to make the source code easy to read. A set is an ordinal number type, so Delphi assigns a numerical value to each expression defined in a set.

One way you can use sets is to compare whether a specified value is contained in a set. To do so, use the reserved word in. If the value is contained in a set, then true will be returned, otherwise false will be returned. This kind of comparison looks something like this:

```
if ANumber in [1..9] then
    MessageBeep(0);
```

The MessageBeep(0) statement will be executed if the value of ANumber lies between one and nine.

3.1.7 Records

A record groups different types of data into one new data type. This gives the programmer enormous flexibility. You could, for example, save an address in one record instead of in several individual variables, making the operations that are carried out with the data record much simpler.

Single record

A record is a data type, so it is declared using the keyword Type, and must then be assigned to a variable:

```
type
   TMyAddress = record
      Name       : String;
      Firstname  : String;
      Street     : String;
      State      : String;
      City       : String;
   end;

var
   MyAddress : TmyAddress;
```

You have now declared a record that can contain all the details for an address. To access the data, simply specify which field you want to access. In technical programming terms, we also say that the name is qualified. For this purpose, a period (full stop) is written between the name of the record and the variable name:

```
MyAddress.Name := 'Eller';
MyAddress.city := 'Dachau/Germany';
```

Record arrays

Records are a data type, so we can also create an array from records. You could, for example, create a small database from addresses that are stored in an array. The declaration would be as follows:

```
type
   TMyAddress = record
      Name       : String;
      Firstname  : String;
      Street     : String;
      State      : String;
      City       : String;
   end;

var
   MyAddress : array[1..10] of TMyAddress;
```

You would access the datasets in a similar way to the single record:

```
MyAddress[1].Name := 'Eller';
```

3.1.8 Pointers

Pointers are a dynamic means of working with data. Usually, you declare a variable and assign it a value. This variable occupies a certain amount of static memory, which varies according to the data type used. It needs exactly the number of bytes necessary for storing the data. For a 32-bit numerical value, for example, this corresponds to 32 bits, or 4 bytes, which is not very much. However, if you use a record or an array, or even an array that consists of records, this can very quickly use up all the available memory.

With pointers, you can reserve memory dynamically. Use the following trick: instead of statically reserving all the memory required for the variable, simply reserve some memory somewhere in the computer's address space for the contents of the variable. The pointer variable only contains this address, so it always uses the same amount of memory (4 bytes) regardless of the amount data saved.

Declaring a pointer

To declare a pointer variable, use the circumflex character (^):

```
var
   PInt : ^Integer;
```

In this line, PInt is declared as a pointer to an integer value. A pointer to a record works in just the same way:

```
type
   TMyAddress = record
      Name       : String;
      Firstname  : String;
      Street     : String;
      State      : String;
      City       : String;
   end;

var
   PMyAddress : ^TMyAddress;
```

Reserving memory and assigning values

The last line of code above declares PMyAddress as a pointer to the record TMyAddress. In the program code, you now need to reserve memory for the data because although Delphi knows how much space the data will require (because the size of the records is known), it has not yet reserved memory for this purpose. To do this, we need the statement new. You also use the circumflex character to assign a value to the pointer variable, but this time you place it after the pointer name:

```
type
   TMyAddress = record
      Name       : String;
      Firstname  : String;
      Street     : String;
      State      : String;
      City       : String;
   end;

var
   PMyAddress : ^TMyAddress;

begin
   New(PMyAddress);
   PMyAddress^.Name := 'Eller';
end;
```

Releasing memory

We have now declared a pointer, reserved memory for it, and assigned a value to it. If the pointer variable, or rather the memory reserved for the pointer variable, is no longer required, then we can use the Dispose command to release the memory:

```
Dispose(PMyAddress);
```

Now the saved value will no longer be available.

Assigning addresses

Delphi also provides functions with which you can assign an address to a pointer variable. For example, if you have declared a variable and want to use a pointer to access the value stored in it, then there are two ways you can do so. Either you declare a new pointer, reserve the right amount of memory for it, and assign the value to the variable, or you simply use the same memory space as the variable already fills. To do this, define the address of the pointer in such a way that the pointer points to the value in the already-declared variable. In Delphi, you can use either the @ (at) character or the addr statement, which has exactly the same function:

```
var
   x    : integer;
   MyPtr: ^Integer;
begin;
   x := 5;
   MyPtr := @x;
   Dec(MyPtr^);
end;
```

In the example program code above, a variable called x is declared to which the value 5 is assigned. Then the pointer variable My Ptr has the address of the variable x assigned to it. This is the address at which the value of x is saved. This value, to which the pointer variable now points, is then reduced by one. As a result, the variable x has a new value of 4.

The line:

```
MyPtr := @x;
```

can also be written like this:

```
MyPtr := addr(x);
```

They both function in exactly the same way.

Working with pointers always takes a little getting used to, since you have to think a bit more abstractly. For example, if you forget the circumflex character, you do not assign a value but a new address that cannot lead anywhere.

Pointers are very important under Windows. Delphi's concept, on the other hand, generally keeps the programmer away from them, although internally all objects and classes are administered dynamically. For this reason, pointers are no longer required very often.

3.1.9 Objects and classes

Objects are the logical extension of records, and classes are a further development of objects. Basically, all classes are also objects, but Delphi handles them differently (e.g. when saving them). For this reason, this section describes mainly objects, although everything in it also applies to classes.

A record has certain disadvantages, especially if you want to extend it. The object model solved that problem by introducing inheritance and polymorphism.

The concept of inheritance

Let's look again at the record for storing address data that we worked on earlier. The declaration was as follows:

```
type
   TMyAddress = record
      Name      : String;
      Firstname : String;
      Street    : String;
      State     : String;
      City      : String;
   end;
```

```
var
    MyAddress : TMyAddress;
```

Now let's assume we want to extend this record, e.g. by adding a telephone number. We could either create a new record that also contained the telephone number, or we could create a new record and simply integrate the old one into it. We cannot simply extend the original record, because the data in it must remain available. The new record would therefore look like this:

```
type
    TMyAddress = record
        OldAddress : TMyAddress;
        Phone      : integer;
    end;
```

```
var
    MyAddress2 : TmyAddress2;
```

It is now a bit more difficult to access the individual fields in the original record:

```
MyAddress2.OldAddress.Name := 'Eller';
```

It becomes even more complicated if we add a fax number to the new data record. If we use the same approach again, we end up with a third record:

```
type
    TMyAddress = record
        OldAddress : TmyAddress2;
        Fax        : integer;
    end;
```

```
var
    MyAddress3 : TmyAddress3;
```

An access to the same field would then look like this:

```
MyAddress3.OldAddress.OldAddress.Name := 'Eller';
```

You could carry on like this for ever, but no doubt you can already see that the assignments become more and more complicated with every field that we add. Eventually, either you will no longer know where you are or you will need several lines of code for a single assignment. Objects solve this problem by using the concept of inheritance.

Inheritance means that an object derives all its data and structures from another object. In the original version, let's begin by changing the word record to object:

```
type
   TMyAddress = object
      Name       : String;
      Firstname  : String;
      Street     : String;
      State      : String;
      City       : String;
   end;
```

```
var
   MyAddress : TMyAddress;
```

To extend the object, we derive a new object from it. The new object then contains all the data structures already present in the original object. Now we can add the TelNr variable:

```
type
   TMyAddress2 = object(TmyAddress)
      Phone : integer;
   end;
```

```
var
   MyAddress2 : TMyAddress2;
```

If you assign a value, you can see the difference:

```
MyAddress2.Name := 'Eller';
```

Compared with the record, the data in the original object are already present here; they have been inherited by the new object. Now let's add the fax number. We declare the new object as follows:

```
type
   TMyAddress3 = object(TMyAddress2)
      Fax : integer;
   end;
```

```
var
   MyAddress3 : TMyAddress3;
```

See how this affects the value assignment:

```
MyAddress3.Name := 'Eller';
```

As we see, nothing about the value assignment has changed. If we had been using records, we would have had to change all the assignments within the entire program. This is not necessary if we work with objects: thanks to inheritance, the assignments remain the same for all objects.

Methods in objects

An object or class not only contains data but can also provide the functions needed to work with these data. The functions and procedures that an object provides are called methods. The methods of an object are defined in the object itself:

```
type
   TMyAddress = object
      Name      : String;
      Firstname : String;
      Street    : String;
      State     : String;
      City      : String;
      procedure SaveAddress;
      procedure LoadAddress;
   end;

var
   MyAddress : TMyAddress;

procedure TMyAddress.SaveAddresses;
begin

   //Place program code here

end;

procedure TMyAddress.LoadAddresses;
begin

   //Place program code here

end;
```

The procedure call is similar to the way in which a variable is assigned. A period (full stop) separates the object name and the method. The methods and variables in an object can be inherited.

Overriding methods

An object or a class can provide virtual or dynamic methods that the successor can override. This may or may not mean that the original method will be hidden.

The methods of a class or object are static by default. To declare a method as virtual, you must use the reserved word `virtual`:

```
procedure MyMethod; virtual;
```

You use the reserved word `dynamic` to declare dynamic methods:

```
procedure MySecondMethod; dynamic;
```

Dynamic and virtual methods can be overridden in descendant classes. To do so, use the `override` directive. The declaration of the overridden method must match up with the method of its predecessor:

```
procedure MyMethod; override;
```

Virtual and dynamic methods generally behave in the same way. They only differ in the way they are optimized for compilation. Virtual methods are optimized for speed. In the case of dynamic methods, Delphi tries to keep their code size to a minimum.

3.2 Loops

A loop is a segment of program code that repeats itself. Loops are used, for example, to run through a database from top to bottom, or to search through the items in a list. When working with loops note that, apart from when you are using a `for` loop, it is your responsibility as the programmer to ensure that the program leaves the loop again – otherwise it would keep running without interruption forever. In the worst case, the whole system would then freeze (something you are no doubt familiar with from the blue screen error that occurs in Windows systems).

3.2.1 The for loop

```
for <run variable> := <initial value>  to <final value> do
begin;
  //Place code here
end;
```

If the list of statements contains only one statement, it does not need to be enclosed by `begin` and `end`.

The variable `i` is known as a run variable. It has the predefined initial value at the start of the loop. The loop will be repeated until the value of the run variable corresponds to the specified final value. Every time the loop runs, the value in the run variable is increased by one. Here is an example of a `for` loop:

```
for i := 1 to 10 do
begin;
    U := U+1;
    X := X+U;
end;
```

The statements between `begin` and `end` will be executed when `i` has reached the value 10. However, with a `for` loop, you can also count backwards. To do so, replace the word `to` with `downto`:

```
for i := 10 downto 1 do
begin;
    U := U+1;
    X := X+U;
end;
```

Then the counting runs backwards.

> **Tip** If you are using a `for` loop and you get results that make it seem that Delphi has counted backwards even though the loop was programmed to count forwards, this is not a compiler error but a "feature". The reason for it is compiler optimization, which is usually switched on (and you should leave it switched on). In fact, in `for` loops that have been programmed to count forwards, Delphi does count backwards after compiler optimization is enabled. According to Borland, counting backwards is faster than counting forwards. If you discover errors, rewrite the program so that it counts backwards anyway. You can also fix the error by switching off optimization. However, that is not recommended, due to the advantages that optimization brings with it.

3.2.2 The `while` loop

```
while < Expression> do
begin;
    //Place code here
end;
```

Here, too, if the list of statements contains only one statement then it does not need to be enclosed by `begin` and `end`.

The expression corresponds to a Boolean value, and therefore produces `true` or `false`. Here is an example of how to use `while`:

```
while i<10 do
begin;
    i := i+1;
    u := u+2;
end;
```

Note that the expression will be evaluated before the statements are executed. In this kind of pretest loop, the program code within the loop does not have to run through completely. If you want to execute the statements at least once, then you should use the `repeat` loop.

3.2.3 The `repeat` loop

```
repeat
    //Place code here
until <Expression>
```

This form of loop, the post-test loop, will also run through until a predefined expression is true. However, the statements will be executed at least once, since the expression is not checked until the end of the loop. When programmed, a `repeat` loop looks like this:

```
repeat
    i := i+1;
    u := u+2;
until i >= 10;
```

The `repeat` loop does not require `begin` and `end`. The statements between the words `repeat` and `until` will be repeated until the checked expression is true.

3.3 Branches

3.3.1 If–then–else branching

```
if <Expression> then
begin;
    // Executed if expression is true
end
else
begin;
```

```
    // Executed if expression is false
end;
```

Branchings are used if statements are to be executed in dependence on a Boolean expression. Once again, if there is only one single statement, the words `begin` and end are not required:

```
if i=10 then
begin
    u := u+1;
    i := i+1;
end;
```

In the construction above, `else` has been omitted since it is not required. After evaluation, the program continues running with the next statement.

> **Tip** If you do use the word `else`, ensure that there is no semicolon in front of it.

3.3.2 Case branching

```
Case (ordinal type) of
    (Value1) : begin;
    //Place code here
            end;
    (Value2) : begin;
    //Place code here
            end;
else begin;
        //This code is executed if none of the
        //above conditions apply
    end;
end; {Case}
```

The syntax is a bit cryptic and hard to understand, so there is an example below to explain it. An ordinal type is a counting type. These include the whole numbers (integers) or self-defined quantities. A variable with this data type is referenced for evaluation. A particular statement (or group of statements) will be executed according to the value of the variables. Usually, a variable of the type `integer` will be referenced for evaluation. Here is an example of the `case` statement in a program:

```
case MyValue of
    1 : OpenFile(FName);
```

```
   2 : begin;
         MainForm.color      := clBlue;
         MainForm.Font.Name := 'Arial';
      end;
   3 : begin;
         MainForm.color      := clBtnFace;
         MainForm.Font.Name := 'MS Sans Serif';
      end;
end;   //Case
```

Again, `begin` and `end` are only required if several statements are present. In the example above, a procedure called `OpenFile` is called if `MyValue` has the value 1. With the values 2 and 3, the main window is assigned a color and a font.

The `case` statement can include a final `else`. Any statements after the `else` programs will be executed if none of the values match up.

3.3.3 Procedures and functions

Procedures and functions are the core of Object Pascal. A procedure executes a particular process, and the required statements are programmed in it. These procedures can be accessed from the program via a call using their name. A function is no different except that it has a return value. You can therefore check, for example, whether the statements within the function have been carried out correctly.

Structure of a procedure

A procedure consists of the procedure header in which both the name of the procedure and the variables, and the procedure body containing the statements, are defined. The procedure header is introduced by the reserved word `procedure`. This is followed immediately by the declarations of the required variables or constants. These are local variables that are valid only for this procedure. The variables are deleted when the procedure is exited. The declarations are followed by the procedure body, introduced by `begin`. The procedure finishes with the word `end`. Between these words are all the statements to be executed within the procedure.

Here is an example of a procedure:

```
procedure CountUp;               //Procedure header
var
   i : integer;
begin;                           //Body
   for i := 1 to 10 do
   begin;
      Label1.Caption := IntToStr(i);
```

```
        Pause(1000);
    end;
end;                                    //End of procedure
```

The procedure is called using its name. The program jumps to the specified procedure, processes the source code contained in it, and then automatically jumps back to the calling location. Actually, that has already happened in the program code above, as the call Pause(1000) is nothing more than a procedure call. The name of the procedure here is Pause, and the value 1000 is a parameter that is passed to the procedure.

Structure of a function

The biggest difference between procedures and functions is that a function returns a value but a procedure does not. In the program code, a call to a function corresponds to the assigning of a value to a variable. The type of the returned value is declared in the header of the function. You use the reserved word function to introduce a function. The example below shows a function that increases a variable passed to it by one and returns it as a result:

```
function MyIncrement(MyValue: integer): integer;
begin;
    MyValue := MyValue+1;
    Result := MyValue;
end;
```

The reserved word Result stands for the result value here. Alternatively, you could use the name of the function:

```
MyIncrement := MyValue;
```

also assigns the result value. Usually, you should use result for reasons of clarity.

3.3.4 Passing parameters

Static or constant parameters

In the function example, we have already passed a parameter (the MyValue parameter). This is a static, or constant, parameter; it can be changed within the function, but the changed value cannot be returned.

Variable parameters

Variable parameters behave differently. They are returned again after they have been changed, so the passed variable contains the changed value after the function or procedure call. The word `var` is used to declare a parameter as a variable parameter. A procedure header with a variable parameter of this kind looks like this:

```
procedure MyIncrement2(var MyValue: integer);
```

After the procedure has changed the value of `MyValue`, the changed value is returned again. After the procedure is exited, the value of the passed variable equals the changed value (parameters of this kind must be variables). Naturally, this procedure also works with functions, so we are not restricted to using the return value present there.

3.3.5 Overloading procedures and functions

Often, you have to write several functions or procedures that basically do the same thing, but you are required to give them different names because they differ in their type and number of parameters. This is shown in the next example, in which three functions all add numbers. However, one function adds three numbers, another adds two numbers, and the third adds four numbers. The code would look something like this:

```
function Add2(v1, v2: integer): integer;
begin;
  Result := v1+v2;
end;

function Add3(v1, v2, v3: integer): integer;
begin;
  Result := Add(Add(v2,v1),v2);
end;

function Add4(v1, v2, v3, v4: integer): integer;
begin;
  Result := Add2(Add2(v1,v2),Add2(v3,v4));
end;
```

To use these three functions, you would have to remember all their names. In this example that is fairly easy, but if the names are harder to remember, or if the problem arises frequently, difficulties start to arise. It would be a lot easier if Delphi could remember which of the functions we want to use. Fortunately, Delphi does this; you just have to tell it which ones you need. You do so with the `overload` keyword. If you have several functions that basically do the same thing, but have different parameters, you can use overload to create `overloaded` functions. They are shown in this example:

```
function Add(v1, v2: integer): integer; overload;
begin;
```

```
  Result := v1+v2;
end;

function Add(v1, v2, v3: integer): integer; overload;
begin;
  Result := Add(Add(v1,v2),v3);
end;

function Add(v1,v2,v3,v4: integer): integer; overload;
begin;
  Result := Add1(Add2(v3,v4),Add2(v3,v4));
end;
```

This overload functionality also applies to procedures. However, you must ensure that the parameters of the functions or procedures differ, as Delphi uses them as a criterion for distinguishing between them.

If you publish the functions/procedures, you simply need to specify the `overload` directive in the function or procedure header declaration in the `interface` section of the unit.

3.4   Units

As a program becomes more complex, its source code can become very hard to follow. To help, the concept of the unit was introduced in Pascal and is also used by Delphi. A unit groups several procedures and functions in files. Units can access functions, procedures or variables in other units. To allow Unit1 to access procedures and functions that are declared in Unit2, Unit 2 must be encapsulated (integrated) in Unit1. In addition, the procedures in Unit2 must be published.

3.4.1 Structure of a unit

A unit is introduced by the reserved word `unit`. The individual sections include the `interface` section, the `implementation` section, and an optional `initialization` or `finalization` section. Note that there can only be a `finalization` section if there is also an `initialization` section. In the source code, it looks like this:

```
unit Unit1;

interface

  {In this section the procedures and functions are
    specified that are published for use in other units}
```

```
uses

  {Here we enter the names of the units whose
  procedures and functions our unit wants to use}

implementation

  {This section contains the source code for the units
  and procedures}

initialization

  {Optional: contains source code that is to be executed
   when the unit is called for the first time}

finalization

{Optional, only needed if an initialization section is
 present. Contains the code that is executed when the unit
 is removed from memory (when the program ends)
  }


end.
```

Procedures and functions are published when the procedure header or function header is repeated in the `interface` section. All functions/procedures that are not published are available only in the unit in which they have been programmed.

3.4.2 Mutual visibility of units

Sometimes, two units need to access each other's functions. People who are new to Delphi programming often attempt this with the following construction, but unfortunately it does not work:

```
unit Unit1;

interface
uses
   unit2;   //Here Unit2 is encapsulated

{Procedure headers}
```

```
implementation

  {Procedure source code}

end.



unit Unit2;

interface

uses
  unit1;    //Here Unit1 is encapsulated, causing an error.
            //Unit1 cannot be encapsulated as
            //Unit1 is attempting to encapsulate Unit2.

{Procedure headers}

implementation

{Procedures source code}

end.
```

In this case, the compiler would show an error. Unit1 would attempt to encapsulate Unit2. However, Unit1 is also encapsulated in the `interface` section of Unit2, which would mean that Unit1 ought to encapsulate itself. Even if you are not exactly sure what that means, you just need to remember this, it doesn't work! Instead, the encapsulation of at least one of the units needs to be moved to the `interface` section. Then the mutual visibility of the units also works. Normally, you should not need to use mutual visibility, which is usually a sign of poor programming (except in some rare cases).

3.4.3 Units in Delphi

Delphi uses the units concept extensively. Every form that is created has its own unit. Delphi provides its basic structure including the `interface` and `implementation` sections. Even when you are actually programming, you scarcely need to bother about the correct structure; Delphi takes care of it for you.

Naturally, you can also program your own units in Delphi, following the methodology shown above, and integrate them into your own program. In the FILE | NEW menu option, you can select UNIT to create a new unit. If you use this functionality to create a unit, Delphi provides you with the basic framework for it.

If you create your own unit, you are also responsible for defining the units that are to be encapsulated. You need to encapsulate different standard Delphi units according to which functions you are implementing in your unit. If you forget to encapsulate them, the compiler displays an error message and places the cursor at the point in the source code that it cannot process. Usually, you will find there is a procedure or data type that is declared in a unit that is not yet encapsulated in your unit. Delphi's online help usually tells you which unit you still need to encapsulate.

If you are working in a unit that contains a form, you can display all self-created units that are not yet encapsulated in the current unit by selecting the FILE | USE UNIT menu option. Alternatively, you can use the keyboard shortcut [Alt] + [F11].

Delphi's base elements

This chapter is intended to provide a small, but useful, overview of the most important components and classes in Delphi. The main part is played by the VCL. This has been maintained and constantly extended since the first version of Delphi was released, and Borland have made sure that it has always remained backwards-compatible.

The Personal Edition of Delphi contains around 85 components with which you can program, mainly under Windows. However, some important features, such as the database and internet functionality and XML support, are missing. This makes the Personal Edition more of a try-out version of Delphi than a programming environment worth taking seriously. This book is based on the Enterprise Edition, but I have tried as far as possible to restrict myself to the components and options that are also available in the Professional Edition.

Some components may not be explained in any great detail, or may even have been left out of the list entirely, due to limited space in this book.

4.1 Visual Components Library

Delphi's Component Palette has a fairly logical structure. Users of a previous version of Delphi will notice that the sequence of the Component Palette tabs (referred to in Delphi as "pages"), and the components located on them, are the same as in previous versions. Usually you will use the Standard, Additional and Win32 pages, and the database components, and possibly also the pages containing the Indy, Internet and FastNet components.

4.1.1 Common properties

Not all properties or events are suitable for all components. However, there are some common properties and events that are valid for many components and also have the same meaning or function. Table 4.1 lists the common properties that are available for all components in Delphi's Component Palette. Many of these have established themselves as standard names, so you will also find them in components provided by other suppliers.

Property	Function
Align	Used to specify how a control element is to be arranged in relation to its superior control element. Control elements with this property can be placed on any edge of their superior control element or can even use up the entire remaining available space.
Alignment	Used for labels and input fields to specify the alignment (justification) of the text within the component. Text can be aligned to the left, right or center.
AutoSize	Defines whether a control element is to change its size to suit its content.
BorderStyle	Specifies the type of border used for a component. The possible settings are bsSingle and bsNone.
Caption	Contains the text that labels the control element.
Color	Specifies the color used to display a control element. The data type is TColor. If you call a ColorDialog at runtime, you can immediately assign the color returned by the dialog.
Constraints	Sets size restrictions for the current control element. You can use the event-handling routine for OnConstrainedResize to check its maximum and minimum sizes.
Cursor	Specifies what the mouse arrow looks like as it passes over a control element. You can select a cursor type from the list or define your own cursor.
DockSite	Specifies whether a window can be docked on to the control element.
DragCursor	Specifies which mouse arrow is to be used while a control element is being dragged during a drag-and-drop operation.
DragKind	Defines whether a control element is moved (dragged) and then docked, or dragged and dropped (without docking).
DragMode	Specifies how a drag-and-drop operation is to start. If you set the property to the value dmManual, you must call the BeginDrag method to start the drag-and-drop operation.
Enabled	Specifies whether the control element is available, e.g. in the case of an input field of the type TEdit, it specifies whether data can be entered in that input field. Control elements for which Enabled is set to false are usually displayed in gray.
Font	Contains the font that is used by the associated control element, and all the font's attributes. If you implement a dialog field for font selection in your application, you can assign directly the returned Font property. Any properties specified by the user in the dialog field can be transferred. Otherwise, you can also change the different attributes of the font individually.

Height	Specifies the height of a control element.
HelpContext	In this property, you can enter a value with which you can later link a particular help topic when you create a help file for your application. This would then provide context-sensitive help.
Hint	Contains a short help text that is displayed, for example, next to a toolbar button when you pass the mouse arrow over it. You can enter both a short hint text and a longer one if you separate them with the "|" character (keyboard shortcut [Alt Gr] + [<]).
Left	Specifies the distance from a control element to the left-hand edge of its superior control element.
Name	In this property, you can define a name for a component. Delphi does not accept extended characters such as accents in names. However, you can use the underscore in names.
ParentColor	Specifies whether a control element inherits the color of its superior control element.
ParentFont	Specifies whether a control element inherits the font from its superior component.
ParentShowHint	Specifies whether a control element inherits the ShowHint property from its superior component.
PopupMenu	In this property, you can specify a TPopupMenu component that is used as a context menu.
ShowHint	Specifies whether the tooltip for a component is to be displayed.
TabOrder	Specifies the sequence in which the tab jumps from one component to the next. If you use the tab key to jump from one element in a dialog window to the next, you will find that they are set in a fixed sequence. You use TabOrder to define this sequence.
TabStop	Specifies whether the user can jump the control elements by pressing the [⇥] key.
Tag	Used for anything you wish. It is an integer value that is not used by Delphi. Every Delphi component has the Tag property. Other components, such as those from the internet, also have the Tag property and do not use it.
Top	Sets the distance between a component and the upper edge of its superior component.
Visible	Specifies whether a component is visible at runtime. If you set the value of this property to false at runtime, the control element will not be displayed.
Width	Specifies the width of a component.

Table 4.1   *Common properties of Delphi components*

4.1.2 Component Palette Standard page

On the Component Palette Standard page (Figure 4.1) you will find the components that are used most frequently in a Windows application. Users of the Personal Edition will immediately miss the first component, the Frames component (shown in Figure 4.1 shown as the second icon from the left), because frames are not available in this edition.

Figure 4.1 *The Component Palette Standard page*

Frames

A frame is not an independent component, but is more like a container for other components. Components, and the sequence in which they are arranged, are saved in a frame so that they can be used later in a form. The advantage of a frame is twofold: the sequence of the contained components is saved in it, and any changes you make to the actual frame are immediately visible everywhere it has been used. Therefore you can, for example, use a frame to create the basic structure of a dialog and then implement it several times in a program. If you have to change this dialog, you only need to make the change once (by changing the frame itself) and then recompile the program.

From this point of view, a frame behaves just like a component. For this reason, frames are also displayed on the Component Palette once they have been created and saved. However, you should not mistake them for real components. Instead, you should see a frame as a special, reusable kind of form. You can find out more about frames in Chapter 7.

TMainMenu

You can use the TMainMenu component to create a main menu. To specify the individual menu options you can use the Menu Designer, the TActionManager component or a TActionList component. The individual menu options are also components with the type TMenuItem. They have properties and can react to events. However, since they are components that are never used alone, but always in combination with a menu component, you will not find them on the Component Palette. To access the properties of a menu option, mark it in the Menu Designer.

The TMainMenu component has two other interesting properties: AutoHotkeys and AutoLineReduction. The effect of the former is that if you set it to true, Delphi automatically checks whether a keyboard shortcut (a letter with an underscore) has been specified twice, for two different menu options. If it has, then Delphi replaces it so that no keyboard shortcuts are duplicated within one menu. If AutoLineReduction is true, then Delphi automatically removes double (redundant) separators. This is a very helpful function for working with menus in which the menu options are displayed and removed dynamically.

The most important event for a menu option is the `OnClick` event, which occurs if the user clicks on the menu option. In the event-handling routine for this event, you enter the program code for the menu option's functionality.

Another way to define the function of a menu option is to use the `TActionList` component, which provides you with other `TAction`-type components. In Delphi 6, there is yet another way to create menus: the `TActionManager`, `TMainMenuActionBar` and `TToolActionBar` components, with which you can produce menus that mimic those of Microsoft's Office 2000 products. This affects not only their appearance but also the way they behave. As a result, a menu option disappears if it has not been selected for some time.

TPopupMenu

The `TPopupMenu` component is also a menu component. It is a context menu that you can link with any component on the form (or even with the form itself). If you then click with the right-hand mouse button on the component, at runtime, Delphi displays the context menu you have specified.

Some components, such as `TMemo`, already have a context menu with basic functionality by default. If you specify a context menu for such components it replaces the default context menu.

The menu options of a context menu are also of the type `TMenuItem`, so the same rules apply as described for the `TMainMenu` component. `TPopupMenu` can be seen simply as another way of displaying a menu.

TLabel

`TLabel` is the simplest, but most frequently used, component provided by Delphi. It is used to create a label for elements such as an input field or title. You enter the text of the label in the `Caption` property. You can also enter the ampersand character (&) to set an underscore under one of the letters. If a user presses the key ⟨Alt⟩ with that letter at runtime, they can select a particular control element, specified by you. You specify this control element in the `FocusControl` property.

TEdit

The `TEdit` component is a single-line input field, and is very simple to use. Using the component's `Text` property, you can access the contents of the input field. You can define a default text and also evaluate any text entered by the user. The `Text` property is passed as a character string.

`TEdit` also offers other options. For example, a context menu has been implemented in it that contains frequently used functions such as copying, cutting or pasting from the Clipboard. Delphi makes this functionality available without you having to type a single line of program code.

Each input field can also be masked so that it behaves like a password prompt field. To activate this, you specify a character in the `PasswordChar` property that is to appear instead of the user's input.

Using the `AutoSelect` property, you can define whether the contents of the input field are marked automatically when they receive the focus. You are probably familiar with this feature from other Windows programs. You can use the `HideSelection` property to specify that selected text is also displayed as selected when the input field no longer has the focus. To do this, set the property to `false`.

TMemo

`TMemo` is the multiline counterpart to `TEdit`. It is a multiline input field that also has many of the properties of `TEdit`. This includes the context menu with which you can carry out the basic functions of an input field. `TMemo`, like `TEdit`, has a `Text` property in which you can enter text or load the text it contains. Within the memo component, however, the text is also arranged in lines saved in the `Lines` property. This property is a string list (see Chapter 7). As a result, all the methods present in a string list are also available.

The `WordWrap` property is used to automatically break lines. The width of the memo field is important for determining where lines break. Another way to wrap unformatted text in lines is to wrap the text into several lines, and then save them by setting the width of the memo field, assigning a character string to the `Text` property, and then setting the `WordWrap` property to `true`. This allows you to assign basic formatting attributes to huge strings.

As the basic version of the `TMemo` component uses `TStringList` for lines of text, it already has all the same properties as the Windows Editor. You can therefore program a replacement text editor very quickly without needing a lot of programming expertise.

TButton

`TButton` is one of the standard buttons under Windows that you usually find in dialogs. There is another component called `TBitBtn`, which can also display a `Glyph` or icon. However, under Windows 98 and 2000, the use of a `TButton`-type component has become the norm.

If you use `TButton` in a self-defined window, which you want to display modally at runtime, you can close this window automatically when the user clicks this button. To do so, simply set the `ModalResult` property to a value other than `mrNone`. Delphi passes the value of the property to the form and then automatically closes the form. Again, you do not need to enter a single line of program code. If you use several buttons, you can assign to each one a different value for `ModalResult` and then evaluate them later to find out which button the user has clicked.

The `Default` and `Cancel` properties are required for extended navigation. If you set `Default` to `true` for a button, you make it the default button, which means that if the user presses ⏎ this corresponds to a click on that button. The `Cancel` property has the same effect with reference to the Esc key. In this simple way, you can therefore define a default button for OK and CANCEL.

TCheckBox

You can use TCheckBox to display or evaluate Boolean values. The value of the Checked property defines whether the checkbox is marked. There are also checkboxes that are displayed in gray if no defined status can be assigned to them. For example, if you are working in Windows, mark a range of files, some of which are write-protected, and then display the Properties page, you can see a grayed-out checkbox of this kind. In Delphi, you can achieve the same thing by setting the AllowGrayed property to true and then using the State property to define the checkbox's appearance.

TRadioButton

You use the TRadioButton component to select an option. You can use this component if you want to offer the user several settings to choose from but only want one of them to be marked at a time.

You can also specify which radiobuttons belong to a group. To do this, group all the buttons that belong together in the same window-oriented control element. Window-oriented control elements include TPanel, TGroupBox or a form. For example, if you place a TGroupBox component on a form and set some TRadioButton components on it, they are then grouped together. At runtime, Delphi automatically ensures that only one of these radiobuttons can be marked. As for a groupbox, you can use the Checked property to evaluate which of these radiobuttons is marked.

TListBox

TListbox is used to display a list on the screen. The list items are saved in the Items property and are of the type TStrings. At runtime, you can add or delete items to or from the list. You can also save the contents of the list in a file if required. You use the methods in the TStringlist class to add, delete or change list items. If the number of list items exceeds the size of the component, Delphi displays a scroll bar with which the user can also move to the hidden entries. You can set up automatic sorting of all items in the list box by setting the Sorted property to true. Additionally, you can use the MultiSelect property to specify whether the user can mark more than one item in the list. You can find out whether an item is marked by using the Selected method to which you must pass the item's index.

TComboBox

TComboBox provides the drop-down selection fields familiar from Windows. Essentially, they are lists represented in a different way. You can only ever choose one item in a TComboBox. Like TListbox, TComboBox has an Items property of the type TStrings, so you can use the methods of TStrings to add, delete or change items.

To find out which item in the combobox list has been selected by the user, you can either use the Text property or the ItemIndex property. Text then contains the selected item as a string and ItemIndex returns the index of the selected item in the list. If no item has been selected by the user, ItemIndex has the value −1.

TScrollbar

TScrollbar provides you with a way to assign a scroll bar to items without an integrated scroll bar. You can use the LargeChange and SmallChange properties to define how far the marking of the scroll bar moves when a user clicks on the bar itself or the buttons in it. However, you are responsible for programming the movement of the content of the component to which the scroll bar applies.

TGroupBox

TGroupBox is used to group control elements that belong together. If you add a TGroupBox, you can visually separate a group of components from the remainder of the form.

TRadioGroup

TRadioGroup looks like the TGroupBox component, but it has extra properties that are designed specifically for groups of radiobuttons. You can, for example, specify the text for the radiobuttons in the Items property. Delphi automatically creates a radiobutton for each line entered in Items. You can use the ItemIndex property to find out which button is marked. Note that Delphi begins counting at zero in this case.

TPanel

TPanel is a window-oriented control element that you can use to separate a group of components from the remainder of the form. The main differences between it and the TGroupBox component are that TPanel does not provide a title, and that you can use the BevelInner and BevelOuter properties to change the frame of a panel. TPanel is often used to visually split up a form.

TActionList

TActionList is a complex component introduced in Delphi 4 that makes life a lot easier for the programmer. TActionList basically groups all the possible actions that the user can carry out in a program into actions. These actions contain all relevant properties, such as menu titles, tooltips, keyboard shortcuts, etc. Once you have created an action, you can assign several control elements to it, such as the buttons on a toolbar or menu options, or any control element that has the Action property.

You program the functionality in the event-handling routine for the OnExecute event for each action. When this event-handling routine is assigned to a control element, it is linked with its default event (in the case of menu options, for example, this is OnClick). You therefore basically define an action in the same way as a menu option. The difference is that you can reuse the action many times.

4.1.3 Component Palette Additional page

On the Component Palette Additional page (Figure 4.2), you will find other standard elements that are not used very often but do provide essential functionality.

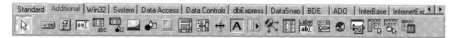

Figure 4.2 *The Component Palette Additional page*

TBitBtn

TBitBtn is a button under Windows. Basically, it has the same properties as the TButton component, but they differ in appearance. TBitBtn can display a graphic together with the text to make the function of the button clearer. Buttons of this kind were very popular in Windows 95 but have since largely disappeared in favor of plain buttons without a graphic.

TSpeedButton

The TSpeedButton component stands for a toolbar button. This component looks different from the usual buttons in dialogs: you can, for example, display it without a frame or make it transparent. I hardly ever use this component because I create my own toolbars using TActionBar or the new TMainMenuActionBar or TToolActionBar components.

TMaskEdit

TMaskEdit is a special kind of input field that allows you to define an input mask, forcing the user to enter data in this field in a particular format (e.g. as a country-specific postal code or telephone number). You define the mask in the EditMask property. If you click the ellipsis button next to the EditMask property, the mask editor opens, in which you can define a mask or select an existing mask.

TStringGrid

TStringGrid is a grid component; it looks like a table whose entries consist of strings. You can specify the number of rows and columns in the table and specify its contents. If required, you can also allow the user to change the contents at runtime. In the FixedCols and FixedRows properties, you can specify fixed columns or rows that are not to scroll when the contents of the table scroll. You can also specify a different color for these fixed columns or rows.

To access the entries in the table you can use the Cells property, which is not published in the Object Inspector. For each field in the table, there is an entry that is defined via the relevant column and row coordinates. The first cell in the table lies at the coordinates [0.0]:

```
Cells[2.3] : 'Column 3, line 4';
```

Since Delphi starts counting at zero, the statement above corresponds to the assignment of a text to the cell in column three, row four. Using the Cells property you can, of course, also evaluate the entries.

TDrawGrid

TDrawGrid is another kind of grid component. Unlike TStringGrid, when using TDrawGrid you must ensure that the table contents are drawn. You are unlikely to use the TDrawGrid component very often.

TImage

TImage is used to display different kinds of images (graphics). You can either specify the graphic that is to be displayed or load a graphic at runtime. The graphic that is to be displayed is saved in the Picture property, which has the type TPicture. TPicture is a class that also provides methods for loading and saving the received data. You can instruct the component to adjust its size to suit the received image. To do so, set the AutoSize property to true. You can also do the opposite. Using the Stretch property, you can size the received graphic to fit into the component. However, note that the proportions of the graphic are not maintained.

TImage also has a new property, Proportional, with which a graphic can always be displayed using the correct proportions. If the actual graphic is smaller than the TImage component, then it will be displayed normally. If it is larger, then it will be scaled down until it is completely visible, while still complying with the defined behavior for the page.

TShape

TShape is used to display geometric shapes in a form. You can use its properties to adjust the appearance of the component in terms of both the outline and the fill. Using the Pen property, you can specify the outline; use the Brush property to specify the color and appearance of the fill.

TBevel

TBevel is a component with which you set a frame round a group of control elements that belong together. The TPanel component is used frequently for this purpose and programmers to tend not to use TBevel. However, Windows handles the two components in different ways. TPanel is a window element that uses resources, whereas TBevel uses (almost) no resources as it is a simple graphical object.

TScrollBox

TScrollBox is a component with which you can define an area in which screen scrolling is enabled. Let us assume you have a graphic that is bigger than the area available in the form. If you set the form's AutoScroll property to true, you can use scroll bars to access and display the invisible part of the graphic. The disadvantage, however, would be that the rest of the form's components, such as the toolbar, would also be subject to the scrolling. To prevent this, use the TScrollBox component. Everything you place within the scrollbox will move during scrolling and all components located outside the scrollbox will remain in their position.

TChecklistBox

TChecklistBox, like the TListBox component, is a list element but it has the additional property of a checkbox next to each item in it. Consequently, you can use this component to check not only whether a list item has been selected but also whether it is marked. For this reason, this component is ideal for use within an option dialog.

Apart from the checkboxes next to the list items, this component and its functionality are identical to TListBox. You can check whether one of the checkboxes is marked by using the Checked property, which you can access at runtime. The same applies to this property as to the list box Selected property.

TSplitter

TSplitter is a splitting component. Within your application, you can use it to provide the same feature as you find in Windows Explorer. Place a component on the form and set the Align property to alLeft. Then place the splitter component on the form and assign it the same alignment. Now all you need is another component, to which you assign the alignment alClient, so that it uses up all the remaining space in the form. At runtime, you can now move the splitter component with the mouse and change the size of the two elements. Using the ResizeStyle property, you can define how the components are displayed during resizing. In the MinSize property, you can specify the minimum size of the component that is aligned on the edge. If this size is exceeded at runtime, it no longer applies. But here too there is an exception. To make the component on the edge disappear if its size falls below the value set in MinSize, set the AutoSnap property to true.

TStaticText

TStaticText, like TLabel, is a component that is used to display text that you specify in the Caption property. The difference between the two is that TStaticText is a window-oriented component.

TControlBar

TControlBar is used to specify the sequence of the components in a toolbar. In it, other components are arranged in zones that the user can move with the mouse at runtime. Usually, TToolbar components are used for this purpose.

Using the ReAlign method, you can instruct the component to rearrange the control elements it contains. You use the AutoDrag property to specify whether the zones in the component can be dragged away when the component is dragged. If AutoDrag is true they can be dragged away, otherwise they remain within the component.

Using the BevelEdges property, you can specify the edges that are to be displayed around the component. BevelKind sets the type of edge. You can use this component to create a toolbar to or from which you can add or remove features, just like in other Windows programs.

TAppEvents

This component is one of the most useful components in Delphi. It contains the most important events that can occur in an application. These are events that affect the application itself, such as `OnDeactivate` if the focus jumps to another application, or `OnMinimize` if the user minimizes the application's main window. You can use the appropriate event-handling routines to react to all these events from this central component.

The component has one property, for its name, and simply provides access to the events in the application. The advantage is that now all events affecting the application can be administered from one place. For example, you can use the event-handling routine in `OnException` to program a central routine for handling any errors that occur; this routine is then also activated if an error occurs in another form instead of the main form. Centralizing the handling of application events makes the program clearer.

TValueListEditor

This component is new in Delphi 6. It is a predefined table element in which a key/value pair can be processed. Using the `Component` and `ComponentProperty` properties, you can link `TValueListEditor` with another component that publishes a string list. If you link `TValueListEditor` with a `TListBox` component, and set the `ComponentProperty` property to `Items`, Delphi will display the list box items in `TValueListEditor`, where they can be processed. You can use this component to create key/value pairs that can then, for example, be saved in the Registry.

The `Strings` property of `TValueListEditor` displays the entries. Each string contains both the key name and the value, separated by the equals sign. The string

```
'Key=5'
```

would display "Key" on the left-hand side and "5" on the right-hand side. You can use the `Names` and `Values` properties to access the names (keys) and values separately.

TLabeledEdit

The `TLabeledEdit` component is new in Delphi 6. It is an example of how two components can be integrated permanently with each other in technical programming terms. The two components are one of the type `TLabel` and one of the type `TEdit`, which both behave as normal. You can use this component to generate an input field that already contains (default) text.

TColorBox

`TColorBox` is also new. It is a combo box from which you can select a color. You can use its `Selected` property to find out which color has been selected. You can also define whether the user has the option of choosing their own color or whether there is to be a default color in the selection list. If the user of the program decides to select their own color, Delphi displays the color-selection dialog box with which you are probably familiar from Windows.

TChart

`TChart` is an extensive component for displaying evaluations. You can use `TChart` to display data graphically in a clear way, in the same way as spreadsheet charts. `TChart` has a large number of properties that influence its behavior and appearance. There is an entire user manual about this component, which tells you something about how extensive it is! This book is not large enough to go into all the options this component provides.

TActionManager

The `TActionManager` component is a powerful tool for creating menus, toolbars or even an Outlook bar. Once again, some individual actions are used more than once. `TActionManager` contains all the information that relates to the layout of self-defined or standard actions. Since you can also use `TActionManager` to reproduce the behavior of Windows 2000 menus (vanishing menu options, etc.), we will come back to this component in Chapter 5 and look at it in more detail. Sadly, this component is one of those missing from the Personal Edition.

TMainMenuActionBar and TToolActionBar

These two components are the actual toolbar and menu bar used with `TActionManager`. They have been created specifically for this purpose. We will describe these components in more detail in Chapter 5. Like the `ActionManager`, these components are missing from the Personal edition of Delphi 6.

4.1.4 Component Palette Win32 page

The Component Palette Win32 page (Figure 4.3) provides components that are typically used in 32-bit Windows applications. Its counterpart is the Component Palette Win 3.1 page, on which you will find the elements that are typically used for Windows 3.x. The components on this Component Palette page are much used and form some of the basic functionality of a Windows program. An example is the `TStatusBar` component, which you can find in every Windows program.

Figure 4.3 *The Component Palette Win32 page*

TTabControl

`TTabControl` provides a sequence of tabs with which you can control the display within a multipage dialog. In contrast to `TPageControl`, `TTabControl` does not provide the tab pages itself, so you are responsible for programming the display to change when the user clicks on a tab.

You specify the tab labels in the `Tabs` property, which is a string list. A tab field is displayed for each line you enter. Using the `TabIndex` property, you can find out which tab is currently active, or you can activate a new tab.

You can place the elements you want to display on `TTabControl`. However, the component only provides a page; you must program in the change of view. The easiest way is to use a `TNoteBook` component from the Component Palette Win 3.1 page. Place the component on `TTabControl` and then specify the same number of pages as the number of tabs present. The code for changing the pages then consists of just one line in the event-handling routine for `OnChange` in `TTabControl`:

```
NoteBook1.PageIndex := TabControl1.TabIndex;
```

This component is useful, for example, if you want to display the contents of different databases on different tabs in the same `TDBGrid` component. In this case, there would be no need to change page; only the contents of the table would need to be refreshed. If you really want to display several independent pages, it is best to use the `TPageControl` component.

TPageControl

You can look at the `TPageControl` component as a big brother of `TTabControl`. `TTabControl` only makes each tab available, but `TPageControl` provides you with a complete page, including the tab. Another difference is at designtime: when you use `TPageControl`, you can simply click on a tab to change the page; when you use `TTabControl`, you have to change the value of `TabIndex`.

To insert a new page in a `TPageControl` component, simply right-click on that component and select the NEW PAGE menu option from the menu. Delphi will insert a new page and a new tab for that page. The individual pages are components that are subordinate to PageControl, and are of the type `TTabSheet`. You can insert all types of visual components into them.

When using `TPageControl`, there are two ways in which you can change pages at runtime. The first is to assign the `TTabSheet` component to the `ActivePage` property, which you will also find in the Object Inspector. `TPageControl` then changes to the specified page, provided it exists. The second way is to use the `ActivePageIndex` property (not published in the Object Inspector) to access the pages. You can also assign this value to the index of the required page, with the result that the `TPageControl` component will change to the relevant page.

`ActivePageIndex` and `ActivePage` always change your value in common, meaning that if you assign a `TTabSheet` component in `ActivePage`, then the value of `ActivePageIndex` will also change correspondingly and display the index of the selected page.

TImageList

The `TImageList` component is a user-friendly graphics list that is usually used in combination with the `TActionList`, `TMainMenu`, `TPopupMenu` or `TListView` components. You can store a number of graphics (images) in this component and access them later via the index. In the case of a menu component, this would mean that you could simply assign the correct icon to each individual menu option via the corresponding index value.

Generally, the `TImageList` component is useful if you use several graphics in the same component. You will find more information about `ImageList` in Chapter 5.

TRichEdit

`TRichEdit` can be seen as the big brother of the `TMemo` component. Although it has the same basic functionality, `TRichEdit` can also process texts in rich text format (RTF) and accordingly offers extended formatting functions. Naturally, you can also use it, like `TMemo`, as a pure ASCII (or ANSI) text processor.

If you want to use `TRichEdit` to process ASCII text, set the `PlainText` property to `true`. The extended formatting functionality is then not available. If you want to process formatted text, note that you should not load it into a normal memo field, otherwise the formatting commands (tags) that are hidden in RTF format will become visible. `TRichEdit` is described in more detail in Chaper 7.

TTrackBar

`TTrackBar` provides a standard Windows sliding control (slider) known as a trackbar in Delphi. Sliders are used frequently in Windows, e.g. there are several in the Windows Volume Control. You can define a settable area for a trackbar, which the user can change at runtime by clicking with the mouse or pulling the slider.

The value of the `Position` property returns the current position of the trackbar. The number of positions is defined by the values in the `Min` and `Max` properties.

If the `TickStyle` property is set to `tsManual`, you can use the `Frequency` property to specify how many tick marks (scale marks) are displayed. For example, if you specify the value 5 for `Frequency`, then a tick mark will be displayed every five units.

TProgressBar

`TProgressBar` is a standard Windows progress display element. Using the `Min` and `Max` properties, you can define the progress bar area. The `Position` property shows the current position of the progress bar. The `StepIt` method in `TProgressBar` is used to advance the display. It is advanced incrementally according to the number of units specified in the `Step` property. Alternatively, you can use the `Position` property to determine the current position of the progress bar.

If you prefer the appearance of the old progress bar (in which the progress bar ran continuously, with no scale), you can use it by setting the `Smooth` property to `true`.

TUpDown

TUpDown is a component that contains two switches for incrementing and decrementing a value. You can use the `Min` and `Max` properties to define the range within which TUpDown is to switch. The current value is returned in the `Position` property. Using the `Increment` property, you can also specify the number of units by which the current value is to be increased if the user activates the switch.

TUpDown itself has no display capability but can be docked on to a component such as TEdit. To implement this, specify the required component in the `Associate` property in TUpDown. TUpDown will resize to suit this component and also align itself to it. With the `AlignButton` property, you can specify TUpDown to align itself relative to the component specified in `Associate`.

THotKey

THotKey is a component with which you can allow the user to define their own keyboard shortcut combination of two or more keys, pressed together or in sequence, unlike a single key (e.g. a function key) that has a macro or other function linked to it and is sometimes, confusingly, also referred to as a "hot key". With THotKey, the user presses the required keyboard shortcut instead of selecting the related menu item from a list. In the properties for the component, you can specify the hotkeys that can be used and specify a default hotkey. The user selects the keyboard shortcut at runtime by pressing the required keys when the input field has the focus.

TAnimate

TAnimate includes the animations that you see in Windows 95, 98 or 2000 in different windows when you are, for example, copying files. Using the `CommonAVI` property, you can specify some of the default animations. TAnimate also allows you to display your own animations. However, it is not possible to output sound files. To display your own animations, specify the required audio video interleaved (AVI) file in the `FileName` property.

TDateTimePicker

TDateTimePicker provides a combo box in which you can enter the date and an input field in which you can use updown buttons to set the time. For the date, the drop-down list is replaced by a typical Windows calendar. Using the property, you can also define the date to be displayed with updown buttons, instead of a combo box, just like the time.

In this component, the format in which the time and date are displayed varies according to the current language (locale) setting. Using the `Date` or `Time` properties, you can query the set date or time. Using `MaxDate` and `MaxTime`, you can restrict the input.

The `Kind` property specifies whether the time or the date is to be displayed. The `DateFormat` property specifies whether the date is to be displayed in a short format or the long format, with the day of the week or the month written out in full.

TMonthCalendar

TMonthCalendar is the calendar that is also displayed in the TDateTimePicker component when you open its combo box. However, the calendar has some other settings. For instance, you can use the MultiSelect property to specify whether several dates can be marked simultaneously, or use the WeekNumbers property to display the number of each week (a value between 1 and 52).

By default, the component shows the current date, written in full, on its bottom edge. You can switch off this display by setting the ShowToday property to false. Using the ShowTodayCircle property, you can also remove the circle that appears by default around the current date.

Using the CalColors property, you can modify the different colors of the component to make them suit the colors used in your application.

TTreeView

TTreeView is used to display a hierarchical structure. You are probably used to this component from Windows Explorer, where it is used to display the folders on the left-hand page. You specify the individual items and subitems in the component in the Items property, which has type TTreeNodes. At runtime, you can use the Add or AddChild methods to add a new node or subitems. For details of the exact procedure, please refer to the example in the Delphi online help.

TListView

The TListView component corresponds to the right-hand page of Windows Explorer. It is a fairly extensive component that contains several display options. The Items property, which is of type TListItems, specifies the items in TListView. The single items there consist of an icon and a label. Since this component can display both small and large icons, you can specify them using an ImageList component. The properties involved are LargeImages, SmallImages and StateImages. In the ViewStyle property, you can also specify the display type. The image (graphics) lists from the LargeImages, SmallImages or StateImages property will be used, depending on which you have specified in the ViewStyle property.

THeaderControl

The THeaderControl component provides a table header for your application, which you can configure in any way you wish. The individual sections in it are of the type THeaderSections. At designtime, you can use the Sections Editor in the Sections property to add new sections. Alternatively, you can add or delete sections or change their properties at runtime.

`THeaderControl` is useful, for example, if you want to create a header row that contains sections on which the user can click for a `TStringGrid` component. The standard header row of a `TStringGrid` or `TDBGrid` component does not provide functionality of this kind, but you can use the `THeaderControl` component to simulate it.

TStatusBar

`TStatusBar` is a status bar with several sections that you will be familiar with from almost every Windows application. You can display the status bar either as a simple bar or with several sections that you specify in the `Panels` property. They are of the type `TPanel` and provide properties with which you can customize the size and various labels and other texts.

Using the `UseSystemFont` property, you can also specify whether the system font is always to be used for the status bar. Alternatively, you can specify a different font. With the `SizeGrip` property, you can specify whether the status bar includes a resizing field. Normally, the status bar is displayed on the bottom window edge, and the top right-hand corner is also the right-hand lower corner of the main window.

TToolBar

The `TToolBar` component provides the complete functionality of a toolbar. All the components that you place on it are arranged automatically. At designtime, you can add toolbar buttons by selecting them from a context menu. The component also has other properties with which you can modify its appearance.

You use the `ButtonWidth` and `ButtonHeight` properties to specify the size of the buttons in the toolbar. Using the `EdgeBorders` property, you can specify which of the component's pages are to have edges. Using `EdgeInner` and `EdgeOuter`, you can also specify their appearance.

You can also display texts (captions) for the individual buttons. To do this, set the `ShowCaptions` property in `TToolBar` to `true`. Delphi then resizes the buttons accordingly.

Use the `Indent` property to specify the size of the gap between the left-hand edge of the toolbar and the first button. If you also want to specify an additional gap above and below, then use the `BorderWidth` property.

You can insert a `TToolBar` into a `TControlBar` or `TCoolBar` component in which it will then be provided with its own section. However, you have to do a lot of programming to make use of this component, especially to control the position of the individual sections.

TCoolBar

`TCoolBar` is a container component for toolbars. It is sometimes also called a rebar. You insert components in a `TCoolBar` and each inserted component is assigned its own section. You can arrange the individual sections in the coolbar component in any way you like. However, if you want to provide different toolbars that the user can "tear off" you should use the `TControlBar` component instead of `TCoolBar`.

I hardly ever use `TCoolBar` because it is quite hard to program. It is basically a standard Windows component and to use it you need Version 4.70 or higher of a file called ComCtrl32.dll. This component is present under Windows 98 and 2000. If you are not sure that the file is also present on the target system for your application, you can obtain more information about supplying the file from Microsoft.

TPageScroller

`TPageScroller` is a component with which you can specify the display area for a component such as a toolbar. If the display area is too small to display all the buttons present, you can use `TPageScroller` to scroll the screen in order to make the invisible elements available. `TPageScroller` can work either horizontally or vertically, but not in both directions at once. For a component whose area is to be enlarged using `TPageScroller`, this means that it must fit into the displaying form in at least one direction.

You can see an example of a `TPageScroller` component in the Delphi IDE if you minimize the main window so that Delphi cannot fit all the components into the Component Palette. The arrow on the right-hand edge shows the `TPageScroller` component in use.

TComboBoxEx

This component is new in Delphi 6. It is a special form of combo box with which you can display not only the usual data entries but also images. To do so, you need to use a `TImageList` component in which the images are contained. The individual entries in the combo box are of the type `TComboBoxExItems`. You can specify which of the images is the default image, which image is to be overlaid if the mouse is passed over the combo box item, and which image is finally displayed when the item has been selected.

4.1.5 The Component Palette System page

On the Component Palette System page (Figure 4.4), you will find some components for programming dynamic data exchange (DDE) and object linking and embedding (OLE). In addition, there are three multimedia components: a paintbox for drawing or painting pixel graphics (bitmaps), a timer (which is, unfortunately, very inaccurate), and an implementation of a media player with which you can run various multimedia device types, including CDs, .AVI files and .WAV files.

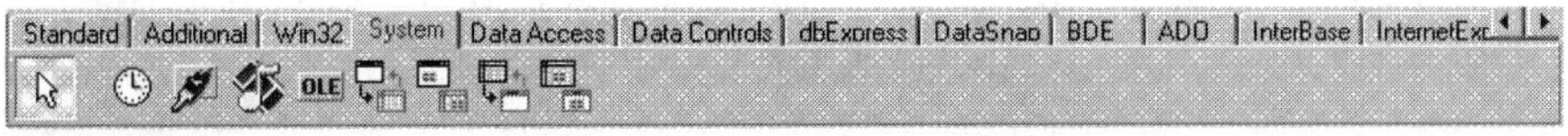

Figure 4.4 *The Component Palette System page*

TTimer

`TTimer` is a component for containing time data. Unfortunately, it is very inaccurate. You can also use it for timed control of events or procedures. For example, you could use this component for switching off a splash screen after a certain period of time. You could also use it for creating one of the nag screens you find in shareware programs.

TPaintBox

`TPaintBox` is used to display or draw an image on the interface. In contrast to `TImage`, the image must be drawn on the interface itself and therefore cannot simply be loaded. Naturally, you can assign an image at runtime, including one that is located on the hard disk. To output an existing image on the drawing area, you can call the `Draw` method in the `Canvas` property in `TPaintBox`.

`TPaintBox` is more suitable for creating your own graphics packages, and almost every book about programming with Delphi uses it as an example. If you only want to display an image, then use the `TImage` component. This also has the advantage that Windows takes over responsibility for drawing the image contained.

TMediaPlayer

With `TMediaPlayer`, you can output almost any multimedia file in your program. `TMediaPlayer` can handle AVI, WAV, CDAudio, videodisc, scanner and many more file types, detailed in the Delphi online help (keyword DeviceType). For example, you can play audio CDs within your program (used in many example programs). You can even play AVI files in a window or in a component of your choice (provided that component contains the `Canvas` property); `TPanel` is a suitable component, for example. You must specify the component concerned in the `Display` property in `TMediaPlayer`.

TOleContainer

`TOleContainer` provides functionality for linking or embedding objects from other OLE-enabled applications. You probably know about it already from other applications. `TOleContainer` automatically combines the menu from its own application with the menu from the OLE application, and also makes the functionality available. There is a set way to implement this. Menus whose `GroupIndex` property is set to 0, 2 or 4 are retained. Menus whose group index is set to 1, 3 or 5 are replaced by menus from the server application of the OLE object.

TDDEClientConv and TDDEClientItem

Using these two components, you can turn your application into a DDE client. A DDE client is a program used to send commands or information to a DDE server and therefore to control the server. The DDE server also sends data back to the client, i.e. they communicate with each other.

TDDEServerConv and TDDEServerItem

Using these two components, you can turn your application into a DDE server. A DDE server responds on requests from a DDE client program. Usually, a program is either a DDE server or a DDE client, but with Delphi you can create programs that are both, a server and a client.

4.1.6 The Component Palette BDE page

Figure 4.5 *Component Palette BDE page*

TDataSource

TDataSource is the component that forms the interface between a data-sensitive control element and a table or query component. It is located on the Data Access page. You will find the data-sensitive control elements on the Data Controls page. The majority of these are well-known control elements to which database functionality has been added.

The only thing you have to specify in the properties of TDataSource is the value of the DataSet property, to which you must assign a data record component. When you do this, the TDataSource component is linked with the data source; you can then use the TDataSource component to link the data-sensitive control element with the data record. Each data-sensitive control element has a DataSource property for that purpose. You can enter the name of the used TDataSource component in it.

There are some real benefits to using TDataSource instead of a direct link between the control element and data source. For example, it makes it easier to change to another table; you simply change the assignment to the DataSet property in TDataSource. You do not need to make any other settings; the control elements linked with the TDataSource component automatically display the values from the newly selected data source.

TTable

TTable is the Borland Database Engine (BDE) implementation of a physical table on the hard disk. Some people call this a complete database, but I prefer to think of it as a table since a database (by definition) can also consist of several tables. In a table you can store data, every data record of which can be uniquely split into individual fields. TTable provides properties for the table name and table type, and also a means to create a link to a database by using an alias. If you do so, all that is needed is the alias; the name of the file and its position are saved in the BDE settings and are automatically called from there.

TTable provides only basic database functionality, such as adding, deleting or changing a data record, functions for sorting and searching, and some rudimentary functions for filtering according to different criteria. Otherwise, you can use this component to create links between databases – so-called *1:n* relationships – in which, for example, a data record in the first database can be assigned to several data records in a second database. You can create relationships of this kind almost without any programming, simply by entering suitable values in the component's properties. However, there is a much more powerful component for working with databases and tables; TQuery.

TQuery

TQuery contains functionality for working with the Structured Query Language (SQL). Although not all SQL functions have been implemented in TQuery, the majority of the command set is available. This makes TQuery much more powerful than TTable, especially in its filtering. The disadvantage is that you have to use the SQL database language. There are many books about SQL and its functionality, containing detailed information about this language's options and advantages. However, this book cannot provide a detailed description of SQL. If you are familiar with SQL, or you need extensive filtered queries in your programs, then TQuery is the component you should choose, assuming you want to use BDE.

TStoredProc

Using TStoredProc you can access a stored procedure in a client/server database. A client/server database has the advantage that the server carries out all the database operations, reducing the amount of data transferred to the client to the minimum possible. The client sends a query to the server. The server filters the appropriate data from the database, or executes the requested operations, and then sends the resulting values back to the client (once again, involving fewer data than if the client was to carry out all operations itself).

It is possible to save frequently recurring tasks as stored procedures on the database server. For the client, this means that they simply trigger the function saved on the database server and then receive the results. I will not discuss the other advantages of a construction of this kind (apart from the low volume of data that has to be transferred) as entire books have been written about this subject. In Delphi, you can use the TStoredProc component to access such stored procedures. If a stored procedure needs parameters to be passed, you can set them in the Params property in TStoredProc.

TDatabase

TDatabase is the component that controls a connection to a database. If you do not insert a database component, Delphi automatically creates an instance called database.

TDatabase also administers transactions. This involves carrying out several database actions simultaneously. If you start a transaction, the data will not be written to the database immediately but will be buffered until you give the command to write to the database. If a conflict occurs, or if you want to interrupt input, then you can undo all the changes you have made.

In Delphi 6, you can also use TDatabase for the following SQL functionality: TDatabase has a method called Execute with which you can use SQL statements without having to use a TQuery component. To do this, when the Execute method is called, the entire SQL statement is passed to it. That statement contains the name of the data source.

This book does not have room for a description of all Delphi's database components, but the most important functions are covered in Chapter 8.

TSession

TSession is one of the components from which Delphi automatically generates an instance if you are working with databases. TSession is used to administer the aliases in a database. These are alternative names that are more convenient for accessing databases. Once an alias has been installed on a system, the programmer only needs to know its name to work with the databases. The real names of the files are no longer required.

If you are working with Paradox databases over a network, BDE creates a file called Pdoxusrs.net. This file exists only once on the network and is used to manage database accesses. The folder in which this file is saved is specified in the NetFileDir property in TSession. All applications that work with the databases must specify the same folder for NetFileDir. You should ensure that you enter the real path (the network path), not just a relative path.

However, in the case of local databases you do not need to bother about NetFileDir or TSession. Delphi creates an instance automatically, and you can use the TTable and TQuery components without making any other settings to access local databases.

TBatchmove

Using TBatchmove, you can move large volumes of data between tables, or change or delete data. Normally, the structures of the source table and target table must be the same. If that is not the case, you can specify an allocation table in the Mapping property in TBatchmove. You use the Execute method to start the operation.

TUpdateSQL

TUpdateSQL is used to update or execute operations on tables that are declared as read-only tables. The user cannot actively change data in databases of this kind, even if the program itself has provided functionality for that purpose. TUpdateSQL can carry out these operations transparently for the user. However, some programmers see this as a failing in the SQL language since it provides a way to get round the read-only restriction.

TNestedTable

You can use this component to insert a complete table into another table as an individual data field. TNestedTable encapsulates the data record of this table, which is then called a nested table. Working with TNestedTable or with nested tables generally, you can rapidly descend into confusion after just a few nestings or encapsulations; it soon becomes impossible to see which table a data record belongs to, whether that table is nested in another table, and so on. For this reason, this component is suitable only for use by experienced database programmers, so I will provide no more details about it.

TBDEClientDataSet

You can use this component, new to Delphi 6, to arrange cached updates over BDE. These are a mechanism that can considerably improve the performance of database applications and are usually used for client/server databases. Changes to a data record are usually made immediately. If the database is being accessed over a network, this logically increases network traffic since actions are executed every time there is a change to a record, meaning data are transferred.

When cached updates are in use, you work locally in your computer's memory. For the time being, no data are transferred. You make your changes and then send them over the network in one go. This speeds up your application, but there are also disadvantages. While you are working with the data that are currently in your computer's memory, the database is unaware of your changes. This means that other users could change the data while you are still busy with your own changes. TBDEClientDataSet is there to let you work with these cached updates. Internally, the component works with a TQuery class and a TDataSetProvider class.

4.1.7 Component Palette Data Controls page

| **Figure 4.6** | **The Component Palette Data Controls page** |

TDBGrid

TDBGrid displays the contents of a database in a table on the screen. A row is reserved for each data record. When designing the database, you can make settings in the properties of the TField components in a TTable or TQuery component to specify which of the table's fields are displayed.

The properties of TDBGrid take more or less the same settings as you find in a TStringGrid component. Using the DataSource property, you can specify the data source (TDataSource component) with which the data source is linked.

TDBNavigator

TDBNavigator is an easy way to provide the user of an application with navigation elements for a database. TDBNavigator is simply linked to a TDataSource and then displays several buttons with which the user can move about within the associated database table.

TDBLabel

TDBLabel has similar functionality to the TLabel component, except that its contents come directly from a table. In the DataSource property you can specify the data source, and in the DataField property you can specify the field whose contents are to be displayed.

TDBEdit

TDBEdit offers the same functionality as the TEdit component, but it is connected to a field in a database. This means that inputs in a field of this kind are only possible if the connected table component (e.g. TTable) is in write or change mode. You will find more details about these modes in Chapter 8.

TDBMemo

The same applies to TDBMemo as to TDBEdit; it is connected to a field in a database table and can also only accept inputs if the connected table component is in write or change mode.

TDBImage

TDBImage is used to display images that are stored in a database. This component is also connected to a database field.

TDBListBox

TDBListBox displays a list field from which the user can select a value for the database field connected to the component. You add values to it using the same procedure as for TListBox. However, if the user selects a value, then it is passed on directly to the database field.

TDBComboBox

TDBComboBox behaves similarly to TDBListBox, but it is a combo box.

TDBCheckBox

TDBCheckBox is another component with which the user can change values within a database. For obvious reasons, you can only change numerical values or texts with a TDBEdit component, but with TDBCheckBox you can display and change Boolean values.

TDBRadioGroup

TDBRadioGroup displays some values, one of which the user can select for insertion into the connected database field. TDBRadioGroup behaves like a TRadioGroup; the value of the marked radiobutton is always the one transferred. You can specify the text that appears for each radiobutton in the Items property in the component. In the Values property, you specify the value that is to be transferred if a radiobutton is selected. If no entry has been made in Values, then a radiobutton's text will be used by default.

TDBLookupListBox

You can use TDBLookupListBox to assign a value that is taken from a database field to a field in another database. To do this, you need a field (such as a customer number) with which you can link the two data sources. You must specify this field in the DataField property for the data volume in which the entry is to be made. For the lookup data source, you specify the appropriate field as a value of the KeyField property. In this way, you create a link between the two databases.

You must also specify which field or fields from the lookup database are to be displayed in the list. Enter these fields in the ListField property in TDBLookupListBox. If the user now selects an item from the lookup list, the value for that item specified in the KeyField field will be taken as a value for the field specified in DataField. Note that it does not matter here which fields are actually displayed in the list box. The display is therefore provided only to make it easier for the user to understand what it going on.

As an example, imagine you are writing an invoice. To do so, you usually require at least two databases: one containing the details for the customers and their addresses, and one containing the actual invoicing data. Only the customer number is saved with the invoicing data, since it does not usually change. Now you would like to select the customers from a list, using their names instead of their customer numbers. You use a lookup list in which you also use the customer number (which is also assigned later) to link the two databases but always display the surname and first name of the customer within the list. That is the purpose of the TDBLookupListBox component.

TDBLookupComboBox

TDBLookupComboBox behaves just like TDBLookupListBox, except that it is a combo box.

TDBRichEdit

Using the TDBRichEdit component, you can save formatted text instead of plain (ASCII) text in a database. This component behaves just like the corresponding non-data-sensitive component TRichEdit, except that it is connected to a database. The same applies to it as to the other data-sensitive control elements, namely that the database component must be in insert or change mode so that data can be entered in it.

If you are using this component, ensure that you are not accessing the database with another application that uses only a TDBMemo component. TDBMemo displays only text, therefore if you used it you would also display the normally invisible formatting codes (tags) used in RTF format. The actual text would then be unreadable.

TDBCtrlGrid

TDBCtrlGrid is a special component that provides another way to display the contents of several data records simultaneously. At designtime, the component provides you with a panel on which you can place different control elements. These can be both data-sensitive and non-data-sensitive elements.

TDBCtrlGrid is linked to a TDataSource component and, at runtime, a panel containing the control elements that you have inserted is displayed for each data record in the connected data source. In this way, you can provide the user with a slightly different overview of the contents of a database.

TDBChart

TDBChart is derived from TChart and consequently has the same properties for displaying diagrams (charts). Charts are arranged in rows, which can contain different data. In the case of TDBChart, the rows receive their data not from the program but from a data source. You can specify a different data source for each row.

4.1.8 Component Palette dbExpress page

The data access components on the Component Palette dbExpress page (Figure 4.7) are aimed primarily at programmers developing applications for use both on Windows and Kylix systems. Kylix does not contain BDE, which works only under Windows. As a result, another means of data access is needed for Kylix. The dbExpress components provide this; they can be used to access different databases such as MySQL, DB2 or Oracle. Unfortunately, you can only access Oracle databases if you have the Enterprise Edition of Delphi.

Figure 4.7 *The Component Palette dbExpress page*

TSQLConnection

The TSQLConnection component creates the connection to a database. When you double-click on the component, a dialog opens in which you can select the required database. Obviously the appropriate database system must also be installed on your system. Figure 4.8 shows the dialog, which in this case uses MySQL as a database link. In the dialog, you simply specify the database server to which the connection is to be created. Delphi creates the actual connection when you set the Connected property to true.

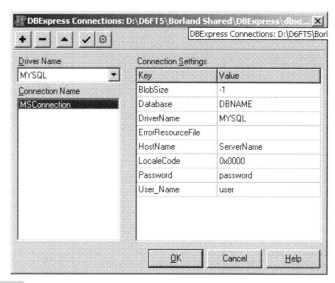

Figure 4.8 *A TSQLConnection to a MYSQL database*

TSQLDataSet

TSQLDataSet is an SQL-based data record component that works in one direction. Unlike human beings, this component cannot work in both directions. If you leave a data record because you have jumped to the next data record, the one you leave is not held in memory and therefore you cannot jump back to it again later. The methods available for navigation are Next and First. Since the data records are not buffered (held in memory), you are also unable to use any features that require them. In addition, there is no automatic support for changing a data record. To do this, you need the Update command, which SQL provides.

You use the TSQLConnection component described above to create the connection to a database.

TSQLQuery

TSQLQuery is used to apply an SQL command to a database table. However, this component is also a unidirectional component, so the same restrictions apply as for TSQLDataSet. You specify the SQL statement that the component is to execute in the SQL property. The SQL statement is executed via the Open method or if you set the Active property to true. You can also use this component to carry out an action that returns no result. To do so, execute the ExecSQL method at runtime.

TSQLStoredProc

TSQLStoredProc, like the two previous components, is a unidirectional database component and is used to execute stored procedures on a database server. Once again, a TSQLConnection component is used to create the connection.

TSQLTable

You can use the `TSQLTable` component to quickly display the contents of a database table. This component generates an SQL query that returns all the data records present in the specified table. As a result, you do not need to enter any SQL statements. This component is also unidirectional, so the limitations mentioned above apply.

TSQLMonitor

`TSQLMonitor` is a logging component used for debugging a database connection. All SQL commands sent to the database engine are saved in a string list and can be displayed. You can therefore use this component to see exactly which commands the database server receives.

TSQLClientDataSet

`TSQLClientDataSet` is similar to `TSQLDataSet`; the difference is that when you use this component, the data records are cached. Unlike the other components, it is not a unidirectional connection. Internally, `TSQLClientDataSet` works with a `TSQLDataSet` component and a `TSQLProvider` component. This file behaves just like a `TClientDataSet` component that is connected to a database via a provider. The only difference is that both `TClientDataSet` and the provider are contained within the component itself.

4.1.9 Component Palette Internet page

You can use the components on the Internet page (Figure 4.9) to write DLLs for your website, which it then uses to react to enquiries from its visitors. An example is the demo supplied with Delphi called WebServ. This is a DLL that can make the contents of databases visible on the web. To create an application with which you can access the features of the internet, use the components on the Component Palette FastNet page.

Figure 4.9 *The Component Palette Internet page*

TClientSocket

You use the `TClientSocket` component to administer a transmission control protocol (TCP)/IP connection. If you use this component, your computer becomes a TCP/IP client. `TClientSocket` provides methods for administering the connection. An example of how to use this component is supplied with Delphi (the Chat demo).

TServerSocket

You can use the `TServerSocket` component to turn your application into a TCP/IP server that other applications can contact, and then manage the connection with them.

TWebDispatcher

`TWebDispatcher` is a powerful component with which you can make a data module internet-enabled. This means that an application can react to Hypertext Transfer Protocol (HTTP) requests and pass them on to the appropriate elements. They then provide a response to the request accordingly.

If you develop a webserver application, Delphi automatically creates a web module. If you later want to integrate a data module that had been implemented using a `TWebDispatcher` component in the application, you must first delete the automatically generated web module. This is because that the web module is also a component for passing on requests, but no application can have more than one of these components.

TPageProducer

`TPageProducer` uses a template to generate a Hypertext Markup Language (HTML) string that a browser can interpret. In this way, `TPageProducer` can convert transparent HTML tags into genuine HTML. `TPageProducer` requires a template, which you can provide either in a file or in the `HTMLDoc` property.

`TPageProducer` only generates the contents of the web page that the user later sees. Before you can really display it, `TPageProducer` must first pass on its result to a `TWebDispatcher` component.

TDataSetTableProducer

The `TDataSetTableProducer` also creates a table in HTML format from the data records in a database but, unlike `TQueryTableProducer`, it cannot process parameters. The data are taken from the data set specified in the `DataSet` property. In that property, the table itself is specified, rather than the `TDataSource` component. The result must be passed on to a `TWebDispatcher` component so that the recipient can see it.

TDataSetPageProducer

The `TDataSetPageProducer` component uses an HTML code template that contains field data to create a string that can process and display a web browser. `TDataSetPageProducer` uses a template in which fields can also be specified. The `OnHtmlTag` event-handling routine is used to generate genuine HTML strings from these fields, which are then passed on to the browser. `TDataSetPageProducer` is able to convert HTML tags that correspond to the contents of fields into the current contents of the field. This means that the component shows the actual contents of the field instead of the field tags. The result must be passed on to a `TWebDispatcher` component so that the recipient can see it.

TQueryTableProducer

The `TQueryTableProducer` component creates a table in HTML format from the data records in a database. `TQueryTableProducer` can also process parameters.

In the `TableAttributes` property, you can specify what the display looks like later. The attributes you set in this property apply to the whole HTML table that is created by `TQueryTableProducer`. In the `DataSet` property, you specify the database table from which the data are to be taken. You do not need to use `TDataSource` in this case as `TQueryTableProducer` generates it internally.

`TQueryTableProducer` can also process parameters for the query, which `TDataSetTableProducer` is unable to do. The parameters come from the object making the query, depending on whether this is a `Get` or `Post` request. The result must be passed on to a `TWebDispatcher` component so that the recipient can see it.

TSQLQueryTableProducer

`TSQLQueryTableProducer` behaves similarly to `TQueryTableProducer`, but it is based on the dbExpress engine rather than BDE.

TTCPClient and TTCPServer

These are TCP/IP components that use the appropriate protocol (TCP/IP) to connect two computers. Among other things, you could use these components to determine whether a TCP/IP connection is present, or to write a server application that you could access using the TCP/IP protocol.

TUdpSocket

Just as you can use the `TCPClient` and `TCPServer` components to program TCP/IP programs, you can also use `TUdpSocket` to program applications that work with a user datagram protocol (UDP)/IP connection.

TXMLDocument

Delphi's Version 6 can now also handle XML. Using this component, you can load and process an XML document and then save it again. Since XML is only plain text, you could also do this with a normal text editor. `TXMLDocument`, on the other hand, can also check the generated XML document to which much stricter rules apply than to an HTML document. Delphi uses an external parser for checking the XML code. You can configure it using the `DOMVendor` property. Under Windows, the Microsoft parser is usually present by default.

TWebBrowser

`TWebBrowser` is a browser component. You can use it to enable your application to display HTML stored either on the internet or locally on the hard disk. `TWebBrowser` uses the browser functions in the Windows System Libraries. Its functionality is so extensive that you could use it to program your own home-made web browser.

4.1.10 Component Palette FastNet page

On this Component Palette page (Figure 4.10) you will find more components for accessing the internet. Using them, you can create your own newsreader or e-mail program, generate a chat program, and much more.

Figure 4.10   *The Component Palette FastNet page*

TNMDayTime

You use the `TNMDayTime` component to call the date and the time from appropriate servers in the internet. The called time is stored in the `DayTimeStr` property. In the `TimeOut` property, you can specify the timeout for the query, in milliseconds. The `Host` property must specify a valid date or time server that can process the query.

TNMMsg

You use the `TNMMsg` component to send a query in ASCII format to a server. That server must obviously also be able to process the query. Suitable components include `TNMMsgSrv` or other components derived from `TNMGeneralServer`.

TNMMsgSrv

You use the `TNMMsgSrv` component to process an ASCII message sent by `TNMMsg`.

TNMEcho

You use the `TNMEcho` component for communication with an echo server in the internet.

TNMFTP

You use the `TNMFTP` component to send files to a file transfer protocol (FTP) server or receive them from one. The component is very easy to use; you simply set the properties whose meaning you already know from using FTP to create a connection (user name, host, password, etc.). Use the `Connect` method to create the connection and the `Disconnect` method to break the connection. The `ParseList` property specifies whether the list of the folders present on the FTP server is to be returned in the `FTPDirectoryList` property. You can then display this list in your application. The folder in which you are currently located is returned in the `CurrentDir` property.

`TNMFTP` also contains other methods with which you can carry out all the operations you expect to find in a standard FTP client. The names of the functions are generally self-explanatory so they are not described in any more detail here.

TNMHTTP

You use the TNMHTTP component for HTTP transfer over the internet. You can receive data from a webserver, send data to a webserver, or generate or delete documents on it. The component provides the following methods for this purpose: Get, Post, Put and Delete. Get and Post are used to receive and send data. The Put method generates a document on a webserver. The Delete method deletes the specified document.

TNMNNTP

Using the TNMNNTP component, you can build your own newsreader. This component contains methods and properties for receiving and sending news posts. Naturally, you can also fetch a list of current newsgroups, otherwise there would be no point. Use the Connect method to create the connection and the Disconnect method to break the connection. After a connection has been created, you can call GetGroupList to fetch a list of available newsgroups.

TNMNNTP also provides methods for downloading the headers of a newsgroup message, the complete message, or a group of message headers on to your computer. If you create your own newsreader, it can have the same functionality as you find in standard programs.

TNMStrm

You use the TNMStrm component to send streams. Just as the TNMMsg component transfers ASCII text, the TNMStrm component transfers streams.

TNMStrmSrv

You use the TNMStrmSrv component to receive streams that have been sent with TNMStrm.

TNMPop3

You use the TNMPop3 component to receive e-mail over the internet. You can write your own e-mail program with it (although to send e-mails, you will need the TNMSmtp component). If you do so, the mail server involved must use the POP3 protocol. Before you can fetch a message, you must use the List method to find out how many e-mail messages are currently present on the server. List also tells you how big each e-mail is. After that, you can use the GetMailMessage method to download individual e-mails, identifying them by their index number.

TNMSmtp

The TNMSmtp component is the other half of an e-mail program. You can use it to send your own e-mail messages with the single network management protocol (SNMP). You specify the message that you want to send in the PostMessage property, and then send it by calling the SendMail method.

You can also check whether a user is logged on to a mail server. They can only send a message if they are. To do so, use the `Verify` method.

TNMTime

The `TNMTime` component works similarly to the `TNMDayTime` component; it fetches the time from an internet server (that supports this kind of query) and stores it in its `TimeStr` and `TimeInt` properties. `TimeInt` records the time in seconds elapsed since 1 January 1900.

TNMUDP

The `TNMUDP` component uses UDP to send data packets over the internet.

TNMURL

The `TNMURL` component codes strings in uniform resource locator (URL) format (a unique internet address) or converts URL details into a readable string.

TNMUUProcessor

The `TNMUUProcessor` component codes and decodes messages in multipurpose internet mail extension (MIME) or UNIX to UNIX encoding (UUencode) format.

TPowerSock

`TPowerSock` is a base component for most FastNet components, and is already implemented in them so you do not usually need to use it. You only need this component as the basis for your own internet components.

TNMGeneralServer

You rarely need to use the `TNMGeneralServer` component as an independent component. Instead, you use it to create your own servers.

TNMFinger

You use the `TNMFinger` component to fetch information about other users or servers in the internet.

4.1.11 Component Palette Dialogs page

Version 6 of Delphi provides ten predefined dialogs that you can use in your applications. They are standard Windows dialogs that are encapsulated in Delphi components.

Figure 4.11 *The Component Palette Dialogs page*

This also means that the appearance of the dialogs varies according to which version of Windows is being used. You simply place the dialog components on the form in which you want to use them. You use each dialog's `Execute` method to call it. `Execute` returns a Boolean value that shows whether the user has left the dialog by clicking [OK] or [Cancel]. If they have clicked [OK], then the component returns `true`; if they have clicked [Cancel], or quitted the dialog, the component returns `false`.

Dialogs for opening and saving files

Delphi provides four dialogs for opening and saving files. Two of these dialogs were developed specifically for opening or saving image files and display a preview of a selected image in the dialog. Table 4.2 gives an overview of the properties in the dialogs used for opening and saving files.

Property	Meaning
DefaultExt	Specifies a default file extension that Delphi uses if the user enters only the file name without a file extension. When you enter a value in `DefaultExt`, enter the file extension without the period (full stop) that divides it from the filename.
FileName	Returns the file name that has been selected or entered. You can also specify a file name that is displayed by default when the dialog is opened.
Filter	Sets the different possible filters for the dialog ("text files", "all files", etc.).
FilterIndex	Fetches from the filter list the index of the filter that is to be active by default when the dialog is opened.
HelpContext	Help context value for calling online help.
InitialDir	Specifies the default directory for the dialog. You can set `InitialDir` yourself, otherwise the current program directory is used as a default (or the My Documents directory, depending on the version of Windows).
Name	The name of the dialog.
Options	Different options that affect the way the dialog behaves and how it is displayed.
Tag	A freely available `integer` value that is not used internally by Delphi.
Title	Title of the dialog, displayed in the title bar.

Table 4.2 *Properties of dialogs for loading and saving*

`TOpenDialog` and `TOpenPictureDialog`

Dialogs for opening and saving files of all types are often used in programs. The dialogs that Delphi provides you with are standard Windows dialogs, so they already contain all the necessary functionality for creating new folders, etc. (as you will see by looking at the dialog buttons). When you look at the dialog, it may be slightly different from the one shown in Figure 4.12, as all the screenshots in this book were made under Windows 2000.

Note that the dialog returns only the name of the file that is to be opened or saved. You have to program the actual loading or saving process. Delphi returns the entire file name including the complete path. Figure 4.12 shows the dialog for opening a file.

The only difference in the dialog for opening an image file, `TOpenPictureDialog`, is that it displays a preview of the image and any predefined filters for different image files. The options or methods are the same.

The `Execute` method for calling the dialog returns `true` if the user clicks the ⟨Open⟩ button, otherwise it returns `false`.

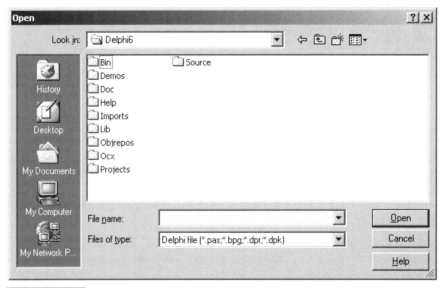

Figure 4.12   *Dialog for opening a file*

TSaveDialog and TSavePictureDialog

These dialogs have almost the same structure as the file-opening dialogs, except that instead of the ⟨Open⟩ button, they have the ⟨Save⟩ button. Accordingly, the properties of the dialogs are also identical. Again, the dialog for saving images differs only through its integrated preview and the predefined filters for different image formats.

TFontDialog

When a user is working with text files, it is useful to provide them with a dialog in which they can select a font. Delphi provides a standard dialog for this purpose, which contains the selected font. The user can also choose different font attributes such as italic, bold or underlined. Figure 4.13 shows the dialog for selecting a font.

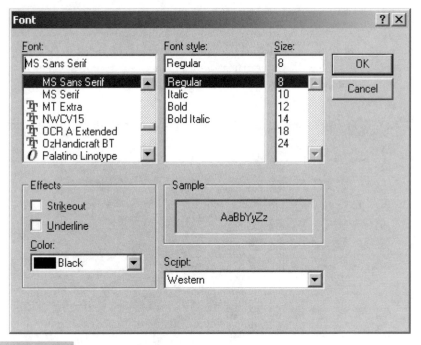

Figure 4.13   *The font dialog*

This dialog also has several properties, which are listed in Table 4.3.

Property	Meaning
Device	Specifies the kinds of fonts that are to be displayed in the selection list. `fdScreen` displays the screen fonts, `fdPrinter` displays the printer fonts, and `fdBoth` displays both kinds of fonts.
Font	In the `Font` property, the selected font is returned with all its attributes. You can specify a font in Font in the Object Inspector before the dialog opens, which is then displayed as the default font.
HelpContext	Enter the value for the help topic context that is to be used to call the help file.
MaxFontSize	Specifies the maximum user-selectable size for the font. Does not apply unless the `fdLimitSize` flag is set in Options.
MinFontSize	Specifies the minimum user-selectable size for the font. Does not apply unless the `fdLimitSize` flag is set in Options.
Options	Different options with which you can customize the appearance and behavior of the Font dialog.

Table 4.3   *Some properties of the Font dialog*

TColorDialog

Using the `TColorDialog` dialog, you can change colors. The color is returned as a value of the type `TColor`, which you can immediately pass on to the `Color` property of a component. Using the Color dialog, you can also define your own colors or allow the user of your application to define them. Figure 4.14 shows the entire dialog.

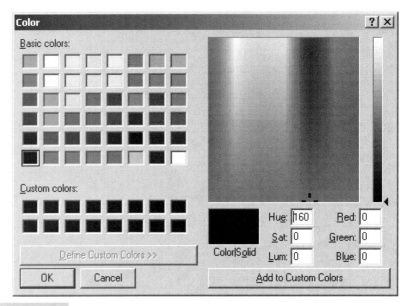

Figure 4.14 *The Color dialog*

The Color dialog also provides some properties, the most important of which are shown in Table 4.4.

Property	Meaning
Color	Contains the color that the user selects after they click the ![OK] button. The default color is `clBlack`, but you can also set a different default color in this property.
CustomColors	Contains the additional, self-defined colors available in the dialog.
HelpContext	Enter the value for the help topic context that is to be used to call the help file.
Name	The name of the dialog.
Options	Different options with which you can customize the appearance and behavior of the Color dialog.
Tag	A freely-available `integer` value that is not used internally by Delphi.

Table 4.4 *The properties of the Color dialog*

Find and Replace dialogs

Every application that processes texts needs a dialog for searching for, and replacing text chunks. Delphi provides two standard dialogs for this purpose, but they do not implement an algorithm for searching or replacing. You must program the search or replace yourself. The two dialogs contain events that occur if a user clicks on the `Find Next`, `Replace` or `Replace All` buttons. In addition, they return the input text for which Delphi is to search, and the text with which it is to be replaced, in a property.

Figures 4.15 and 4.16 show the dialogs for searching for and replacing text.

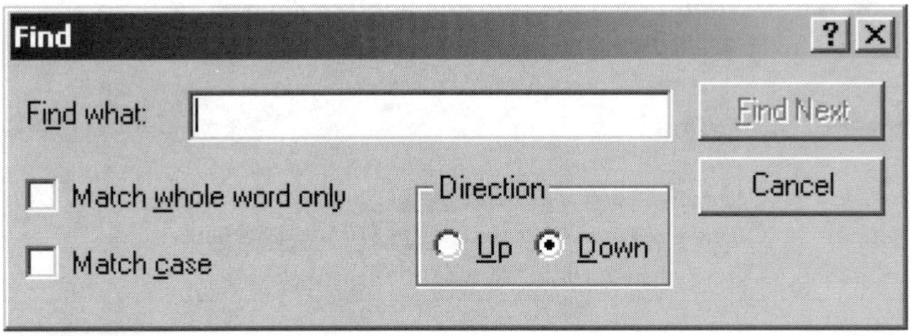

Figure 4.15 *The Find dialog*

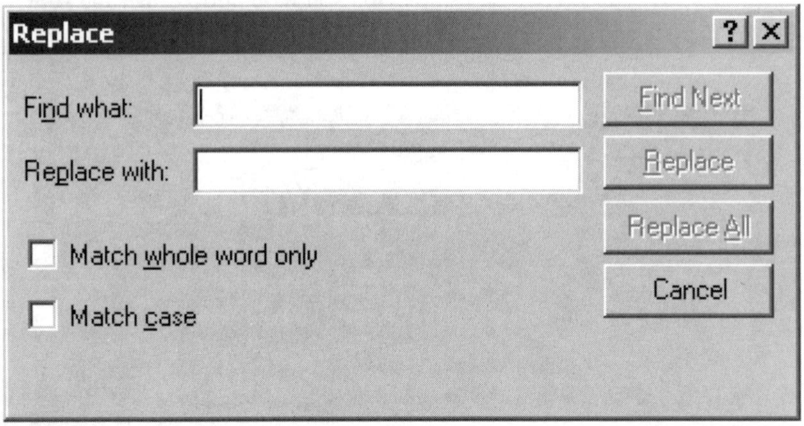

Figure 4.16 *The Replace dialog*

Table 4.5 lists the properties of the two dialogs. Note that not all properties listed apply in both dialogs.

The dialogs provide three important properties in whose event-handling routines you must program the dialogs' functionality. They occur when the user clicks the associated buttons in a dialog. However, this does not close the dialog. Table 4.6 shows these events and when they occur.

Property	Meaning
FindText	Contains the text that is to be found.
HelpContext	Enter the value for the help topic context that is to be used to call the help file.
Options	Different options with which you can customize the appearance and behavior of the two dialogs.
ReplaceText	The text with which the found text is to be replaced.

Table 4.5   *Properties of the Find and Replace dialogs*

Event	Meaning
OnFind	Occurs if the user clicks the [Find Next] button.
OnReplace	Occurs if the user clicks the [Replace] or [Replace All] button.
OnClose	Occurs when the dialog closes.

Table 4.6   *The events used in the Find and Replace dialogs*

These dialogs have another special feature. You will have noticed that the same event occurs for Replace and Replace All. Delphi differentiates between them by using two

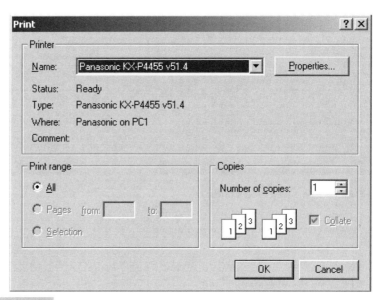

Figure 4.17   *The Print dialog*

flags in the dialog's options. If the user clicks on the [Replace] button, Delphi sets the `frReplace` flag and deletes the `frReplaceAll` flag. The opposite happens if the user clicks on [Replace All] button; Delphi sets the `frReplaceAll` flag and deletes `frReplace`. You therefore have to evaluate these flags if you use the Replace dialog.

The Print dialog

Delphi also provides a standard Windows dialog for printing a file (Figure 4.17). In it, you can make a variety of settings, but the dialog does not take control of the actual print process.

Any settings you make within the dialog are returned in its properties so you can easily evaluate them. Table 4.7 lists the properties of the Print dialog.

Property	Meaning
Collate	Is `true` if the COLLATE checkbox is selected in the Print dialog.
Copies	Contains the number of copies specified in the dialog.
FromPage	Contains the value in the (PAGES) FROM: field in the dialog.
HelpContext	Enter the value for the help topic context that is to be used to call the help file.
MaxPage	Specifies the maximum number of pages that the user can enter for printing.
MinPage	Specifies the minimum number of pages that the user can enter for printing.
Options	Different options with which you can customize the appearance and behavior of the Print dialog.
PrintRange	Indicates which print range has been specified in the dialog (ALL, SELECTION or PAGE(S) FROM: & TO:).
PrintToFile	This property is `true` if the PRINT TO FILE checkbox has been selected in the dialog. If you want the checkbox to be selected by default, set this property to `true` before calling the dialog.
ToPage	Contains the value entered in the TO: field in the Print dialog.

Table 4.7   *The properties of the Print dialog.*

Print Setup dialog

Using the Print Setup dialog (Figure 4.18), you can select a printer for use. However, if you change the settings for the printer, they do not permanently override the system control settings; they apply only during this session with your application. When you work with other dialogs, you have to program other actions; but that is not necessary here. The printer is reconfigured and you can simply start printing.

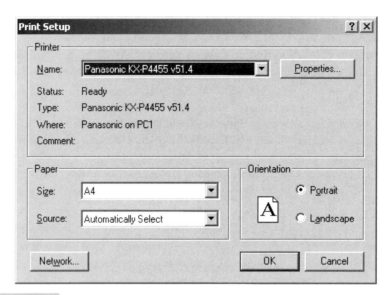

Figure 4.18 *The Print Setup dialog*

As the settings in this dialog apply immediately, it has no special properties. It has only the `Name`, `HelpContext` and `Tag` properties, with which you are already familiar, and the `CTL3D` property, which is provided for backwards compatability with early versions of Windows.

4.1.12 Component Palette Samples page

The Component Palette Samples page in Delphi 6 contains examples of customized components. Four of these were omitted in the last few releases, although they were very useful and had to be created separately, over and over again, requiring much time and effort. For this reason, this page is described in detail below.

TShellTreeView

`TShellTreeView` displays a representation of the directory structure of the hard disk and behaves just like the left-hand pane of the Windows Explorer window. You can use the `ShellListBox` and `ShellComboBox` properties to integrate the components with other components that are optimized for file access.

TShellComboBox

`TShellComboBox` behaves like the drop-down list that you see in the dialogs for loading and saving files. It also displays a list of disk drives or folders. This component can also be integrated with the other control elements that are optimized for file access, such as `TShellTreeView`.

`TShellListView`

`TShellListView` behaves like the right-hand pane of the Windows Explorer window. You can use its properties to specify how the contents of a particular folder are to be displayed, or to open the displayed folders or files, or to start displayed programs. If you use a `TShellTreeView` component together with a `TShellListView` component, you can very quickly program your own replacement Explorer without having to type much program code; the majority of the functionality is already contained in the components. For example, if you click with the right-hand mouse button on an element such as a folder, you will see exactly the same context menu as in Windows Explorer.

`TShellChangeNotifier`

`TShellChangeNotifier` is a component for monitoring a folder. If something in that folder changes, such as a file name or the size of a file, this triggers an event in which you could, for example, load a new file tree structure. The component can also monitor all subfolders in just the same way; so you can, for example, check all changes made on one drive.

4.2 Base classes of a program

For every program, Delphi provides some classes that you will not find in the Component Palette. They are generated automatically and are made available for you to use at runtime. You can use these classes for a variety of tasks, such as evaluating system characteristics and reacting to system events.

4.2.1 `TApplication` class

The `TApplication` class is the basis for every Delphi program. The tasks that `TApplication` deals with include the administration of Windows messages, online help calls and exception administration. Delphi automatically creates an instance of `TApplication` for each program so you can access the methods, properties and events in this class at runtime. To access the events, you can use the `TAppEvents` component. This makes available the events of `TApplication` just like a normal component. When generated, the class is automatically assigned the name `Application`.

`TApplication` properties

You must access the properties and methods directly. However, some properties are available only for read-only access. For example, you cannot change the value of the `ExeName` property in `TApplication`, since it is the name of the executable file for your application. In the online help in Delphi, you will find more information about the individual properties; Table 4.8 lists their most important properties.

Property	Function
ExeName	To find out the name of the current application. Delphi returns the entire application name, including the complete path.
Title	To change the name of the application for display, e.g. when its window is minimized. You can also make this setting in the Project Options for the application.
Hint	If the user moves the mouse over a control element, its Hint property is assigned to the Hint property in TApplication. Consequently, you can use Application.Hint to find out the hint text of the control element over which the mouse is currently passing.
HintColor	In this property you can specify the color of an application's hint windows. To do so, simply assign a value of the type TColor to the property.
HintHidePause	Specifies how long a hint text is to be displayed for if the mouse pointer remains over a control element.
HintPause	Specifies how long Delphi waits before displaying a hint text if the mouse pointer remains over a control element.
Icon	Specifies which icon is to be displayed if the application is minimized.
MainForm	Specifies which window is the main window of the application. You can also specify the main window yourself, but you should do so in the Project Options.
ShowMainForm	Specifies whether the main form of the application is displayed when the application starts. To suppress the main form display, set the form's Visible property to false, and set the ShowMainForm property to false in the source code, before the Application.Run call.

Table 4.8   *The properties of the* TApplication *class*

TApplication methods

As this class also deals with Windows messages and exception handling, it also contains some methods that access the Windows system. These are not the same methods as are used to access the Windows API. Table 4.9 lists the methods in TApplication.

The most frequently used method is probably Application.MessageBox. This method contains only a call to a Windows API routine, which you could obviously also call directly.

4.2.2 TScreen *class*

At runtime, each Delphi application provides an instance of the TScreen class called Screen. You can use this to access the properties of the screen, the current form and

Method	Function
Terminate	Ends a program in the normal way. You can use this command to end a program before it has completed.
Minimize	Reduces the application's main window to an icon on the Windows task bar.
Restore	Restores the application's main window if it has been minimized.
MessageBox	Displays a Windows message window in which you can customize the title and message and specify which buttons it contains.
ProcessMessages	Allows Windows to process messages from other applications or processes. This is useful because it means the system is not inactive when you execute an action that requires a lot of resources (e.g. printing) in your program.
BringToFront	Brings the last active window to the front.
HelpCommand	Sends a command to Windows help.
HelpJump	Specifies the ID of a help topic to display its contents.

Table 4.9 *Some methods in the TApplication class*

its components, and also the installed fonts or mouse pointer. Table 4.10 lists some of the properties of TScreen. Note that some of them are read-only. For more details, look in the online help using the keyword TScreen.

Property	Meaning
ActiveForm	Tells you which form currently has the input focus.
Cursor	Changes the mouse cursor setting globally. In the default setting, crDefault, the appearance of the mouse cursor changes according to the control element over which it is located.
Cursors	Lists all cursor shapes available for the application.
Fonts	Contains all fonts supported by the screen.
Height	Contains the height of the screen in pixels.
Width	Contains the width of the screen in pixels.
MenuFont	Sets the font used for menus.
HintFont	Sets the font used for hints.
IconFont	Sets the font used for icon labels in dialog fields for loading or saving files.

Table 4.10 *The main properties of the* TScreen *class*

You can access the properties to get information about the user's system. The values for the width and height of the screen are useful, for example, if you want to make the size of the main window display dependent on the screen resolution. The system font details are useful if you want to list all fonts in a menu or list for selection by the user. The names of the system fonts are provided in a `TStringList`-type list so they can be used immediately.

4.2.3 `TPrinter` class

Delphi automatically creates an instance of the `TPrinter` class, but you must integrate the corresponding unit, called `Printers`, in which the class is defined in your program. To do so, simply insert it in the `Uses` clause of the unit from which you want to address the printer. The name of the generated instance is `Printer`.

`TPrinter`, besides allowing you to access the printer, supplies information about the installed printers. You can use it to select a printer. Usually, however, you use the Print Setup dialog as it carries out the selection of a printer for you.

`TPrinter` properties

Like the other base classes, `TPrinter` also provides some properties that you can access at runtime. Some are read-only properties. Table 4.11 lists the properties and their functions.

Property	Meaning
Aborted	Shows whether the user has interrupted the print job.
Canvas	Represents the surface of the sheet that the printer prints. Using Delphi's drawing methods, you can output graphics directly on the printer's `Canvas`. However, these operations may fail on printers that do not support graphics.
Capabilities	Shows the current properties of the printer driver.
Copies	Returns the number of printed copies.
Fonts	Contains a list of the installed printer fonts.
Handle	Accesses the printer object's handle.
Orientation	Contains details of the orientation of the page, either vertical (`Portrait`) or horizontal (`Landscape`).
PageHeight	Returns the height of the page in pixels.
PageNumber	Returns the number of the page that has just been printed.
PageWidth	Returns the width of the page in pixels.
PrinterIndex	If several printers are installed, this returns the index of the selected printer.
Printers	Contains a list of the installed printers.
Printing	`true` if the printer is currently printing.
Title	Specifies which text appears in the Print Manager (Owner column).

Table 4.11 *The properties of the* `TPrinter` *class*

TPrinter methods

You can use the methods provided by `TPrinter` to control, start or cancel printing. Two of these methods, `BeginDoc` and `EndDoc`, are very important. If you call `BeginDoc`, all write and drawing procedures are diverted to the printer; if you call `EndDoc`, this starts the actual printing. This means that if you start a printout, you will not see any results on the printer until you call `EndDoc` to end the print job. Table 4.12 lists the most important methods in `TPrinter`.

Method	Function
Abort	Interrupts the current print job, cancelling all unprinted data.
BeginDoc	Starts the print job. After it, data can be sent to the printer. However, the data are not actually printed out until the `EndDoc` method has been called.
EndDoc	Ends the sending of data to the printer. After `EndDoc` has been called, the actual printing starts.
GetPrinter	Obtains informaton about the current printer.
NewPage	Forces a page break and increments the PageNumber property.
Refresh	Updates the `Fonts` and `Printers` properties for the class.
SetPrinter	Changes to another printer that is installed but currently inactive.

Table 4.12 *The methods of the* `TPrinter` *class*

For more details, look in the online help using the keyword `TPrinter`. There, you will also find an informative example of how to use the class.

Basic elements of an application

Forms are the basis of every Delphi program. In each application, there is always one main form that Delphi generates automatically which, unlike all other forms, is also displayed automatically on the screen.

5.1.1 Main form of the application

The main form provides the interface between the user and the program functions. It usually contains three main elements that you find in almost every application under Windows: a main menu, a toolbar and a status bar. As a Delphi application always has one main form, if you create a new application, the first form that Delphi provides you with is set automatically as the main form. However, if you want to specify another form as the main form, you can simply change the setting in the application's Project Options.

5.1.2 Displaying forms

If you have created several forms, you can display them in two different ways at run-time: modal and non-modal. The difference between these is that modally displayed windows, such as dialogs, stop the program until they have been closed, whereas non-modally displayed windows are displayed (and can also contain and run functions) but the program still runs on while they are doing so. You can use these commands to display a window on the screen:

```
Form2.ShowModal;   //Modal display
```

or

```
Form2.Show;        //Non-modal display
```

To remove a window from the screen again, call one of these methods; Close or Hide:

```
Form2.Close;   //Closes the window
```

If a window is displayed modally, you first need to know when the user has clicked one of the buttons for closing it. Since a modal window stops the program, you must program this functionality into the unit of the displayed window. Simply add the `Close` command to the button's `OnClick` event-handling routine:

```
procedure Button1Click(Sender: TObject);
begin
  close;
end;
```

It is even easier to use the button's `ModalResult` property. You use this property to determine which button in the dialog has been clicked by the user. You can set one of the predefined values, such as `mrOk` or `mrCancel`. Delphi will then close the window automatically if the user clicks the button so you do not need to write an event-handling routine. In the routine that has called the window, you can then evaluate the form's `ModalResult` property to determine which button has been clicked.

Tip You are not restricted to evaluating the value of `ModalResult`. `ModalResult` returns a numerical value, which you usually use to determine which button the user has clicked. However, you can also directly return a string or another data type. Declare the string in the `public` section of the called form so that you can use the same variable name for different forms. Assign the appropriate value to the variables when the form closes. When the form closes, it is still present in memory, so the contents of the variables are still present and can be queried within the calling unit. In this example, I have called the relevant variable `ModalString`:

```
procedure TForm1.Button1Click(Sender: TObject);
var
   MyValue: String;
begin
  //Form1 is the calling form
  //Form2 is the called form
  //This source code naturally comes from Form1

  Form2.ShowModal;
  MyValue := Form2.ModalString;
    ...
end;
```

5.1.3 Creating forms at runtime

Delphi usually creates all forms in memory when their program runs; you only have to write program code to display them. However, this has a disadvantage; each generated form, regardless of whether it is displayed, uses up memory. For this reason, you can also choose to create a form yourself at runtime, in a very simple way, at the time you need it. However, you must also then ensure that the form is removed from memory again:

```
procedure TForm1.Button1Click(Sender: TObject);
begin;
   Form2 := TForm2.Create(Application);  //Create
   Form2.ShowModal;                      //Display
```

(It is assumed that the buttons on the form have had values for ModalResult assigned to them so that the form closes automatically if the user clicks on a button.)

```
   if Form2.ModalResult=mrOk then        //Evaluate
   begin;
      //Statements if Ok has been clicked
   end
   else
   begin;
      //Statements if Ok has not been clicked
   end;

   Form2.Release;    //Remove form from memory
end;
```

The procedure above generates a form provided you have previously created it. The form is displayed modally, Delphi evaluates which button has been clicked, and then the form is removed from memory.

> **Tip** If you want to access the contents of components in this self-generated form, such as an input field, you must do so before you remove the form from memory, otherwise the components (and the data they contain) will no longer be available.

5.1.4 Evaluating form contents

You can access a component in a form in the normal way provided you also specify the name of the form on which the component is located. The reason for this is that different forms can contain components with the same names. If you do not reference via the form name, then you can only access components that are declared within the calling form:

```
procedure TForm1.Button1Click(Sender: TObject);
var
    MyString : String;
begin;
    Form2.ShowModal;
    if Form2.ModalResult=mrOk then
        MyString := Form2.Edit1.Text;
end;
```

Tip You can use API functions to define a different appearance for forms. For example, you can create a form that is always on top. To do so, call the SetWindowPos function (you cannot do so by setting the FormStyle property to fs_StayOnTop, as this applies only to the application in which the form is located):

```
procedure TForm1.Create(Sender: TObject);
begin;
    SetWindowPos(Handle,
                 HWND_TOPMOST,
                 Left,
                 Top,
                 Width,
                 Height
                 SWP_SHOWWINDOW);
end;
```

The Windows API also offers other options for creating effects. Using the SetWindowLong and GetWindowLong functions, you can also remove a title bar from a form. GetWindowLong returns a form's display attribute and SetWindowLong sets it:

```
procedure TForm1.FormCreate(Sender: TObject);
begin
  SetWindowLong(Handle,
                GWL_Style,
                GetWindowLong(Handle,GWL_Style) and
                (not WS_Caption));
  Height := ClientHeight;
  Refresh;
end;
```

Naturally, you can also access other components. However, you must ensure that the form whose components you are accessing has been generated. It need not necessarily be visible on screen, but it must be generated in memory.

5.1.5 Transparent forms

In previous releases of Delphi, it took a great deal of effort to generate a transparent or half-transparent form, but with Delphi 6 this is no longer a problem. The TForm component now has a property called AlphaBlend with which you can specify whether the form is transparent when it is displayed. Using the AlphaBlendValue property, you can define how transparent the form is. The lower the value, the more transparent the form. These properties are useful for a variety of effects, such as making a form appear or disappear. The following program code shows how you could make a form appear slowly at runtime:

```
procedure TForm1.FormActivate(Sender: TObject);
var
  i: integer;
const
  u = 10;
begin
  if self.AlphaBlendValue<255 then
  begin;
    for i:=0 to (255*u) do
    begin;
      AlphaBlendValue := i div u;
      Application.ProcessMessages;
    end;
  end;
end;
```

Naturally, the result of this code cannot be displayed as an image. The form appears from nothing and seems to become more and more substantial until it has finally materialized completely. In this example the form appears very slowly but still in an acceptable way.

The for loop, in which the value constantly increases, is responsible for the speed at which the form appears. AlphaBlendValue is changed in accordance with this value. You can speed it up or slow it down by changing the value of the u constant.

You can make the form disappear in a similar way simply by running the loop the other way and counting backwards.

5.2 Menus

Menus are an important element in Windows applications since they provide users with a way to access all the functions in a program. An application has a main menu and context menus to which you can assign individual components. A form can only ever have one main menu, but each component on the form (and the form itself) can have a context menu like the small menus you often see when you right-click on an element in Windows.

5.2.1 Menu Designer

If you place a menu component on the main form and double-click on it, the Menu Designer opens. It does not matter whether the menu component is a `TMainMenu` component for a main menu or a `TPopupMenu` component for a context menu. Figure 5.1 shows the Menu Designer for a main menu.

You can easily define new menu options by marking them in the Menu Designer and then adding a value for their `Caption` property. Delphi uses the text typed in `Caption` to create the name of the menu option, but you can also define your own name. The empty fields with a dotted border are new menu options that are not in use yet.

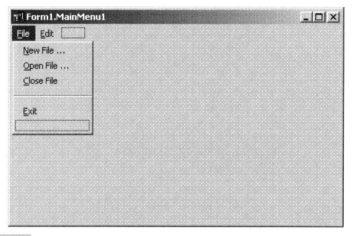

Figure 5.1   *The Menu Designer*

Separators

A menu usually contains separators. You can create a separator by typing a minus sign in the `Caption` property. Delphi then inserts a horizontal line for the separator.

Submenus

In many applications, you will see subitems in a menu option. You can also generate such submenus with Delphi. To do so, right-click on an existing menu option and select CREATE SUBMENU from the context menu.

Keyboard shortcuts

You can also define the usual Windows keyboard shortcuts (hotkeys). These are shown as underscored characters in a menu or a menu option. In the Caption, you simply enter the "&" character in front of the letter you want to underscore. That letter then appears with an underscore in the menu or menu option. Note that this is not the same as the keyboard shortcut you define in the ShortCut property.

Defining menus

Each form can display one main menu, but you can define more than one. The form itself (and each component in it, if appropriate) can also have a context menu.

The form's main menu is displayed only if the FormStyle property in the form has the value fsSizeable. There is not much point in having a main menu in dialog windows. In contrast, you can assign a context menu to every form or component by means of the PopupMenu property. In this way, you can also assign several components to the same context menu.

Property	Function
AutoHotkeys	Set to true so that Delphi checks the keyboard shortcuts used in the menu. Delphi then ensures independently that no keyboard shortcut appears twice.
AutoLineReduction	Set to true if you want Delphi to check whether two separators follow each other immediately. One of these separators is then removed automatically.
AutoMerge	If you are using subforms in a single-document interface (SDI) application and want to link their menus to the application's main menu, set AutoMerge to true. This happens automatically for multiple-document interface (MDI) applications.
BiDiMode	Used if you are writing a program in a language that is not written from left to right, such as Hebrew or Arabic.
Images	Specifies which TImageList component is to be used for the images that are to appear in the menu.
Items	Contains the names of the individual menu options.
OwnerDraw	Set to true to influence how the elements in a menu are to be drawn, e.g. in a color menu you could display colored bars instead of the color names.
ParentBiDiMode	If this is true, then the value of the BiDiMode property is taken from the superior element (usually the form).

Table 5.1 *Properties of the* TMainMenu *component*

5.2.2 Menu templates

In the Menu Designer's context menu, you can access complete, predefined menus stored as templates. To open the context menu, right-click in the Menu Designer. To transfer a complete, predefined menu to the Menu Designer, select the INSERT FROM TEMPLATE menu option. Delphi provides a number of these menus as standard.

You can also store one of your own menus as a template. The context menu contains the menu option SAVE AS TEMPLATE for this purpose.

5.2.3 Important properties

Table 5.1. lists the menu properties.

5.3 Toolbars

Another vital component of a program is the toolbar, which usually includes the program's most important features. Often, these toolbars can also be modified, i.e. you can specify which components they are to contain. The toolbar component is called `TToolbar`. When you place this component on a form, it is positioned automatically under the main menu.

You use the context menu to assign new buttons to a `TToolbar` component. The button components are `TToolbutton` components, which have their own properties. You can also insert separators in the same way to group buttons together.

5.3.1 `TToolbar` properties

The `TToolbar` component has a large number of properties, most of which you can ignore. The most important properties are listed in Table 5.2.

5.3.2 `TToolbutton` properties

The buttons in `TToolbutton`-type components also have a few properties; Table 5.3 lists them.

5.3.3 Grouping buttons

You can combine the buttons in a toolbar into a group. However, in this group, only one button can be clicked at once, so the others automatically remain unclicked. Before a button can belong to a group, the following properties must be fulfilled:

➜ the button's `Grouped` property must be set to `true`;

➜ the button's `Style` property must be set to `tbsCheck`.

Property	Meaning
BorderWidth	Indicates the width of the space around the buttons. Usually, the toolbar is as high as the buttons, but you can use this value to increase the space as required.
ButtonHeight	Specifies the standard height of a button.
ButtonWidth	Specifies the standard width of a button.
DisabledImages	If necessary, you can specify a TImageList component with the images that are to be used if a button is unavailable ("disabled").
EdgeBorders	Specifies which sides of the toolbar are drawn, and which have edges (top, bottom, left, right).
EdgeInner	Sets the border style for the inner part of a drawn edge.
EdgeOuter	Sets the border style for the outer part of a drawn edge.
Flat	If you set this property to true, the toolbar and its buttons are transparent and the frame around the buttons is visible only when the mouse pointer is moved over it.
HotImages	Specifies a TImageList component that is to contain the images to appear on the buttons when the mouse pointer is moved over them.
Images	Specifies an image list that contains the images for the buttons.
Indent	Enter a value for the left indent of the toolbar. This value specifies how far to the right the first button appears.
List	Changes the way in which a button is displayed, i.e. whether image and text are to be shown. If you set this to false, then the image and text appear under each other; if you set it to true, then they appear next to each other.
ShowCaptions	If this property is set to true, then the button captions are displayed.
Transparent	Specifes whether the toolbar is displayed transparently.
Wrapable	If this is set to true, then any elements for which there is not enough space in the current line are displayed on the next line.

Table 5.2 *Properties of the* TToolbar *component*

If you have three buttons next to each other that all have these properties, you will notice that only one of them can be clicked at any one time. The default setting is that one of the three must be clicked. However, you can deactivate this with the AllowAllUp property.

The start and end of the group are defined by buttons whose properties do not have the tbsCheck value. Here, you should use tbsDivider or tbsSeparator buttons as they act as clear separators.

Property	Meaning
AllowAllUp	Defines whether buttons in the same group can be unselected at the same time. If it is set to false, then one of the buttons in a group must always be selected ("clicked").
Down	Shows whether the button is clicked. If there are several buttons in a group, then it is a good idea to check whether one of the buttons is clicked, or to have the program "click" one without involving a user action.
DropDownMenu	If you want the button to act like a menu option, then you can specify a popup menu here that opens when the button is clicked. Do not confuse this with a context menu that appears when the user right-clicks on a component. Here, you use a normal left-click. However, the same TPopupMenu component is used.
Grouped	If this is set to true, then the button is one of a group of buttons, only one of which can be clicked at any one time. These are neighboring buttons that have the value true for the Grouped property and whose style is set to tbsCheck.
ImageIndex	Shows the index in the image list of the image displayed on the button. However, the image list itself appears in the toolbar.
Indeterminate	Indicates a button's status when it is neither clicked nor unclicked.
Marked	Specifies whether a button is marked (indicated by its shaded surface).
MenuItem	Specifies the menu option to which the button is to correspond.
Style	Specifies how the button is to appear on screen.
Wrap	If this property is set to true, then a new line opens after this button, so the toolbar is wrapped. Used to specify a button as the last button in a row.

Table 5.3   *TToolbutton* **component properties**

5.4 Status bar

A status bar is the kind of feature you'd expect to find in a good program. You should always keep the user informed, either by providing hints about things such as button functions, the time and the date, or with information about what the program is currently up to. The status bar is ideal for this. To create it, use the TStatusBar component on the Component Palette Win32 page. When you place the TStatusBar component on a form, it is assigned automatically to the bottom edge of that form.

5.4.1 Splitting the status bar

The status bar can be split into different areas. To access these areas, use the `Panels` property in the `TStatusBar` component. You can simply divide the status bar into several sections and then customize how they are displayed. To do this, double-click on either the status bar or the ellipsis button next to the `Panel` property in the Object Inspector. A small window appears in which you can create the panels. To do this, either click on the top left-hand button or press (Ins).

In the Object Inspector, you can modify the appearance of the individual panels. The properties are pretty much self-explanatory.

5.4.2 Modifying panels at runtime

As users often change the size of the main window when a program is running, it is a good idea to modify the size and position of panels at runtime as well. If you do this, you only need to create the panels. Do not change any of the other options in the Object Inspector.

The event we use is `OnResize` from our main form. We shall now add program code to its event-handling routine to modify the appearance of the status bar. The advantage of this event is that it occurs not only when the size is changed but also when the form is displayed for the first time, when the program starts:

```
procedure TForm1.FormResize(Sender: TObject);
begin;
   { Set Values for Statusbar }
   with StatusBar1 do
   begin;
      Panels[1].Width := 80;
      Panels[1].Bevel := pbRaised;
      Panels[2].Width := 80;
      Panels[0].Width := Width-160;
   end;
end;
```

The statements shown above set both right-hand panels with the index values 1 and 2 to a width of 80 pixels. The left-hand panel with the index value 0 (Delphi starts counting at 0) is made so wide that it takes up the rest of the status bar. Later on, you can display information in this panel. Both the right-hand panels are used to display, for example, the number of data records in a file or the number of lines and columns in a word-processing program.

5.4.3 Filling the status bar with text

SimpleText property

There are two ways to write text in the status bar. The first is to define no panels for the status bar and to use the `SimpleText` property in the `TStatusBar` component to define which text is to be displayed. If no panels have been defined, then the text contained in `SimpleText` is displayed in the status bar:

```
procedure DisplayHint;
begin;
   StatusBar1.SimpleText := Application.Hint;
end;
```

Using panels for display

The other way to write text to the status bar applies if you are using panels and you therefore want to split the status bar. In this case, use the panels' `Text` property to display the text. The advantage is that the program looks much more professional and you can also accommodate more information on the status bar:

```
procedure FillStatusBar;
begin;
   with StatusBar1 do
   begin;
      Panels[0].Text := Application.Hint;
      Panels[1].Text := TimeToStr(now);
      Panels[2].Text := DateToStr(now);
   end;
end;
```

Once again, the source code uses three different panels: the first displays a short help text, the second contains the current time, and the third contains the current date. However, in the example above, the time is not updated, so you would need a timer component in whose `OnTimer` event the time is written to the status bar. But we can add it later. Place a `TTimer` component from the Component Palette System page on to the form and enter the following source code in the event-handling routine for `OnTimer`:

```
procedure Timer1Timer(Sender: TObject);
begin;
   Statusbar1.Panels[1].Text := TimeToStr(now);
end;
```

Now the time display will be updated constantly.

This component has been available since Delphi 4. **5.5** `TActionList` **component**
It has produced enormous increases in programming efficiency. With a `TActionList` component, you can define all actions in one place centrally and then assign them to several control elements. To administer the program functions, you use `TAction` components grouped in the `TActionList` component. The advantage is that you need to declare all functions and programs only once. After this, you simply assign them.

5.5.1 ActionList Editor

You will find the `TActionList` component on the Component Palette Standard page. Place it on the form and open the ActionList Editor by double-clicking on the component. Figure 5.2 shows the ActionList Editor.

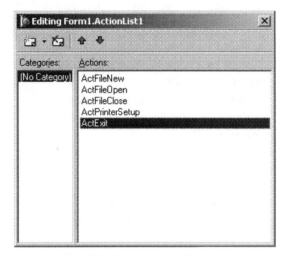

Figure 5.2   *The ActionList Editor*

In this window, you can specify the different actions that are to be available in the program. To do so, add a new `TAction` component to the list for each action. Either click the top left-hand button or press Ins. In the Object Inspector, you can then make the necessary settings. All relevant settings, such as the `Caption`, `Hint` or `Shortcut`, are transferred later when the action is assigned to a menu option or a toolbar button; this is what saves so much time when you use action lists.

You can also assign the individual actions to categories to make them easier to manage. To do so, simply assign a value to the `Category` property in the Object Inspector. A sensible approach would be, for example, to categorize actions to suit the menus they will be used in, using expressions such as File, Edit, etc.

There are also predefined standard actions for the ActionList. To access these actions, select the NEW STANDARD ACTION menu option from the ActionList context menu. The standard actions are the usual actions, such as cutting, inserting or copying, along with some others. In Delphi 6, some more standard actions have been added to those provided in Delphi 5. You can save a lot of time by using these predefined actions, since some of them provide very useful functionality, e.g. the action for closing a program does so without you having to write a single line of program code.

5.5.2 `TAction` properties

The properties of the `TAction` component are largely the same as those of a menu option since, among other things, `TAction` provides the functionality for a menu option. Table 5.4 lists the properties.

Property	Meaning
Caption	The text that is transferred later for the control element.
Category	A freely definable category in which you can store the action in the action list. Helps you see what belongs where.
Checked	Sets the value of the `Checked` property for the control element to which the action will be assigned.
Enabled	Specifies whether the action can be executed.
HelpContext	Enter the value for the help topic context that is to be used to call the help file.
Hint	Enter a hint that provides the user with information about the action. This will be transferred later to the control element to which the action is assigned.
ImageIndex	Specify the index of the image in the `TImageList` that is to be assigned for this action. However, you must assign the image list to the `TActionList` component.
ShortCut	Specify a keyboard shortcut for direct access by the user; it will be transferred to the relevant control element later. Do not confuse this with the keyboard shortcut that you can define by inserting the "&" character in the `Caption` property.
Visible	Specifies whether the action (and therefore the control element to which it is assigned) is visible.

Table 5.4 **Properties of the** `TAction` **component**

5.5.3 Defining the functionality of actions

To define the function that is to be executed when a particular `TAction` component is called, simply insert the relevant program code into the event-handling routine of the `OnExecute` event. If you later assign the action to a menu option or toolbar button, then its `OnClick` event will be diverted automatically to the `OnExecute` event in the `TAction` component.

5.5.4 Adding images

You use the `ImageList` property to add images to a `TActionList`. However, you must have already created an image list component in which the individual images are defined. Using the `ImageIndex` property in the `TAction` components, you can then add an image to each action.

The images added do not appear immediately in the menus; only the `ImageIndex` values are transferred for the menu and the toolbar buttons. To display the images, use the `ImageList` property to assign the correct image list to the menu or toolbar.

No doubt you have recognized that working with the Actionlist can reduce your programming effort considerably. Even the fact that you only have to enter the texts for the hints once saves a lot of time. Additionally, it is a lot easier to make changes to the source code or a particular function since you always know exactly where the function is located. All this adds up to great clarity, which few programming systems offer.

5.6 `TImageList` component

This component provides a list of images of the same size as are usually used for buttons or (since Windows 98) in menus. The advantage of an image list is that an image is loaded only once, in the list, and can then be used several times in the program if you assign the image list to the appropriate control element and then use the `ImageIndex` property to access the images in it.

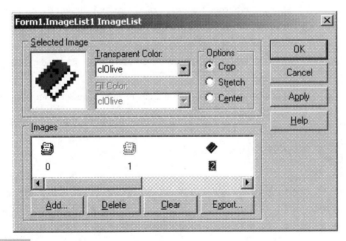

Figure 5.3 *The ImageList Editor in use*

5.6.1 ImageList Editor

Figure 5.3 shows the ImageList Editor.

By clicking [Ins] you can load new images into the image list. The images must be the same size as defined in the `Width` and `Height` properties in the image list, otherwise they will be cut off, stretched or centered. A special case occurs if you have specified, for example, an image list size of 16×16 pixels but the graphic is 16×32 pixels. Delphi then prompts you to make two graphics out of one.

You can click the DELETE button to delete an image from the list. The CLEAR button deletes the entire contents of the image list. You should therefore be careful with using this, as it is very easy to click the wrong button.

5.6.2 `TImageList` properties

The image list has a number of properties, listed in Table 5.5.

Property	Meaning
AllocBy	Specifies how many images the image list is to be enlarged by if it needs to be made bigger so that new images can be added to it.
BkColor	Specifies which background color is to be used when an image is displayed. Normally, you do not need to change this value.
BlendColor	Specifies which foreground color is used when an image is displayed.
DrawingStyle	Specifies the style used to draw the image.
Height	Specifies the height of the images in the image list. Images that are too tall will be cut off or squashed.
ImageType	Specifies whether the image or the mask is drawn during drawing.
Masked	Specifies whether the image list has a mask that is to be mixed with the images.
ShareImages	Specifies whether the image list also releases its handle when it is released.
Width	Specifies the width of the images in the image list. If an image is too wide, it will be squashed or split.

Table 5.5   **Properties of** `TImageList`

Usually, you do not need to change any of the properties of the image list, except perhaps the properties for the size of the images in it. You will find more information about the other properties in Delphi's online help.

A completely new feature in Delphi 6 is the `TActionManager` compo-
nent, which makes it much easier to create a menu structure. However, due to all the things
you can do with this component, working with it takes a bit of practice, and it provides
such a large number of settings that you will probably never remember them all at once.

> **Tip** The `TActionManager` component is not provided in the Personal Edition of Delphi. If
> you are using this version of Delphi, you must restrict yourself to the menu components
> already described.

Among other things, you can use the Action Manager for the following: integrating
an existing menu structure, customizing the toolbars and menus present in it, and
generating menus that look and act like those in Office 2000. It is therefore a really
powerful component. Let us begin with some of the properties provided by
`TActionManager` (Table 5.6).

Property	Meaning
ActionBars	Used internally. Provides you with all the action bars with which the Action Manager is integrated. You can add an action bar to this list by placing one of the actions defined in the Action Manager on it or by adding it manually.
FileName	Specifies a file in which the Action Manager stores its layout data.
Images	Specifies a `TImageList` component that contains the images that are used later in the menu or on the buttons in a toolbar.
ImportMenu	If you have already created a menu structure, e.g. in a main menu, then you can use this to load it, saving you from having to declare menu options twice.
PrioritySchedule	`TStringList`-type property that specifies how long Delphi waits before marking a menu option as unused. With `TActionManager`, you can program your applications to behave like Windows 2000 and suppress menu options that are not required.

Table 5.6 *Properties of* `TActionManager`

TAKE THAT!

5.7.1 Adding actions

The `TActionManager` component and `TActionList` use the same Actionlist Editor. Unfortunately, you cannot integrate an existing list of actions at designtime. However, you can copy the actions from an ActionList into the `TActionManager` component's ActionList Editor.

You create actions in the same way as in the `TActionlist` component. However, here it is even more important to use categories as they are used at runtime in the Customize dialog to simplify selection. Figure 5.4 shows the Actionlist Editor with some actions.

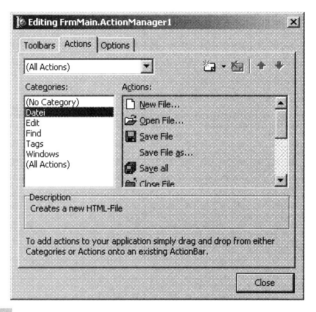

Figure 5.4   *The* `TActionManager` *action list with standard actions*

5.7.2 Using actions

Once an action has been inserted into the `TActionManager` component, it can be used everywhere that you need it, and not just once. However, to optimize their usage, I recommend you use the ActionManager `TToolActionBar` and `TMainMenuActionBar` components.

First, we need actionbars provided by these two components. The first method is to use the components on the Component Palette and add the required actionbars to the form. If you then add actions to an actionbar, Delphi automatically links it to the ActionManager. Alternatively, you could add an actionbar on the Toolbars page of the ActionList Editor. The effect is the same in both cases. I prefer the first method as I can then specify at the same time what kind of actionbar I want to insert.

You can now simply drag and drop to add the required actions to the actionbars. If you use `TMainManuActionBar`, you are not restricted to single actions; you can also insert a complete category of actions. All actions will then be inserted in sequence under the current menu option. Figure 5.5 shows a form with actionbars that already contain actions.

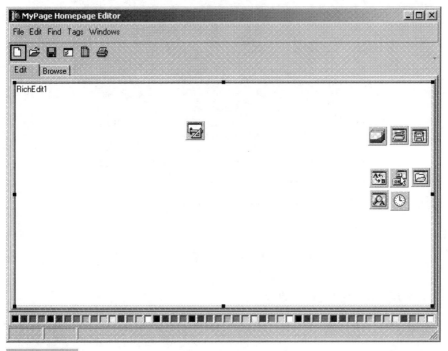

Figure 5.5 *Form with actionbars and actions*

5.7.3 Modifying actions

Neither `TActionManager` nor the toolbars that belong to it – `TToolActionBar` or `TMainMenuActionBar` – provide a way to modify toolbars. However, you could obviously also call the dialog used at designtime to modify the toolbars. The first and simplest approach is to implement the `CustomizeActionBars` standard action. If you implement this, and click on it, Delphi loads the dialog automatically and you can modify (customize) the toolbars or the menu.

Alternatively, you can use the `TCustomizeDlg` dialog. In its `ActionManager` property, you must specify the Action Manager whose actions are to be used for modification. However, at runtime you must then use the `Show` statement rather than `Execute` (which you would use for other dialogs) to call this dialog, as the dialog is no longer modal; instead, both forms are active.

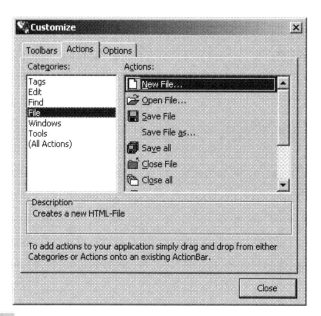

Figure 5.6 *Dialog for customizing the toolbars*

You can see the customization dialog in Figure 5.6.

5.7.4 Mimicking Office 2000

You are no doubt familiar with the way the menu options in Office 2000 behave. Like it or not, the Office applications suppress unused menu options after a set period of timeout. Menus created using TActionManager will behave in the same way unless you run the program from the development environment; then the entire menu will always be displayed. The property with which you control this behavior is called PrioritySchedule. In this, you specify when a menu option disappears and when it reappears. The property contains a string list with two values. The way this property works is rather confusing.

Each action has a property called UsageCount. In it, a value is saved to record how often that particular action has been called. At runtime, Delphi compares the value in the left-hand column of PrioritySchedule with this UsageCount. If UsageCount is higher than the highest value entered in the left-hand column, then that left-hand column value is used.

Now, Delphi checks on the right-hand side, which also contains a value. This specifies how long an action can go without being executed before it disappears. The value counted is the number of sessions, each of which corresponds to one program start. The default setting is that a menu option that has been selected once will disappear if it is not selected during the next three sessions.

Naturally, there are also menu options, such as CLOSE, that are always displayed. To specify that a menu option is always to be displayed, set the value in the appropriate `UsageCount` property to –1. This applies also only to menus. In a toolbar, Delphi will always display as many actions as there is room for.

As a final example, Figure 5.7 shows a menu in which the unused menu options have just been dropped down.

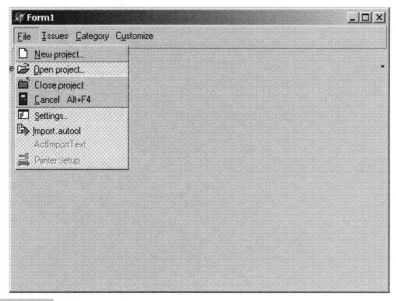

Figure 5.7 *Office 2000-style menu*

Functions and procedures

6

This chapter contains an overview of the important and most frequently used functions and procedures that you will find most useful in day-to-day programming.

6.1 Dialog and message windows

Some of the available Windows dialogs have not been integrated in components. Instead, you use a Windows API function to access these dialogs. For some reason a Windows API function uses C format for character strings, requiring constant data conversions. Delphi helps you get round this by using the Dialogs unit to define many of the functions for calling a standard dialog window.

6.1.1 *ShowMessage*

procedure ShowMessage(**const** Msg: string);

ShowMessage displays a message window with a message. The title of the window is the same as the title of your application. The message window has only a single OK button, which the user must click to leave the window. The message is passed simply as a string constant. Figure 6.1 shows a message window of this kind.

Figure 6.1   *Example of a message box*

6.1.2 *InputBox*

function InputBox(**const** ACaption, APrompt, ADefault: string): string;

The InputBox function displays a dialog window in which the user can enter data. The ACaption parameter contains the title of the dialog window, APrompt contains the input prompt, and ADefault contains a default text that is displayed for the user to see. InputBox provides the user with an OK button and a CANCEL button. If the user clicks the CANCEL button, then the function returns the default value, otherwise it returns the value entered by the user. However, in this function you cannot evaluate whether the user has clicked OK or CANCEL. Figure 6.2 shows an input box in use.

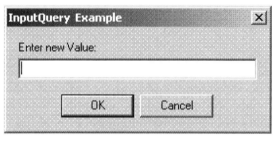

Figure 6.2 *Example of an input box showing an InputQuery*

6.1.3 *InputQuery*

function InputQuery(**const** ACaption, APrompt: string; **var** Value: string): Boolean;

Using the InputQuery function you can evaluate which button the user has clicked. The function returns true if the user has clicked OK, otherwise it returns false.

The rest of the parameters are the same as in the InputBox function. The Value parameter returns the user's input. If you assign a string to Value before calling it, then that string will be displayed as a default to the user. However, you cannot use InputQuery in the same way as Inputbox to return a default value. The two dialogs look identical.

6.1.4 *MessageDlg*

function MessageDlg(**const** Msg: string; DlgType: TMsgDlgType; Buttons: TMsgDlgButtons; HelpCtx: Longint): Word;

Using this function, you can display a message window and evaluate the reaction of the user. Using the `DlgType` parameter, you can select the type of dialog you require. Using the `Buttons` parameter, you can specify how many different buttons are to be displayed in the dialog, and what types of button are to be used. The dialog's return value is dependent on which button is pressed, so you can easily evaluate the user's action.

Delphi provides values for the dialog type and the buttons. Table 6.1 shows the different dialog types.

Constant	Dialog type
mtWarning	Dialog with an exclamation mark icon.
mtError	Dialog with a Stop icon.
mtConfirmation	Dialog with a question mark icon.
mtInformation	Dialog with a small "i" in a circle (the standard Windows information icon).
mtCustom	Window without an icon.

Table 6.1   *Dialog types for the* `MessageDlg` *function*

In a message dialog, you can display several buttons at the same time. In the passed parameter `TMsgDlgButtons`, you specify how many buttons you want to display. This is a call to the function specifying that three buttons are to be displayed:

```
Value := MessageDlg('Hello world',mtInformation,
                [mbYes,mbNo,mbIgnore],0);
```

Table 6.2 lists the individual values for the different buttons.

Constant	Button label
mbYes	YES
mbNo	NO
mbOk	OK
mbCancel	CANCEL
mbAbort	ABORT
mbRetry	RETRY
mbIgnore	IGNORE
mbAll	ALL
mbNoToAll	NO TO ALL
mbYesToAll	YES TO ALL
mbHelp	HELP

Table 6.2   *Buttons available in the* `MessageDlg` *function*

Finally, you still need the return values for the function, since you also want to evaluate how the user leaves the dialog. Delphi provides a constant for each button for this purpose. The names of the constants for the return value resemble the names of the constants for the buttons but begin with `mr` instead of `mb`. For example, the return value `mrOk` would therefore mean that the user had clicked the OK button.

Figure 6.3 shows how a `MessageDlg` dialog might be used. You have probably already seen many dialogs of this kind in different applications. The figure shows a dialog with three buttons.

Figure 6.3 *Example of a message box window*

6.1.5 `Application.Messagebox` and `Messagebox`

The `Messagebox` function in `TApplication` encapsulates the corresponding function from the Windows API (which is also called `Messagebox`). For this reason, you must also arrange qualification if you call the encapsulated function instead of the API function. The difference is that the API function prompts for a form's handle, but the encapsulated function in `TApplication` does not do so.

You must transfer the character strings as `PChar` values, but this is not a problem. If you use variables to store the character strings, you simply need to arrange type conversion from the `PChar(variable name)` type, otherwise the character string is treated as a `PChar` value.

To specify the type of message window and the buttons displayed, you use flags, which you must pass to the function. Windows provides these flags with default values. Table 6.3 shows you the different values and their meanings. You use "+" to link together the flags for the dialog window type and the buttons.

You can use the return value to find out which button the user has clicked. There are also default values for the different return values. These are shown in Table 6.4.

To find out more about these flags, look in the online help under the keyword `MessageBox`; there are many options available. Delphi provides two `Messagebox` functions; `TApplication.Messagebox` and `Messagebox`. The latter is the API function and it contains the flags. They are identical in appearance. You can see the Message Box in use in Figure 6.4.

Flag value	Meaning
mb_Ok	OK button will be displayed.
mb_OkCancel	OK and CANCEL buttons will be displayed.
mb_YesNo	YES and NO buttons will be displayed.
mb_YesNoCancel	YES, NO and CANCEL buttons will be displayed.
mb_AbortRetryIgnore	CANCEL, REPEAT and IGNORE buttons will be displayed.
mb_RetryCancel	REPEAT and CANCEL buttons will be displayed.
mb_IconExclamation or mb_IconWarning	Exclamation mark will be displayed as an image in the dialog.
mb_IconInformation or mb_IconAsterisk	An "i" (for "information") with a blue background will be displayed as an image in the dialog.
mb_IconQuestion	A question mark will be displayed as an image in the dialog.
mb_IconStop or mb_IconError or mb_IconHand	A Stop sign will be displayed as an image in the dialog.

Table 6.3 *Flags for the* Messagebox *function*

Return value	Meaning
IDYes	YES button has been clicked.
IDNo	NO button has been clicked.
IDOk	OK button has been clicked.
IDCancel	CANCEL button has been clicked.
IDAbort	ABORT button has been clicked.
IDRetry	REPEAT button has been clicked.
IDIgnore	IGNORE button has been clicked.

Table 6.4 *Return values for the* Messagebox *function*

Figure 6.4 *Test using a MessageBox from the Windows API*

6.1.6 *SelectDirectory*

The syntax for this is:

```
function SelectDirectory(const Caption: string; const Root:
WideString; out Directory: string): Boolean; overload;
```

or

```
function SelectDirectory(var Directory: string; Options:
TSelectDirOpts; HelpCtx: Longint): Boolean; overload;
```

Using the `SelectDirectory` dialog, you can select a folder with the standard Windows folder selection dialog. You can use whichever function syntax you wish; Delphi selects the syntax that suits your call.

In the first syntax example, you can see that the `Caption` parameter contains the title of the dialog window, and the `Root` parameter contains the root folder in which the dialog is located when it is opened. In the `Directory` parameter, Delphi returns the selected folder. This function returns `true` if the user has selected a folder and con-

Figure 6.5 *Dialog for the first syntax example*

firmed the selection by clicking OK. Otherwise, the return value is `false`. Figure 6.5 shows the dialog in use.

Different parameters apply for the second syntax example. Here, too, the selected folder is returned and the initial folder is specified in the `Directory` parameter. The difference is that you also can set parameters here that influence the appearance of the dialog and its behavior. The `HelpCtx` parameter contains the help context value for the dialog.

The return values are the same as in the first syntax example: `true` is returned if the user has selected a folder, and `false` is returned if they have clicked on the CANCEL button.

However, the two dialogs look very different. The first looks like a typical Windows folder selection dialog, but the second syntax example displays a dialog that is reminiscent of the world of 16-bit computing (Figure 6.6).

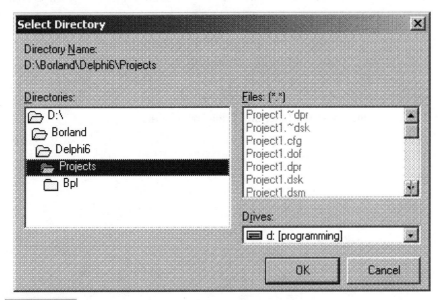

Figure 6.6 *Dialog for the second syntax example*

6.2 Arithmetical functions

Delphi can calculate and compute, and has a very large number of functions and procedures for doing so, some of which are described in this section.

function Abs(X);

The `Abs` function returns the absolute value of X. X can be a real number or an integer value. Mathematically, the absolute value is also called the amount of a number. This means that if X has the value –5, then the `Abs` function returns the value 5.

```
function Ceil(X: Extended):Integer;
```

The `Ceil` function rounds up the value of a variable, so 2.5 becomes 3, but −2.8 becomes −2.

```
function Floor(X: Extended): Integer;
```

The `Floor` function rounds down the value of a variable; it is the counterpart to the `Ceil` function.

```
function Frac(X: Extended): Extended;
```

The `Frac` function returns the fractional part of a real number (after the decimal point).

```
function Int(X: Real): Real;
```

`Int` returns the whole number part of a real number. `Int` does not round off; you must use the `Ceil` or `Floor` functions for that purpose. `Int` cuts off the fractional value of the transferred value (after the decimal point) instead.

```
function IntPower(Base: Extended; Exponent: Integer):
Extended register;
```

The `IntPower` function returns the value of `Base` times `Exponent`.

```
function Ln(X: Real): Real;
```

The `Ln` function returns the natural logarithm of the number `X`.

```
function Log10(X: Extended): Extended;
```

The `Log10` function returns the decimal logarithm (logarithm in base 10) of the number `X`.

```
function Max(A,B: Integer): Integer; overload;
```

The `Max` function returns the greater of two transferred values. `Max` is a function that is overloaded several times because of the possibility of overloading. For this reason any value is permitted for calling `Max`.

```
function Min(A,B: Integer): Integer; overload;
```

The `Min` function returns the smaller of two transferred values. Like the `Max` function, `Min` is also overloaded and therefore valid for all values.

```
function Pi: Extended;
```

The `Pi` function returns the value of pi (π), which is approximately 3.1415926535897932385. As π has an infinite number of decimal places, this is only an approximate value, but it is more accurate than a pocket calculator.

```
function Sin(X: Extended): Extended;
```

The `Sin` function calculates the sine value of an angle in radians.

```
function Cos(X: Extended): Extended;
```

The `Cos` function calculates the cosine value of an angle in radians.

```
function Tan(X: Extended): Extended;
```

The `Tan` function calculates the tangent value of an angle in radians.

```
function DegToRad(Degrees: Extended): Extended;
```

The `DegToRad` function converts an angle from degrees to radians.

```
function GradToRad(Grads: Extended): Extended;
```

The `GradToRad` function converts an angle from centisemal degrees to radians. In centisemal degrees, a circle is divided into 400 grads.

```
function RadToDeg(Radians: Extended): Extended;
```

The `RadToDeg` function converts an angle from radians to degrees.

```
function RadToGrad(Radians: Extended): Extended;
```

The `RadToGrad` function converts an angle from radians to centisemal degrees.

6.3 Files and folders

Delphi provides a wide range of procedures and functions for working with files and folders. Version 6 of Delphi contains even more than previous versions.

```
procedure ChDir(S: string);
```

Using the ChDir procedure, you can change the current directory (even to another drive).

```
function CreateDir(const Dir: string): Boolean;
```

You use the CreateDir function to create a new folder with the name you specify. If you are successful, the function returns true; if the folder cannot be created, it returns false. CreateDir can only create one folder at once.

```
function DeleteFile(const FileName: string): Boolean;
```

Use the DeleteFile function to delete a file from the hard disk. If the file is deleted, then the function returns true, otherwise it returns false.

```
function DirectoryExists(Name: string): Boolean;
```

Use the DirectoryExists function to check whether the specified folder exists. If it does, then the function returns true, and otherwise it returns false.

```
function DiskFree(Drive: Byte): Int64;
```

The DiskFree function returns the number of free bytes on a drive. The passed parameter is a number, i.e. 0 for the current drive, 1 for drive A, 2 for drive B, etc.

```
function DiskSize(Drive: Byte): Int64;
```

The DiskSize function returns the size of the specified drive. You use the same parameters as for the DiskFree function.

```
function FileExists(const FileName: string): Boolean;
```

Use the FileExists function to check if the specified file exists. You can enter the entire file name, including the complete path. If the file exists, then the function returns true, otherwise it returns false.

```
function FileGetAttr(const FileName: string): Integer;
```

The FileGetAttr function returns the attributes of a file in the format also used in the TSearchRec record for finding a file. This is just a single Integer value. For more details, look in the online help with the keyword TSearchRec. There, you will find a list of the different file attributes.

You can use the and operator to check the file attributes. For example, you can use the following to check whether a file is hidden:

```
MyAttributes := FileGetAttr(MyFileName);
if (MyAttributes and faHidden)>0 then
  ShowMessage('File is hidden!');
```

```
function FileSetAttr(const FileName: string; Attr:
Integer): Integer;
```

You use the FileSetAttr function to set the attributes of a file. Where you use the and operator to read file attributes, you use the or operator to set them. Otherwise, the procedure is the same as for FileGetAttr.

```
function FindFirst(const Path: string; Attr: Integer; var
F: TSearchRec): Integer;
```

Use the FindFirst function to search for the first occurrence of a file in the specified folder. Any specified attributes will also be applied during the search. The result of the search is returned in the F parameter. If the search is successful, the return parameter contains 0; if it is unsuccessful, the return parameter contains a Windows error code.

```
function FindNext(var F: TSearchRec): Integer;
```

FindNext finds the next occurrence of the file found with the FindFirst function. As TSearchRec already contains all necessary details, they simply need to be passed (by first calling FindFirst). This function also returns 0 if successful and an error code if it is unsuccessful.

```
function ForceDirectories(Dir: string): Boolean;
```

You can use the ForceDirectories function to create several folders simultaneously. The CreateDir function can create only one new folder at a time, but ForceDirectories can create an entire list of folders simultaneously. This function replaces time-consuming programming in previous versions.

```
function GetCurrentDir: string;
```

Use the GetCurrentDir function to return the current folder.

```
function RemoveDir(const Dir: string): Boolean;
```

The `RemoveDir` function deletes an empty folder. If deletion is successful, then the function returns `true`, otherwise it returns `false`.

```
function RenameFile(const OldName, NewName: string):
Boolean;
```

The `RenameFile` function renames a file from `OldName` to `NewName` provided no file already exists with the name `NewName`. If the renaming is successful, then the function returns `true`, otherwise it returns `false`.

```
function SetCurrentDir(const Dir: string): Boolean;
```

Use the `SetCurrentDir` function to set the current folder. The function returns `true` if the change to a different folder is successful, otherwise it returns `false`.

```
function ChangeFileExt(const FileName, Extension: string):
string;
```

The `ChangeFileExt` function renames a file's extension. However, it only generates a new string and does not rename the file. To do this, you can use the `RenameFile` function.

```
function ExpandFileName(const FileName: string): string;
```

The `ExpandFileName` function extends a native file name by adding the current folder name to it. However, the function does not check whether the file actually exists.

```
function ExtractFileDir(const FileName: string): string;
```

The `ExtractFileDir` function extracts the folder name from a specified file name. If the file name contains no folder details, then the function returns an empty string.

```
function ExtractFileDrive(const FileName: string): string;
```

The `ExtractFileDrive` function extracts the drive name from the passed file name if it contains a complete path. This function also works with universal naming-convention (UNC) paths (and therefore with network paths). If the passed file name contains no drive name, then the function returns an empty string.

```
function ExtractFileExt(const FileName: string): string;
```

The `ExtractFileExt` function extracts the file extension from the passed file name. The return value also contains the period (dot) that separates the file name from the file extension.

```
function ExtractFileName(const FileName: string): string;
```

The `ExtractFileName` function returns the file name and the file extension from the passed parameter.

```
function ExtractFilePath(const FileName: string): string;
```

The `ExtractFilePath` function returns the path from the passed file name. If the file name contains no path details, then the function returns an empty string.

```
function ExtractRelativePath(const BaseName, DestName:
string): string;
```

The `ExtractRelativePath` function returns the relative part of the path, the `DestName`, in reference to the `BaseName`. You use this function to convert an absolute path into a relative path.

```
function ProcessPath(const EditText: string; var Drive:
Char; var DirPart: string; var FilePart: string);
```

The `ProcessPath` procedure splits up a specified file name, including the path, into its individual parts. The file name is passed in the `EditText` parameter. The returned values are the drive, the path and the file name itself.

```
function IncludeTrailingBackslash(const S: string): string;
```

`IncludeTrailingBackslash` adds a backslash to a path if one is not present at the end of the path. If the passed string already contains a final backslash, then no action is carried out. `IncludeTrailingBackslash` also works with 16-bit character sets.

```
function ExcludeTrailingBackslash(const S: string): string;
```

`ExcludeTrailingBackslash` is the counterpart to `IncludeTrailing-Backslash`. If the passed string ends in a backslash, then this function removes it.

```
function MatchesMask(const Filename, Mask: string): Boolean;
```

You use the `MatchesMask` function to check whether a passed file name matches the criteria of any filter present. If it does, then it returns `true`, otherwise it returns `false`. If the passed string for the mask contains a syntax error, then this triggers an exception. You do not have to use `MatchesMask` to check file names. The function actually compares a passed string with a mask. For example, if you are looking for someone called "Smyth", but you do not know how to write the name correctly, you could use `MatchesMask` to find all names that are written in a similar way:

```
if MatchesMask(TheName,'Sm??th') then
  (Name is OK)
```

The wildcards you can use with `MatchesMask` are the same as you use for file searches: "?" to represent any letter at the specified place, and "*" if it does not matter what the string contains from that point onwards.

6.4 Type conversions

In Delphi, there are two kinds of conversion: value conversion and type conversion. In type conversion, the passed parameters are converted into another data type. Type conversions are needed over and over again in programming, e.g. when numerical values need to be displayed in `TEdit` or `TLabel` components.

```
function FloatToStr(Value: Extended): string;
```

The `FloatToStr` function converts a floating point value into a string. During conversion, the floating-point number format with 15 significant places is used.

```
function StrToCurr(CONST S: string): Currency;
```

The `StrToCurr` function converts a numerical value that is a character string into the format used for a currency value.

```
function StrToFloat(const S: string): Extended;
```

The `StrToFloat` function converts a numerical value that is a character string into a floating-point number.

```
function CurrToStr(Value: Currency): string;
```

The `CurrToStr` function converts a value in the format used for a currency value into a character string.

```
function IntToStr(Value: Integer): string; overload;
```

The `IntToStr` function converts an integer value into a character string.

function IntToHex(Value: Integer; Digits: Integer):
string; **overload**;

The IntToHex function converts an integer value into a hexadecimal number and returns it in a string. The Digits parameter specifies the minimum number of hexadecimal places to be returned.

function StrToInt(**const** S: string): Integer;

The StrToInt function converts a number that is a character string into an integer value.

function DateTimeToStr(DateTime: TDateTime): string;

The DateTimeToStr function converts a date or time value into a string. The way the conversion is carried out (i.e. the way the value is displayed as a string) is specified by the global variables ShortDateFormat and LongDateFormat.

procedure DateTimeToString(**var** Result: string; **const**
Format: string; DateTime: TDateTime);

The DateTimeToString function has the same effect as the DateTimeToStr function, except that it allows you to specify a display format when you call it. For details of the different kinds of formatting available, look in the online help using the keyword FormatDateTime.

function DateToStr(DateTime: TDateTime): string;

Use the DateToStr function to convert the date part of the passed date/time value into a string. The way the conversion is carried out (i.e. the way the value is displayed as a string) is specified by the global variable ShortDateFormat.

function TimeToStr(Time: TDateTime): string;

Use the TimeToStr function to convert the time part of the passed date/time value into a string. The way the conversion is carried out (i.e. the way the value is displayed as a string) is specified by the global variable LongTimeFormat.

function StrToDate(**const** S: string): TDateTime;

The StrToDate function converts a date value that is currently a string into a date. If the string contains no valid date, then this triggers an exception.

```
function StrToTime(const S: string): TDateTime;
```

The StrToTime function converts a time value that is currently a string into a date/time value of the type TDateTime. Again, if the string does not contains a correct time format, then this triggers an exception.

```
function ColorToString(Color: TColor): string;
```

The ColorToString function converts a color value into a string.

```
function ColorToRGB(Color: TColor): Longint;
```

The ColorToRGB function converts a color value into a red–green–blue (RGB) value. In RGB format, the color is saved as a mixture of red, green and blue shades. It is necessary, for example, for passing values to API functions.

```
function ColorToIdent(Color: Longint; var Ident: string):
Boolean;
```

The ColorToIdent function attempts to convert a specified color value into the symbolic constant to which it corresponds (e.g. clBlack, clWindow, clBtnFace). If the function is unable to carry out conversion, then it returns false, otherwise it returns true.

```
function IdentToColor(const Ident: string; var Color:
Longint): Boolean;
```

Using the IdentToColor function, you can convert a symbolic color constant such as clBlack or clWindow into a color value.

```
function StringToColor(const S: string): TColor;
```

The StringToColor function converts a string value into a color value.

```
function Trunc(X: Extended): Int64;
```

The Trunc function converts a floating-point value into a whole number by cutting off anything after the decimal point; it does not round off.

```
function Date: TDateTime;
```

The Date function returns the current date.

```
function DayOfWeek(Date: TDateTime): Integer;
```

The DayOfWeek function returns the day of the week in a date as an Integer value. A return value of 1 corresponds to Sunday, 2 corresponds to Monday, etc.

```
procedure DecodeDate(Date: TDateTime; var Year, Month,
Day: Word);
```

The DecodeDate procedure splits a date into its day, month and year.

```
function EncodeDate(Year, Month, Day: Word): TDateTime;
```

The EncodeDate function returns a date/time value of the type TDateTime formed from the passed parameters for the day, month and year.

```
function EncodeTime(Hour, Min, Sec, MSec: Word): TDateTime;
```

The EncodeTime function returns a date/time value of the type TDateTime formed from the passed parameters for the hour, minute, second and millisecond.

```
function IncMonth(const Date: TDateTime; NumberOfMonths:
Integer): TDateTime;
```

The IncMonth function returns a date value, which Delphi increases or lowers by the specified number of months. It reduces the value if the NumberOfMonths parameter contains a negative value.

```
function IsLeapYear(Year: Word): Boolean;
```

The IsLeapYear function returns true if the year specified in the Year parameter is a leap year, otherwise it returns false.

```
function Now: TDateTime;
```

The Now function returns the current date and time.

```
function Time: TDateTime;
```

The Time function returns the current time.

```
procedure ReplaceDate(var DateTime: TDateTime; const
NewDate: TDateTime);
```

The `ReplaceDate` procedure converts the date into a date/time value of the type `TDateTime` in which the time part of the value remains unchanged.

```
procedure ReplaceTime(var DateTime: TDateTime; const
NewTime: TDateTime);
```

The `ReplaceTime` procedure converts the date into a date/time value of the type `TDateTime` in which the date part of the value remains unchanged.

```
procedure DecodeTime(Time: TDateTime; var Hour, Min, Sec,
MSec: Word);
```

The `DecodeTime` procedure splits the time part of the passed date/time value into hours, minutes, seconds and milliseconds.

6.6 Other functions and procedures

This section lists procedures and functions that do not fit into one of the earlier categories but are useful to know.

```
procedure Beep;
```

The `Beep` procedure outputs a standard tone on the computer's loudspeaker. You call `Beep` in exactly the same way as you call `MessageBeep(0);` in the Windows API.

```
function Chr(X: Byte): Char;
```

The `Chr` function returns the character with the specified ASCII value.

```
procedure FillChar(var X; Count: Integer; Value: Byte);
```

The `FillChar` procedure fills a particular number of bytes with a specified value. You can use this command, for example, to empty a record by passing the record, its size and a null byte. After this, you can reinitialize the now-empty record.

```
FillChar(MyRec,SizeOf(MyRec),#0);
```

```
function Low(X);
```

The `Low` function returns the lowest value of an ordinal type. `Low` is used mostly with arrays whose size is not known. The statement

```
Low(MyArray);
```

returns the lower index of the passed array.

```
function High(x):Integer;
```

The `High` function returns the highest value of an ordinal type. `High` is used mostly with arrays whose size is not known. The statement

```
High(MyArray);
```

returns the upper index of the passed array.

```
function SizeOf(X): Integer;
```

The `SizeOf` function returns the size of the passed parameter `X` in bytes. Here, `X` can be of different data types.

```
function UpCase(Ch: Char): Char;
```

The `UpCase` function converts a character into a capital letter.

```
function UpperCase(const S: string): string;
```

The `UpperCase` function converts a string into capital letters.

```
procedure Abort;
```

The `Abort` procedure ends the current process without outputting an error message. `Abort` triggers a silent exception.

```
procedure Break;
```

The `Break` procedure quits a loop. If you want to cancel a `For`, `While`, or `Repeat` loop before it has completed, then use the `Break` procedure.

```
procedure Continue;
```

The `Continue` procedure uses the next statement to continue a loop. Do not call `Continue` outside a loop construction otherwise you will cause a runtime error.

```
procedure Exit;
```

The Exit procedure ends the current procedure or function and returns to the calling location.

```
procedure Halt [(Exitcode: Integer)];
```

The Halt ends a program by interrupting it. To end a program in the normal way, call the Terminate procedure. You can pass an Exitcode, which can be an error code, to the Halt procedure, which is then used to end the program.

```
procedure Application.Terminate;
```

Use the Application.Terminate procedure to close a program in the normal way. This procedure does not act directly but triggers the ending of the program. If you call Terminate, you can end a program in a controlled way without the user needing to carry out any action.

```
procedure RunError [(Errorcode: Byte)];
```

The RunError procedure stops program execution with a runtime error, which you can pass. If you do not pass an error code, then the errorcode is 0.

```
procedure Dec(var X[;N: Longint]);
```

The Dec procedure reduces the value of a variable by the value specified in the N parameter. If no value is specified for N, then the value of the variable will be reduced by 1.

```
procedure Inc(var X [; N: Longint]);
```

The Inc procedure increases the value of a variable by the value specified in the N parameter. If no value is specified for N, then the value of the variable will be increased by 1.

Part II

Go ahead!

Program development techniques

This chapter deals with some of the basic techniques of program development with Delphi. Although the actual range of the Object Pascal language is not too great, its performance and capabilities are extremely extensive. Delphi provides a great number of predefined functions and procedures that you can use. However, before you can use them, you must know what they are. For this reason, this section of the book describes some of the most important techniques that you can use again and again in developing your own programs. You will also find information about how to work with texts, strings, lists, input fields and much more.

7.1 String lists

Delphi makes extensive use of lists in its components. Many things, are stored in lists, e.g. the lines in a memo field, the entries in a listbox or a combo box, and even the components in a form. The most commonly used lists are string lists. Components contain the `TStrings` type for this purpose, which, although it is a string list, provides only abstract methods. The best idea for your own string lists is to use the `TStringList` class.

In components, lists declared as `TStrings` are classes that have already descended (been derived) from existing classes, for which functional methods have already been declared for the abstract methods. This is why it is so easy to work with string lists in components.

7.1.1 List components

Delphi has numerous components that work with string lists, e.g. the `TComboBox` and `TListBox` components. However, list items are usually stored in the `Items` property. `TComboBox` and `TListBox` provide the same methods, which you can use to work with `Items`.

Nevertheless, list fields are not the only way you can use string lists in Delphi. The `TMemo` and `TRichEdit` components also use lists internally, because each individual line in the input fields is nothing more than a list item that you can access via the `Lines` property. More about this subject later. We are going to concentrate on the basic functions that you require to work with list items, such as `TListBox` or `TComboBox`.

Adding and deleting list items

To call a list item, call one of the `Add` or `Insert` methods. The `Add` method adds the item to the end of the list; with the `Insert` method, you can specify where the item is to be added to the string:

```
ListBox1.Items.Add('Hello');
ListBox1.Items.Insert(2,'Hello');
```

However, to delete a list item you also require the index value, the location of the item. You should note that Delphi always starts counting at 0, therefore an index of 2 corresponds to the third list item in the list. You use the `Delete` method to delete a list item:

```
ListBox1.Items.Delete(2);
```

This statement therefore deletes the third item in the list. If you want to delete the entire list, simply call the `Clear` method:

```
ListBox1.Items.Clear;
```

Sorting list items

To sort the contents of a list component, simply set the `Sorted` property to `true`. Obviously, this does not apply to memo fields in this context. If the `Sorted` property is set to `true`, then the list items in a list component are sorted alphabetically. If accented characters are present, they are displayed immediately after their base vowel, e.g. "ä" is sorted after "a".

Moving list items

You can also rearrange the sequence of items in a list. Of course, you can only do this if you have set the `Sorted` property to `false`, otherwise Delphi will automatically sort the list alphabetically. You use the `Move` command to move a list item within a list:

```
ListBox1.Items.Move(1,0);
```

This statement moves the second item in the list into the first position (remember, Delphi begins counting at 0). If you want to move a list item to the last position, no matter how many entries there are, use the following statement:

```
with ListBox1 do
begin;
   Items.Move(ItemIndex,Items.Count-1);
end;
```

This statement moves the current, marked item to the last position in the list.

Loading and saving list items

`TStrings` contains two methods in which you either enter a file name to save list items to a text file, or load list items from a text file. These methods are `LoadFromFile` and `SaveToFile`. Here, Delphi takes over all the file operations, such as opening and closing the file or loading the items. However, you should still check that the file from which the items are to be loaded actually exists, and that it is a text file. Delphi does not check the file extension.

The `SaveToFile` method does not check whether a particular file already exists; it simple overwrites the existing file. The programmer is responsible for checking this. The only code parameter is the file name, including the complete path:

```
Memo1.Lines.SaveToFile(MyFileName);
Memo1.Lines.LoadFromFile(MyFileName);
```

7.1.2 *TStringList* class

`TStrings` only declares the basic functions of a string list as abstract methods, so each method's name is declared but the method itself does not contain any functions. With `TStringList`, in contrast, all the necessary methods are integrated. Therefore, if you want to manage a string list you can use the `TStringList` class.

It should be pointed out here that although the `Items` property for list fields or the `Lines` property for memo fields are declared as a `TStrings`-type properties, internally, even for components, they are an implementation of a string list.

`TStringList` provides all the methods described above. This means you can manage a list of character strings by creating an instance of `TStringList` and saving the list items in it. The type of `TStringList` is therefore compatible with the `Items` property in a list box (or combo box), so you can assign the entire contents of a string list with one command:

```
procedure TForm1.Button1Click(Sender: TObject);
var
  MyList: TStringList;
begin
  MyList := TStringList.Create;
  MyList.Add('First item);
  MyList.Add('Second item');
  MyList.Add('Third item');
  ListBox1.Items := MyList;
  MyList.Free;
end;
```

This example creates a string list called `MyList`, adds three items to it, and then assigns all the items to a `TListBox` component. After this, the string list is removed from memory.

Obviously, the `TStringList` class has all the methods described above. You can therefore use them in the same way as the `Items` property of a list box or combo box.

7.2 Working with one-line strings

GO AHEAD!

Strings are the data format for character strings. Over the years, these have been developed extensively in Delphi. Data types whose capacity is limited only by the amount of available memory have evolved from the original "short" strings that could contain a maximum of 255 characters. In addition, Delphi can handle the C-type string format `PChar`, which is often needed to call Windows functions. For example, all Windows API functions work exclusively with `PChar` data types instead of strings.

7.2.1 String formats in Delphi

ShortString

As already mentioned, Delphi uses various types of strings. The first type, which is only kept to provide backwards compatibility, is `ShortString` from the 16-bit world with a maximum length of 255 characters. In this data type, the first byte contains the length, followed by the individual characters, byte by byte. As you can count from 0 to 255 in one byte, this is therefore the maximum length of the string.

AnsiString

Things were done somewhat differently with `AnsiString`. These strings no longer contain a length specification. They are created dynamically in memory and therefore always occupy as much space as they actually require. More precisely, the actual character string is created somewhere in memory and the variable contains a pointer to the string's location. However, this has no effect on how you use it. The final character of the string is a null.

The maximum size of an `AnsiString` is 4 GB, which is also the maximum memory size that Windows can address. It is therefore true to say that the size of an `AnsiString` is limited only by the random-access memory (RAM) available.

Delphi's default settings automatically use the `AnsiString` data type when you assign the `String` type to a variable. You shouldn't change this setting. If you are confused by the explanation that an `AnsiString` is actually a pointer, don't worry; Delphi can cope with this. You can work with an `AnsiString` in the same way as a `ShortString`.

PChar

The only reason for developing this string type is that Windows operates internally with it, and it ends in null. Basically, it is an array of characters, of which the final character is null (hence the term "null-terminated"). As the `AnsiString` data type is also null-terminated, it is not difficult to convert one data type to the other. However, when you convert the data types, you should ensure that the string you want to convert is initialized (already has a value). If you want to convert an empty string into a `PChar`, this is known as a null pointer and may cause a program crash.

WideString

The `WideString` data type is required if you want to use Unicode characters. ASCII format was created when the very first character sets were created. It was originally a 7-bit format, so it could represent 127 characters. This was entirely sufficient for the American character set. An additional bit was added so that special characters could also be represented. Now there was a byte for every character, so 256 characters could be represented. This was more than enough for European languages.

However, the internet brought with it a huge problem; 256 characters are not enough for the Chinese language, and China has a large internet presence. Therefore, there was a need to represent more characters. The Unicode character set was developed to do this. A Unicode character uses two bytes. This now provides space for more than 65 000 different characters, which should be enough for any language. Windows 2000, Windows ME and Windows XP use the Unicode character set, and some functions also expect `WideString` parameters. Delphi can handle this, so you shouldn't have any problems with it.

The `WideString` data type is also null-terminated and can vary in size, limited only by the amount of RAM available.

7.2.2 String functions

Delphi has a large number of functions and procedures for strings, some of which are described below.

Conversion functions

As already mentioned, type conversion is an easy way of converting a `String` to a `PChar` (or vice versa). You call the procedure like this:

```
var
    s,MyString: String;
    p,MyPChar:  PChar;
begin;
    p := 'PChar string';
```

```
s := 'String';
//Casting
MyString := String(p);   //Casting to String
MyPChar  := PChar(s);    //Casting to PChar
end;
```

However, sometimes one string is not enough, e.g. numerical values sometimes must be converted into strings before they can be displayed in an input field. Both the TEdit component and the Caption property have String-type property texts. This is why Delphi also has functions for converting numerical data types into string types, and vice versa. Here are some examples:

```
var
  s: String;
  i: integer;
  r: Float;
  d: TDateTime;

begin;
  s := IntToStr(i);     //Integer to String
  i := StrToInt(s);     //String to Integer
  r := StrToFloat(s);   //String to Float
  s := FloatToStr(r);   //Float to String
  d := StrToDate(s);    //String to Date
  s := DateToStr(d);    //Date to String
  d := StrToTime(s);    //String to Time
  s := TimeToStr(d);    //Time to String
end;
```

You will find more conversion routines for strings in Delphi's online help.

Formatting strings

In many situations, you will need to combine strings and number values into a single string, which you can, for example, transfer to a function that will display it on screen. Because of the numerous conversion functions that you then require, this kind of string declaration can get pretty big. This is why Delphi has the Format function, which you use to format the output of a string. You can also use it to pass floating-point numbers, integer values and other variables to the function, and then use arguments in the string to format them. As this all sounds a bit cryptic, here is an example:

```
var
  s: String;
```

```
begin;
    s := 'The item with number %d costs %m .';
    ShowMessage(Format(s,[5,129.95]));
end;
```

results in the output:

Product number 5 costs USD 129.95.

There are a number of arguments for formatting that can be used for the `Format` function. You will find them in the online help with the keyword `format strings`.

Other string functions

The following list contains some more useful string functions:

→ `s1 := UpperCase(s);` converts all the characters in a string into capital letters.

→ `s1 := LowerCase(s);` converts all the characters in a string into lower-case letters.

→ `i := Length(s);` returns the length of a string as an `integer` number.

→ `i := Pos('.',s);` returns the position of a point in the string s as an integer value.

→ `Delete(s,5,3);` removes three characters from the string s from the fifth character onwards. If you want to delete more characters than still remain in the string (in the example shown above, if the string is only six characters long, for instance), all the remaining characters are deleted without causing an error when you use this procedure.

→ `s1 := Copy(s,5,3);` returns three characters from the fifth character of the string s onwards. After you call the function, s1 contains the three characters.

→ `s3 := Concat(s1,s2,s);` links the transferred partial strings into one string. You can use any number of strings.

→ `s1 := TrimLeft(s);` removes all blanks on the left-hand side of string s.

→ `s1 := TrimRight(s);` removes all blanks on the right-hand side of string s.

→ `s1 := Trim(s);` removes all characters on the left and right of string s.

→ `s1 := QuotedStr(s);` sets the transferred string in quotation marks and returns it.

→ `i := CompareText(s,s1);` compares strings s and s1 and returns a value. This function does not distinguish between capitals and lower-case letters. If s is greater than s1 a positive value is returned; if s is smaller than s1 then a negative value is returned. If the return value is 0, then both strings are the same.

➜ `i := CompareStr(s,s1)` compares strings `s` and `s1` and returns a value. This function distinguishes between capitals and lower-case letters. If `s` is greater than `s1`, then a positive value is returned; if `s` is smaller than `s1`, then a negative value is returned. If the return value is 0, then both strings are the same.

7.3 Working with multiline text

Delphi offers two components for working with texts: `TMemo`, which has roughly the same functionality as Windows Notepad, and `TRichEdit`, which is an input field used to edit RTF texts. Like `TMemo`, `TRichEdit` can also handle ASCII format texts.

7.3.1 *TMemo* **component**

`TMemo` is a multiline input field. You can access the input field's contents in two ways: via the `Text` property, which returns the entire contents of the memo in a single string, or via the `Lines` property, which is a string list. In the latter case, each line of the memo field corresponds to a list item.

Lines **property**

The fact that the `Lines` property involves a string list means that you can also use all of a string list's methods. You can therefore use `Add` or `Insert` to insert lines, use the `Delete` command to delete lines, and call `Clear` to delete the entire contents of the memo field. In addition, the memo field already has the options for loading and saving text files.

Implemented features

`TMemo` offers more than this, however. It also contains all the functions that you recognize from Windows Notepad. By default, `TMemo` has methods for using the Clipboard, selecting text, undoing the previous action, and much more. So, if you add a `TMemo` component to an empty form and then start the application, the input field already has a context menu that contains the most commonly used functions of the EDIT menu in a word-processing program. Despite its unassuming appearance, this makes `TMemo` a very powerful component.

TMemo **properties**

When you reach the right-hand end of the input field, you have the option of inserting an automatic line break. To do this, simply set the `WordWrap` property to `true` and Delphi does the rest.

You use the `ScrollBars` property to specify whether the component displays scroll bars or not. You can select either horizontal or vertical scroll bars, or display both, as required. If you have set `WordWrap` to `true`, then you should display only a vertical scroll bar.

If you want to display something other than the standard context menu, you can specify your own specially designed menu in the `PopupMenu` property. The integrated context menu then no longer appears.

You can use `ReadOnly` to prevent inputs being made in the `TMemo` component, in the same way as you can in the usual one-line input field. After this, the component can only be used to display text.

The `WantTabs` property specifies whether the component will accept the tab key as an input key. You will be familiar with how this works under Windows; you press the ⇥ key to jump to the next input field. As we are dealing with a multiline input field here, which more or less operates as a word-processing function, you can instruct `TMemo` to accept the ⇥ key as an input key. The default setting for this property is `false`. To use the ⇥ key, you must set it to `true`.

The `WantReturns` property, whose default setting is `true`, behaves in a similar way. If the form on which you have placed the `TMemo` component has a standard button (which is defined by default), the normal behavior under Windows would be that this input key corresponds to a click on that standard button. If the `WantReturns` property of the `TMemo` component is set to `true`, then a line break is inserted in the text instead.

TMemo methods

You can, of course, access all the `TMemo` functions via methods. The methods used for inserting, deleting, moving, loading, and saving lines are already familiar because they are implemented in the `Lines` property and, as already mentioned, involve a string list. However, you can see from the context menu that there are other methods. For example, `TMemo` has a method called `Undo`, which undoes the previous action. You can check the `CanUndo` property to see whether you can undo an action. If this property is set to `true`, then you cannot call `Undo`:

```
if Memo1.CanUndo then Memo1.Undo;
```

There are also methods that you can use to work with the Windows Clipboard: `CutToClipboard` cuts the currently marked text and places it in the Clipboard; `CopyToClipboard` copies the marked text to the Clipboard; and `Paste-FromClipboard` inserts the text from the Clipboard at the current cursor position. You do not need to worry about whether the Clipboard contains text or not, as Delphi does this for you. If the Clipboard does not contain text, then `PasteFromClipboard` does nothing. The `CopyToClipboard` and `CutToClipboard` methods work in the same way; they only perform their actions if text has actually been marked.

Use the `SelText` property to evaluate the marked text. If text is marked, and you call the `PasteFromClipboard` method, then this text is overwritten (obviously this only happens if the Clipboard actually contains text that can be inserted). Use the

SelectAll method to mark all the text in the component. To deselect text, set the SelLength property to 0. You can also reverse this and select text automatically by assigning a value to SelLength.

By using all these methods and properties, you can quickly create a relatively user-friendly program for editing text files. This is because Delphi carries out the majority of the functions. The TRichEdit component described in the next section makes things even more user-friendly.

Tip There are two ways of displaying a margin (just like in some professional applications) in a TMemo component. The first way is not really a technical programming option, but more of a design issue. Here, you use a TPanel component that is wider than the memo and assign it the same color as the memo field. Then place the TMemo component on the label, right justify it, and display it without any borders (BorderStyle property).

The second option is an API function that you use to restrict the input area of a TMemo component. In the example below, each click on the button increases the left-hand margin by 10 pixels:

```
procedure TForm1.Button2Click(Sender: TObject);
var
  Rect: TRect;   //Editable Area
begin
  SendMessage(Memo1.Handle,EM_GetRect,0,Integer(@Rect));
  Inc(Rect.Left,10);
  SendMessage(Memo1.Handle,EM_SetRect,0,Integer(@Rect));
end;
```

Logically enough, this trick works both with the TMemo component and with TRichEdit.

7.3.2 TRichEdit component

TRichEdit is basically an extended memo field that gives you the option of formatting text. Where TMemo allows you to format an entire text, but does not let you save the formatting, TRichEdit has formatting functions that are the same as those in the most commonly used word-processing programs. As these formatting functions are part of the RTF format, they can be saved along with this format. TRichEdit provides the methods for this, but you have to program the calls yourself.

Editing standard ASCII text

You can use the TRichEdit component in the same way as a TMemo component, without the extended formatting options. For example, this may be useful if you want to edit a standard ASCII text and also need to handle formatted text. In this case, you can use one component to edit both text types instead of having to toggle between the components required to do this. Using fewer components also means using fewer resources and spending less time and effort programming.

To edit ASCII text, simply set the PlainText property in TRichEdit to true. The component then behaves like a TMemo component, and has the same functionality.

Editing formatted text

TRichEdit uses the RTF format for formatting. However, although the actual formatting commands are present in the text, they are not displayed. Instead, you see the effects in the text itself.

To assign formatting attributes, TRichEdit introduces the unpublished properties DefAttributes and SelAttributes. These properties have the type TTextAttributes. They are only available at runtime. DefAttributes contains the settings for standard text, and SelAttributes contains the properties for marked text or for newly entered text.

If you now want to change the format, simply assign the new values to the SelAttributes property. If you then enter text, this will automatically contain the attributes you selected. Table 7.1 lists the most important properties in the TTextAttributes class.

Property	Function
Color	Specifies the foreground color of the text.
Height	Enter the font size in pixels in this property. If you need to enter the size in points, use the Size property.
Name	Enter the name of the font you want to use in this property.
Pitch	Specifies whether a font with a variable distance between characters (fpVariable) or with a fixed distance between characters (fpFixed) is to be used. The default value is fpAutomatic, where the distance between characters is defined by the font. However, if you set the value fpFixed but use a font with a variable distance between characters, then Delphi attempts to use the most suitable font that has a fixed distance between characters.
Protected	Specifies that a part of the text is to be protected (cannot be processed). Any attempt to edit protected text triggers the OnProtectChange event. If no event-handling routine is present for this event, the text cannot be processed.
Size	Enter the height of the text in points in this property.
Style	Specifies how the text is to appear (bold, italic, underlined, etc.). There is a large number of properties here, and therefore you must either add the property you require for your text to this number or delete the property you do not require from it.

Table 7.1 *The most important properties of TTextAttributes*

You will notice that many of these properties are the same as those in the `TFont` class for a character set. This is why you can make the following assignment:

```
RichEdit1.SelAttributes.Assign(FontDialog1.Font);
```

In this case, the `Assign` method assigns all the right-hand values to the left-hand side because all the `FontDialog1.font` properties are also present in the `TTextAttributes` class.

You must use a special type of assignment for the `Style` property. This property is a quantity (e.g. the options in a dialog where you must also assign options at runtime). The text's style always corresponds to all the style types present in the quantity represented by the `Style` property. To display a text in bold type (or remove the bold style from a text):

```
with RichEdit1.SelAttributes do
begin;
    if BoldButton.Down then
        Style := Style+[fsBold]
    else
        Style := Style-[fsBold];
end;
```

Finding text in a `TRichEdit` component

`TRichEdit` already provides several methods for finding text within a component. The method you require here is called `FindText`. To call the method, you must enter the text you want to find. You must also enter the starting point and the end point of the area to be searched. The `FindText` method returns the starting point of the text it is looking for when it finds it. This makes it easy to mark the text, because you know how long it is:

```
procedure TForm1.Button1Click(Sender: TObject);
var
  SText          : String;
  MyStart,MyEnd  : integer;
  Found          : integer;
begin
  SText   := 'Search text';
  MyStart := 0;
  MyEnd   := Length(RichEdit1.Text)-1;
  Found   := RichEdit1.FindText(SText,MyStart,MyEnd);
  if Found<>-1 then
  begin ;
```

```
    SelStart  := Found;
    SelLength := Length(SText);
  end;
end;
```

The routine shown above searches for the "Search text" text in the TRichEdit component and then marks the place where this text is found. Ideally, you should use this type of routine together with a search dialog or a search-and-replace dialog. The correct search string will then be returned along with the OnFind event.

To replace the text you found, simply assign the new text to the SelText property. The place at which the text was found is already marked. This text is then replaced when you make the assignment to SelText.

Printing with TRichEdit

Word-processing also involves a print function. TRichEdit provides the Print method for this purpose. This method formats and prints the text that is present in the component. The only transfer parameter you must (or can) enter is a string that is to appear as a title in the print manager:

```
RichEdit1.Print('MyPrintout');
```

Loading and saving text

Although the methods for loading and saving text have already been explained in the TMemo component, I repeat that this method is part of the string list in which the lines are stored. To load or save texts, you simply call the LoadFromFile or SaveToFile methods in the Lines property:

```
RichEdit1.Lines.SaveToFile(MyFileName);
```

```
RichEdit1.Lines.LoadFromFile(MyFileName);
```

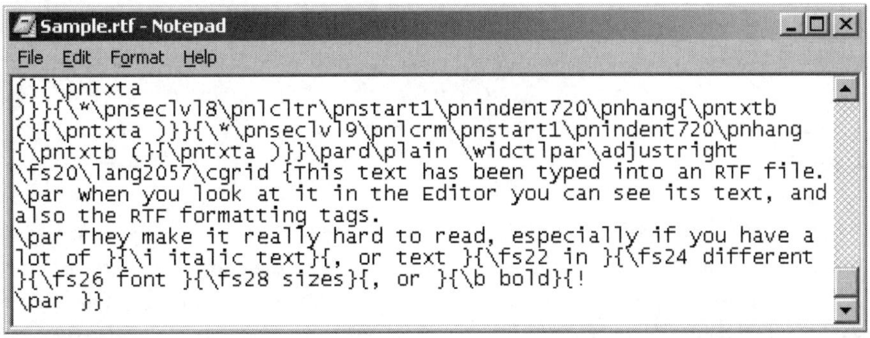

```
Sample.rtf - Notepad                                    _ | □ | X |
File  Edit  Format  Help
{}{\pntxta
)}}{\*\pnseclvl8\pnlcltr\pnstart1\pnindent720\pnhang{\pntxtb
(}{\pntxta )}}{\*\pnseclvl9\pnlcrm\pnstart1\pnindent720\pnhang
{\pntxtb (}{\pntxta )}}\pard\plain \widctlpar\adjustright
\fs20\lang2057\cgrid {This text has been typed into an RTF file.
\par when you look at it in the Editor you can see its text, and
also the RTF formatting tags.
\par They make it really hard to read, especially if you have a
lot of }{\i italic text}{, or text }{\fs22 in }{\fs24 different
}{\fs26 font }{\fs28 sizes}{, or }{\b bold}{!
\par }}
```

Figure 7.1   *RTF-formatted text in the Windows Editor*

It is also easy to display the formatting commands of `TRichEdit` in the text. To do this, just save a formatted text in `TRichEdit` and then load it into the Windows editor. Figure 7.1 shows what this looks like.

7.4 Forms and components

We have already met forms in Chapter 5, where we described how to generate and display a form dynamically, and how to evaluate the components that are present in a form. However, because components are little more than classes, you can, of course, also use these specific functions.

7.4.1 Finding components

If you put a component in a certain place, the component becomes subordinate to the form. The form is therefore the owner of the component. This means that the form itself generates the components that it contains. All the components are therefore stored in a list called `Components`. The `ComponentCount` property shows you how many components are present in a particular form.

Before you can work with components effectively, you still need a way of defining the component type. You already know how to do this; you use the `is` operator, which you saw in the source codes in section 7.1.

Thanks to polymorphism, we can use direct type conversion to access the relevant component. In the next example, we are looking in a form for a component that contains the string "Frank Eller" as a value in the `Text` property:

```
procedure TForm1.Button1Click(Sender: TObject);
var
    i: integer;
begin
  for I:= 0 to Form1.ComponentCount-1 do
  begin;
    if Components[i] is TEdit then
      if TEdit(Components[i]).Text='Frank Eller' then
        ShowMessage(TEdit(Components[i]).Name);
  end;
end;
```

Although the source code might look a bit complicated, it is actually very logical when you look beyond the functions. First, we run through all the components in the form. These are stored in a list called `Components`, which is present in every form. Then each component is checked to see whether it is a `TEdit` input field (if `Components[I]` is TEdit). If so, the text in the input field is checked. To do this, you carry out a type conversion because the entries in the components list are TComponent-type (base type) entries. This is carried out by the line IF TEdit(Components[i]).Text. If the check is positive, then the component's name is displayed.

7.4.2 *Sender parameter*

You will find this parameter in every event-handling routine. It is a TObject-type parameter that contains the component used to call the event. In Delphi, you can assign several components to the same event, e.g. the OnKeyPress event for input fields. This means that several input fields share the event. The OnClick event is another good example. In this case, components of the TButton, TSpeedButton, TPanel or TLabel types can share the same event. In this kind of situation, it is a good idea to find out which component was used to call the event. You can use the Sender parameter to do this.

Once again, you will require the is operator to identify the type of component that called the event. Another operator that is used in this context is the as operator:

```
procedure TForm1.Label1Click(Sender: TObject);
begin
  if Sender is TButton then
    if (Sender as TButton).Name = 'Button1' then
      //Do something
  if Sender is TLabel then
    if (Sender as TLabel).Name = 'Label1' then
      //Do something else
end;
```

> **Tip** Do you remember the Tag property, which every component has? As Delphi does not use this property, you can implement it for your own purposes. The TSpeedButton components in a toolbar are examples of this. If all these components are linked with the same OnClick event, you can use the Tag property to implement various function calls for the individual speed buttons. To do this, you require only one event-handling routine.

7.4.3 *Generating components dynamically*

Forms are not the only thing you can generate dynamically; you can also generate components in this way. However, you still have to specify the attributes (such as the height and width) of components that will generate themselves.

Creating a component

This example generates and removes a TEdit component dynamically when you click on it with the mouse. The example assumes that several input fields already exist, and that the newly generated field will be assigned under the last input field and have the same width and height:

```
var
  Form1:  TForm1;
  MyEdit: TEdit;


implementation


{$R *.DFM}


procedure TForm1.Button2Click(Sender: TObject);
begin
  MyEdit           := TEdit.Create(Self);
  MyEdit.Parent := Form1;
  MyEdit.Name      := 'MyEdit';
  MyEdit.Top       := Edit5.Top+24;
  MyEdit.Left      := Edit5.Left;
  MyEdit.Width     := Edit5.Width;
  MyEdit.Text      := 'Created at runtime';
end;
```

If you want to generate a component dynamically, you must also assign its basic properties. One of the most important properties here is Parent. This property displays the "owner" of the component, which is the superior or higher-level component. In the example shown above, this is the form itself, which means that the values of the properties Left and Top refer to the top left-hand corner of the form.

However, more often you will want to generate a component on to a TPanel component or a TToolbar instead of directly on a form. Here, the TPanel or TToolbar must function as the higher-level component and therefore contain the Parent property as a value. Obviously, Left and Top will then refer to the TPanel that is functioning as the owner.

Deleting a component

Just as you can create a component, you can, of course, delete it again. To do this, simply call the Free method, which is provided in every component. After you call this method, the component and all the data it contains are deleted from memory:

```
procedure TForm1.Button3Click(Sender: TObject);
begin
```

```
try
  MyEdit.Visible := false;
  MyEdit.Free;
except
end ;
end;
```

These were a new feature in Delphi 5, and in Delphi 6 they have become indispensable. Be careful not to confuse them with the frames used on the internet; this function in Delphi is completely different. A `frame` is a container component that can include other components and make them available in a program. The purpose of the `frame` component is to put components in a sequence that, although it can be repeated within one or more programs, needs to be created only once. All the set properties remain within the frame.

Using frames to repeat sequences of components has another advantage. If you want to expand your program or change the component sequence, you only need to do this in the original frame and then generate the project again. The change become visible immediately in every position where you used the frame.

7.5.1 Creating a frame

Although you will see a frames icon on the Standard Component Palette page, you must select the FILE | NEW | FRAME menu item before you can create a new frame. The icon in the Component Palette is only used to select frames that have already been created to insert them in an application.

Delphi displays an empty frame to which you can add your components. If required, you can also define event-handling routines or variables within the frame. All the routines and variables involved in the frame are stored in their own specific unit. When you add a frame to a project, this unit is integrated along with it.

7.5.2 Properties and events

The frame also provides you with its own properties and events. Here, the properties are similar to the properties of a visual component. Therefore, you can, for example, specify how the frame is to appear (later on in the application). A form does not have this property. The `Caption` property is also missing, quite simply because a frame does not have a title bar when it is used. Although when you design it a frame appears to be a special type of form, it is nevertheless merely a container for other components.

The properties and events have the same functions as they do in all other standard elements. So, you can write as many routines as you want that involve the frame. Frames are used in just the same way as components. This means that you never know which variables will be used in the project in which you implement a frame, or which functions and procedures are defined there. This is why a frame must function entirely independently, so that it can do its job properly and be implemented in any application.

7.5.3 Example of a frame

I use the following example in my own projects because it is a very simply constructed frame that does not have many functions. It is a dialog button, which should always appear in the same place in a program and look identical in every dialog. When this appears in a dialog, it should automatically be aligned on the lower margin. The buttons should always be the same distance from the margin (in this case, the right-hand margin). The frame should provide the OK and CANCEL buttons.

Frame structure

Logically, the frame we need for this task should not be too high – 40 points should be enough. You can simply position the buttons (in this case, `TButton`-type buttons) on the frame. They will be arranged exactly at runtime because the frame adjusts its width to the dialog in which it is inserted. When you are finished, the frame should look pretty much like the one in Figure 7.2 (as already mentioned, the actual position of the buttons makes no difference).

Figure 7.2 *A draft frame*

Basic functionality

As with a component, you still need to add a few basic functions. First of all, when the frame is inserted, it should appear on the lower margin of the form. You implement this function via the `Align` property by setting its value to `alBottom`. The buttons should also be ready to function. You set their `ModalResult` properties to `mrOk` or `mrCancel`. This ensures that these buttons will close the form later on without you having to write another line of source code for this purpose.

Another basic function concerns the button sequence, because the buttons should always appear in the same place. Once again, you will need to write a few lines of program code.

We shall use the `OnResize` event, so that the buttons can occupy their original place again even if the size of the form is changed. In the event-handling routine, the only thing you need to do is assign the correct values to the `Top` and `Left` properties, depending on the width of the frame. This ensures that the buttons will always be located in the same position relative to the right-hand margin of the frame (and therefore also the form in which the frame is used). You then simply place the second button relative to the first button. The following listing shows you how easy this is:

```
procedure TButtonFrame.FrameResize(Sender: TObject);
begin
  Button1.Left := width-80;
  Button2.Left := Button1.left-80;
end;
```

Now, we have everything we need. The frame automatically aligns itself to the bottom edge of the window, and adjusts itself to any changes in size. The buttons also always occupy the same location relative to the right-hand margin of the frame or the form. Now we can add the frame to our Component Palette

Adding to the Component Palette

Right-click on the frame and select the ADD TO PALETTE menu item from the context menu. A dialog appears in which you can enter more data about your frame. At this point, you can also see that Delphi handles frames in the same way as it does components. All the control elements on the frame are subordinate to the frame itself (the frame is the owner of the components). This is important later on if you want to access components. Figure 7.3 shows the dialog you use to add a frame to the Component Palette.

Figure 7.3 *Adding a frame to the Component Palette*

As you see, you can select both the icon and the Component Palette page into which you want to insert the frame. You can, of course, also specify a Component Palette page that does not exist yet. In this case, Delphi will create it. Once you have added the frame to the palette, you can save the unit and close it.

Inserting the frame into a project

As you have now added a frame to the Component Palette, you can use it like a normal component and simply insert it into a form. Delphi will ask whether you want to insert the unit that contains the frame into the project. Just click on YES. The dialog at designtime will then look pretty much like the one in Figure 7.4.

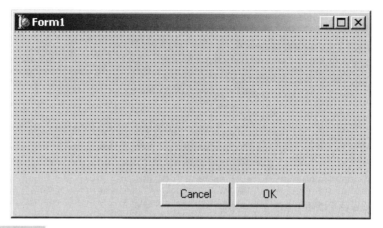

Figure 7.4 *The dialog with the frame at designtime*

Don't worry about the positions of the buttons, because this will sort itself out at runtime. Just start the program; the dialog appears. If you click on a button, the dialog closes. The buttons appear where you wanted them to. Figure 7.5 shows the same dialog at runtime.

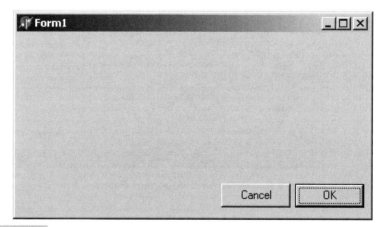

Figure 7.5 *The dialog at runtime*

7.5.4 Accessing a frame's components

As the components located on the frame are subordinate to the frame, the frame itself represents a component for Delphi. This component is, in turn, subordinate to the form.

As a result, it is harder to access the properties than it would be if the component were simply placed on a form. More precisely, the frame must still be inserted between them.

For example, to access the `Caption` property of `Button1` in our example, you need to use the following program code:

```
Form2.ButtonFrame1.Button1.Caption := 'Yep!';
```

In technical terms, the components contained in the frame need to be qualified. However, you will quickly get used to this when you start using frames. In any case, this is a useful and practical extension of the Delphi concept.

7.6 Checking entries

Every program needs data input. However, you will often need to check these entries before you process them. For example, you may need to prevent the user from inputting alphanumeric characters if you are working with number values, or you may want to arrange for the user to enter data in a particular format, e.g. for date values.

7.6.1 Input field restrictions

`TEdit` provides a number of events that you use to check keyboard actions: `OnKeyPress`, `OnKeyDown` and `OnKeyUp`. The `OnKeyDown` and `OnKeyUp` events use virtual key codes. In contrast, in the event-handling routine for `OnKeyPress`, you can evaluate the ASCII (or ANSI) value of the key that has been pressed. Obviously, these events are also present in other input fields, such as `TMemo` or `TRichEdit`.

The virtual key codes also allow you to evaluate special keys, such as Ctrl, ⇧, ↑ and ↓. The following example illustrates how to use `OnKeyPress` and `OnKeyDown`:

```
procedure TForm1.Edit1KeyPress(Sender: TObject; var Key:
Char);
begin
  if not (Key in [#8,#48..#57]) then Key := #0;
end;

procedure TForm1.Edit1KeyDown(Sender: TObject;
                              var Key: Word;
                              Shift: TShiftState);
begin
  if (ssCtrl in Shift) then
    if Key=Ord('5') then
      Edit1.SelText := 'Ctrl+5';
end;
```

Here, the first routine checks whether a number key has been pressed. The second routine checks whether the (Ctrl) and (5) keys were pressed simultaneously, and if so passes the value "Ctrl+5" to the input field. The `SelText` property represents the currently selected text. If `SelText` is assigned a value, then this value appears in the input field. Here is a similar routine:

```
procedure TForm1.Edit2KeyDown(Sender: TObject;
                              var Key: Word;
                              Shift: TShiftState);
begin
  if (ssCtrl in Shift) then
    if (Key in [48..57,65..90]) then
      Edit2.SelText := 'Ctrl+'+Char(Key);
end;
```

This routine also checks keys (A) to (Z) as well as the number keys. You can use this type of routine, for example, to check the input of keyboard shortcuts.

7.6.2 Predefined input masks

You use the `TMaskEdit` component in Delphi to draw the user's attention to a particular input mask. Delphi has a range of predefined masks for this purpose, which you can implement in the Input Mask Editor (Figure 7.6). You can, of course, also define your own masks. The property in which a mask is defined is called `EditMask`.

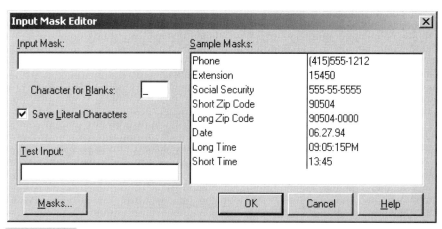

Figure 7.6 *The Input Mask Editor*

You enter your own definitions in the Input Mask field. Table 7.2 lists the characters that you can use in the mask.

Character	Meaning
!	Indicates that optional literal characters are to appear as leading blank spaces. If it is not present in the mask definition, then the optional characters appear as concluding blank spaces.
>	After this, all the characters that the user enters are converted into capital letters.
<	After this, all subsequent characters are converted into lower-case letters.
<>	After this, no check is carried out to see whether the characters are capitals or lower-case.
\	Followed by a literal character. This means you can also display the special characters used to define the mask in the input field.
L	You must enter a letter where you see this character.
l	You can only enter one letter where you see this character. However, this is not a mandatory entry.
A	Where you see this character, you must enter an alphanumeric or numerical character (A–Z, a–z or 0–9).
a	You can only enter an alphanumeric character (A–Z, a–z or 0–9) where you see this character. However, this is not a mandatory entry.
C	You must enter a character.
c	When you see this character, you can enter a character. However, this is not a mandatory entry.
0	You must enter a numerical character.
9	Enter a numerical character. However, this is not a mandatory entry.
#	When you see this character, you can only enter a numerical character or one of the "+" or "–" signs. However, this is not a mandatory entry.
:	When you enter time data, this character is used to separate hours, minutes and seconds. If another character is defined in the country-specific (locale) settings for separating time entries, then it is used here instead.
/	Separates days, months and years. If another character is defined in the country-specific (locale) settings for separating date entries, then it is used here instead.
;	Separates the three fields in the mask.
_	Adds blank spaces to the text in the input field. When you enter data, the cursor jumps over these blank spaces.

Table 7.2 *Characters used for defining masks*

The mask consists of three parts, each separated by a semicolon. The first part is the mask itself. The second part specifies whether the literal character is saved along with the text in the input field. For example, if the `Text` property of the input field is queried, then the literal characters are also transferred with the text. The third part specifies the character that appears at those places where entries are still to be made.

To define the second and third parts of the mask in the mask editor, activate the SAVE LITERAL CHARACTERS field or make an entry in the CHARACTER FOR BLANKS field.

7.6.3 Global hotkeys query

In Delphi, you can query all the hotkeys that are used in a form globally. This means, for example, that you do not need to program a key check for every single input field. Like the input components, each form provides the `OnKeyDown` and `OnKeyUp` events. However, to ensure that a keyboard action is first passed to the form and then to the input field, you must set the form's `KeyPreview` property to `true`. If, for example, you have placed several input fields on one form, you can globalize the key query for all input fields. Here is an example:

```
procedure TForm1.FormKeyDown(Sender: TObject; var Key:
Word; Shift: TShiftState);
var
   MyStr: String;
begin
   MyStr := '';
   case Ord(Key) of
      48: MyStr := 'Zero ';
      49: MyStr := 'One ';
      50: MyStr := 'Two ';
      51: MyStr := 'Three ';
      52: MyStr := 'Four ';
      53: MyStr := 'Five ';
      54: MyStr := 'Six ';
      55: MyStr := 'Seven ';
      56: MyStr := 'Eight ';
      57: MyStr := 'Nine ';
   end;
   if MyStr<>'' then
      Application.MessageBox(PChar('Key: '+MyStr),
                              'Key',mb_Ok);
end;
```

Handling files is the most basic function that a Windows program must be able to carry out, even if this only involves handling text files or typed files for storing data for which it would take too much time and effort to integrate an entire database. Delphi provides you with easy-to-use functions and procedures for accessing data.

7.7.1 Typed files

It is a good idea to use typed files, for example, for storing options. A typed file is not a file that has been typed (entered), but a file that is of a specific type. In a typed file, the size and structure of every entry correspond to the data type assigned to the file. This means you can use both standard data types and data types that you define yourself. This routine stores integer numbers in a file:

```
procedure SaveNumber(Nr: integer; FN: String);
var
  MyFile: file of integer;
begin;
  AssignFile(MyFile,FN);
  {$I-}
  if FileExists(FN) then
    Reset(MyFile)
  else
    ReWrite(MyFile);
  {$I+}
  if IOResult=0 then
  begin;
    System.Seek(MyFile,SizeOf(MyFile));
    Write(MyFile,nr);
  end;
  CloseFile(MyFile);
end;
```

The line

```
System.Seek(MyFile,SizeOf(MyFile));
```

sets the file pointer to the end of the file to attach another entry. The data in a file are always saved sequentially, one item after the other. You use the file pointer to specify which element is to be read or written. To read an element, you must replace the statement

```
Write(MyFile,nr);
```

with the statement

```
Read(MyFile,nr);
```

Here, we will address one of the fundamental structures found in Pascal; records. Data, which can consist of different data types, can be combined to form records. Records are also the basic structure from which Delphi develops objects and classes. However, you cannot store procedures or functions in records. Therefore, once you have combined (grouped) a few pieces of data in a record, you can then store this data in a typed file. Although a record is merely a (combined) data type, it is nonetheless a data type and can therefore be used for typed files.

The compiler directive that is used here originates from the earliest days of Pascal, and is still present in Delphi today. The {$I-} command deactivates the monitoring of file input and output, and therefore any errors cannot be detected and dealt with. After the file operation (opening or creating the file), you must switch the monitoring function on again and query the IOResult variable. This is 0 if no error occurred; if an error has occurred it is not 0. This is therefore an error query.

You must then execute the IOResult query. After this query, IOResult is reset to 0 so that no further errors can occur. If you do not query the value, you run the risk of an error still being present.

Alternatively, you can use a resources exception block, as described in Chapter 11. You could also use IOResult again.

7.7.2 Non-typed (text) files

In Delphi, you can also open files without knowing the precise format of their data. You write data to these files, or read data from them, in a slightly different way to typed files. The reason for this is that there is a fixed data format for typed files, and Delphi knows how big they are. For non-typed files, you need to tell Delphi the size of the data block you want to read. Fortunately, this is not too complicated.

To read data from non-typed files, use the BlockRead procedure; to write data to them, use the BlockWrite procedure. In each case, you must tell Delphi the size of the block of data that is to be read or written.

The transfer parameters for BlockRead and BlockWrite are the file variable, a buffer variable for the block that is to be read, the size that is to be read, and, optionally, a control variable that returns the size of the block that was actually read. Usually, the contents of these variables are identical to the block size you predefined. If there is a difference, it means that the file end has been reached.

A standard use for this kind of access is when you want to copy a file. Here, you can specify any size of copying buffer (the size of the block that is to be read and written):

```
procedure MyCopyFile(FN1,FN2: String;
                     MyBufSize: integer);
var
  Source,
  Target  : file;
  MyBuffer: Pointer;
  BytesRead,
  BytesWritten: integer;
begin;
  GetMem(MyBuffer,MyBufSize); //Find out buffer size
  AssignFile(Source,FN1);
  AssignFile(Target,FN2);
  Reset(Source,MyBufSize);
  ReWrite(Target,MyBufSize);
  repeat
    BlockRead(Source,MyBuffer^,MyBufSize,BytesRead);
    BlockWrite(Target,MyBuffer^,BytesRead,BytesWritten);
  until (BytesRead=0) or (BytesRead<>BytesWritten);
  CloseFile(Source);
  CloseFile(Target);
end;
```

This procedure does not contain any error-handling routines, so if you use it exactly as it appears above you may be faced with errors. The procedure simply illustrates a method for handling non-typed files.

7.7.3 Streams

Both versions of the file-handling procedures described in sections 7.7.1 and 7.7.2 come from the earliest days of Pascal and are also still implemented in Delphi 6. However, there is also a purely object-oriented alternative; streams. In contrast to the first two file-handling procedures, which do not use any objects or classes, streams use Tstream-type classes that provide the appropriate methods for saving data.

In general terms, the TFileStream type is responsible for handling files. There are other types that are used with strings, binary fields, or for reading or writing data via a COM interface, but they will not be described here.

Generating a file stream

As TFileStream is a class, you must create an instance of this class before you can start working with it. Because TFileStream works with files, you will need a file name in every case. In addition, when you create the instance, you must also specify how you want to open the file (to read it, to write data to it, write-protected, etc.). Different constants have been defined for file open mode, used to open and use a file. Tables 7.3 and 7.4 list some of the possible values.

Open mode	Meaning
fmCreate	Creates a file with the predefined file name. If this file exists already, it is opened so that you can read the data.
fmOpenRead	Opens an existing file as read-only.
fmOpenWrite	Opens an existing file as write-only. In this case, the existing contents are replaced.
fmOpenReadWrite	Opens a file for both writing and reading procedures, without replacing the existing contents.

Table 7.3 *Filestream open modes*

Access mode	Meaning
fmShareCompat	Compatible with the method used to open the file control blocks (FCBs).
fmShareExclusive	Prevents other applications from opening the file at the same time.
fmShareDenyWrite	Allows other applications to open the file, as read-only.
fmShareDenyRead	Allows other applications to open the file, as write-only.
fmShareDenynone	Allows other applications to open the file without any restrictions.

Table 7.4 *Filestream access modes*

You require both modes to open a file using a TFileStream. However, they are passed together (as a single parameter) so they are linked by a logical "or".

If a file cannot be opened, then the call to TFileStream.Create triggers an exception. You can counter this by using a resources exception block.

Reading and writing data in a file stream

To read data from a file stream, use the ReadBuffer method; to write data to a file stream, use the WriteBuffer method. When you call one of these methods, you also specify the number of bytes to be read. This means you can also read or write to data structures that have a fixed size:

```
type
   TMyAddress = record
      Name      : String;
      Firstname : String;
      Street    : String;
      State     : String;
      City      : String;
   end;


procedure SaveToStream(MyAddress: TAddress);
var
  MyStream  : TFileStream;
  MyFileName: String;
begin;
  if OpenDialog1.Execute then
  begin;
    MyFileName := OpenDialog1.FileName;
    try
        MyStream :=  FileStream.Create(MyFileName,
                     fmOpenReadWrite);
        MyStream.WriteBuffer(MyAddress,SizeOf(TAddress));
    except
        ShowMessage('Exception during file creation');
    end;
      MyStream.Free;
  end;
end;
```

The example shown above writes a data structure to a file stream. In a similar way, you can use the ReadBuffer statement to read data from the stream:

```
procedure LoadFromStream(MyAddress: TAddress);
var
  MyStream  : TFileStream;
  MyFileName: String;
begin;
  if OpenDialog1.Execute then
  begin;
    MyFileName := OpenDialog1.FileName;
    try
      MyStream :=  FileStream.Create(MyFileName,
                   fmOpenReadWrite);
      MyStream.Position := 0;
```

```
      MyStream.ReadBuffer(MyAddress,SizeOf(TAddress));
    except
      ShowMessage('Exception while opening the file');
    end;
    MyStream.Free;
  end;
end;
```

Saving data in a stream

As streams work with buffer variables, you can save different data formats one after the other and load them again. You cannot do this with the methods described in sections 7.7.1 and 7.7.2 because there the file format must be the same as the data format. Streams have no limitations in this respect. As a result, you can use streams to read any file format as long as you know the file's structure. Even files whose headers have a different data format from the data itself are not a problem:

```
type
  THeaderRec = record
    width,
    height     : integer;
    resolution : word;
    colors     : word;
    Lines      : integer;
  end;

  TDataRec = record
    NrOfBits : Word;
    Bitmask  : word;
  end;

var
  HeaderRec: THeaderRec;
  DataRec  : TDataRec;

procedure SaveToStream;
var
    MyStream  : TFileStream;
  MyFileName: String;
  i         : integer;
begin;
  if OpenDialog1.Execute then
  begin;
    MyFileName := OpenDialog1.FileName;
    try
```

```
    MyStream := FileStream.Create(MyFileName,
               fmOpenReadWrite);
except
    ShowMessage('Error when creating the file');
end;
//The write is carried out here
with MyStream do
begin;
    Position := 0;
    WriteBuffer(HeaderRec,SizeOf(THeaderRec));
    for i := 1 to HeaderRec.Lines do
        WriteBuffer(DataRec,SizeOf(TDataRec));
    end;
    MyStream.Free;
end;
end;
```

This procedure might be a bit complicated for beginners, so I shall explain the most important parts. First of all, two different data types are declared: THeaderRec and TDataRec. You want to write both of these to one file, where the HeaderRec variable is to be the file header and DataRec is for the data. The crucial part of the procedure (writing to the file itself) is concealed in these lines:

```
with MyStream do
begin;
    Position := 0;
    WriteBuffer(HeaderRec,SizeOf(THeaderRec));
    for i := 1 to HeaderRec.Lines do
        WriteBuffer(DataRec,SizeOf(TDataRec));
end;
```

Then the stream is generated in the usual way; the file is opened with read and write accesses. Now the header is written; among other things, this specifies how many DataRec-type records are to be written to the file. These are then written to the file one after the other by means of a For loop. The stream is not bothered by the fact that these records have a different format from the header, but simply writes the entire contents of the buffer to the file.

The same procedure is carried out in reverse when loading data from the file. First of all, the header is read. After this, Delphi then also knows how many records are to be read. You must therefore only read as many records as defined in the header. Once again, you can use a simple For loop to do this.

Streams are an object-oriented way to load and store data. They provide a great degree of flexibility, which you should take full advantage of in your programs. The alternative method involving typed file variables is old-fashioned, and I have only mentioned it to give you the complete picture and to highlight the differences. The actual way in which data are saved is completely transparent for the user; anyone using your program will be unable to identify whether the data are saved or loaded in a structured or object-oriented way.

7.8 Registry

The Registry database is a very important element of the Windows operating system. All the files that are relevant to the operating system and the installed applications are stored in the Registry. This means that the Registry database triggers all the old familiar *ini* files from the 16-bit world. Delphi can handle both *ini* and Registry files. However, under Windows 95, 98, NT, ME or 2000, you should only use the Registry.

7.8.1 Structure of the Registry database

The Registry consists of several databases, which contain the individual settings for the operating system and applications. The settings that affect users who are currently logged on are also saved in the Registry. You use the Regedit program to access the Registry so that you can change values there. Regedit displays the contents of the various databases in such a way that they look like a single file.

Anyone using your program would not expect to have to do anything to Registry entries. In contrast, as an application programmer, you will need to know how to evaluate and write entries in the Registry. Delphi has the TRegistry class, which provides you with methods for accessing the Registry database.

The Registry database is arranged by keys. The most useful main key for programming options is the HKEY_CURRENT_USER key. Another interesting main key is HKEY_CLASSES_ROOT, in which the application associations with file types, and the file types themselves, are registered. You can use this key if, for example, your program can access image files and you want to implement access to a particular file type, such as .jpg files, as a default program setting. Table 7.5 lists the various Registry keys.

In Delphi, you can make changes to all of these keys. However, you should always be aware that any changes in the Registry could also prevent the system running as a result. Be careful! In contrast, the options for saving your own program in the Registry do not involve any risks. It can become catastrophic only if you change existing values without knowing what these values involve.

7.8.2 *TRegistry* class

Delphi has a base class called TRegistry, which you use to access the Registry database. However, you will need to generate an instance of this class before you can start working with it. The TRegistry class provides you with methods for opening and

Key	Use
HKEY_CLASSES_ROOT	Registers the classes, different file types, and the applications used to open those file types.
HKEY_CURRENT_USER	Settings for the current user.
HKEY_LOCAL_MACHINE	Information about hardware and the installed software.
HKEY_USERS	Information about the people who use the computer.
HKEY_CURRENT_CONFIG	Current configuration.

Table 7.5   *Registry keys*

generating keys, and for writing and reading different values. This class also has properties which, for example, restrict access to or accelerate the process of writing values to the Registry. Nevertheless, you should not use the property called `LazyWrite` because it takes up unnecessarily large resources when you write values to the Registry.

Writing values to the Registry

To write values to the Registry, one key must be open. Use the `OpenKey` method to open a key. This passes the name of the key that is to be opened and a Boolean variable that specifies whether the key to be opened should be created if it does not already exist.

If you only want to create a key, use the `CreateKey` method. To delete a key, use the `DeleteKey` method. Both methods return a Boolean value that signals that the operation has been successful.

The following shows how to write a value to the Registry:

```
procedure InsertValueToRegistry;
var
   Reg : TRegistry;
begin;
   Reg := TRegistry.Create;
   try
      Reg.RootKey := HKEY_CURRENT_USER;
      if OpenKey('TestKey',TRUE) then
         WriteString('TestString','This is a test');
   finally
      CloseKey;
      Reg.Free;
   end;
end;
```

In this example, a `try...finally` statement ensures that the key and the Registry are always closed again if an exception occurs. If you use this method to write a value to the Registry, then the value is not actually written until `CloseKey` is called. Before this, the value is simply held in a buffer.

Reading values from the Registry

You use the same method to read values from the Registry. The only difference is that the `WriteString` statement is replaced by `ReadString`:

```
procedure ReadValueFromRegistry;
var
    Reg : TRegistry;
begin;
    Reg := TRegistry.Create;
    try
        Reg.RootKey := HKEY_CURRENT_USER;
        if OpenKey('TestKey',TRUE) then
            MyString := ReadString('TestString');
    finally
        CloseKey;
        Reg.Free;
    end;
end;
```

These options enable you to write all the options in your applications to the Registry, and to read them again as required.

7.9 Threads

You can run different threads simultaneously within the same program. Threads run transparently for the user without requiring a specific action to be executed. An example of a thread is the way in which the contents of a directory are checked. In your program, you can use a thread to implement a function that shows the contents of a directory immediately if these contents change. Similar functionality is implemented in Windows Explorer.

7.9.1 *Synchronize* method

Although threads run independently of the rest of the program, they do use the same address space or memory area. For this reason, you must be careful not to overwrite memory. Use the `Synchronize` method to prevent this.

In Delphi, each program already has one thread, the main VCL thread. This is used to handle messages that originate from your program's components. However, some components do not use this thread; these are known as thread-safe components. If, for example, you use a method of one of these components, you may overwrite a shared memory range by mistake, which could cause a program crash.

In the `Synchronize` method, you simply instruct Delphi to use the main VCL thread. This method therefore ensures that all the messages and actions in your program are synchronized with each other, so that no memory conflicts arise and the program can run smoothly. This may slow down the execution speed a little, but it shouldn't make much difference to modern computers.

Some Delphi components are also thread-safe, e.g. graphics components that still use the VCL main thread to access things like the `Font` property. Despite this, for safety's sake you should always use the `Synchronize` method and put up with the slight reduction in execution speed.

As its transfer parameter, `Synchronize` requires a method that is specified in the thread. This means that you cannot call it directly by, for example, clicking on a button in the `OnClick` event-handling routine. You need to use a wrapper instead; this is a method that calls the event-handling routine. An example of this is shown below, where a click on the `TButton`-type button triggers synchronization:

```
procedure TMyThread.ButtonClick;
begin;
    Button1Click();
end;

procedure TMyThread.Execute;
begin;
    Synchronize(ButtonClick);
end;
```

7.9.2 Declaring a thread

To declare a thread, you can select FILE | NEW | OTHER to display a view of the Object Repository. Then click on the Thread Object icon at the bottom of the new page. Alternatively, declare the thread yourself in your own program. If you use the Object Repository option, then Delphi creates a unit with a complete thread framework. The most important method in a thread is the `Execute` method, in which the actual thread function is implemented. The structure of a thread looks like this:

```
unit Unit2;

interface

uses
    Classes;

type
```

```
TMyThread = class(TThread)
private
  { Private declarations }
protected
  procedure Execute; override;
end;

implementation

{ TMyThread }

procedure TMyThread.Execute;
begin
  { Place thread code here }
end;

end.
```

7.9.3 Initializing a thread

You can initialize a thread yourself by overwriting the Create method of the TThread object. The Create method expects a Boolean value as its transfer parameter, which specifies whether the thread is to be started immediately or after Resume is called. In the Create method, you can, for example, specify the thread's priority and whether the thread should be removed automatically from memory once it has been completed.

Usually, you should not need to overwrite the Create method. You simply call this method, specify the priority, and then start the thread. In the next example, TMyThread is a user-defined descendant of TThread, a thread you have created yourself:

```
procedure StartThread;
var
  MyThread : TMyThread
begin;
  MyThread := TMyThread.Create(true);
  MyThread.Priority := tpLower;
  MyThread.FreeOnTerminate := true;
  MyThread.Resume;
end;
```

If you call Create with the parameter true, then the thread is generated but not executed immediately. Now set the priority to a low value and use the FreeOnTerminate property to specify that the thread is automatically deleted from memory after it is finished. After this, call Resume to start the thread.

At any time, you can call Suspend to stop a thread that has been started or call Resume to restart it.

7.10 Dynamic link libraries

DLLs were introduced as a feature of the Windows operating system. They are basically files that contain compiled, executable program code. The Windows System folder contains a large number of DLLs. However, you cannot run DLLs like programs. Instead, programs access the functions that are contained in a DLL, i.e. a DLL is a library of functions that can be used by a number of programs.

This is the great advantage of a DLL. Not only can it be used by any program that runs under Windows, but frequently-used functions can be moved into a DLL that only needs to exist once, later on, on the target system. If you need to change or extend the functions in a DLL, then all you need to do is generate a new version of the DLL. The actual program, which merely calls those functions, remains unchanged.

In addition, DLLs are independent of the programming language. This is why in a program created in Delphi, you can call functions from a DLL that was created in C++, and you can also write DLLs with Delphi and make their functions available to other programmers who are working with C++. You can also, of course, use Visual Basic to access DLLs.

7.10.1 Structure of a dynamic link library in Delphi

The basic structure of a DLL is similar to that of a unit, with the difference that the reserved word Library is used instead of the reserved word Unit. DLLs also contain a section that is not present in a unit (because it doesn't make sense there). This is a section in which the functions contained in the DLL are exported. The basic structure of a DLL looks like this:

```
library DLLName;

uses
   SysUtils,
   Classes;

{$R *.RES}
```

This is where the functions and procedures present in the DLL are declared.

```
exports
```

The functions that the DLL makes available to other programs are named in this section.

```
begin
```

This is where the DLL's main program is located. In contrast to a Delphi program, no forms are created here because the DLL is called externally.

```
end.
```

As you can see, the DLL is structured in a similar way to the main program in a project. You can, of course, also insert other units into a DLL – even units that contain forms. If, when you load the DLL, you want it to execute initialization functions, then you can program these functions in the DLL's main program.

Exports section

In the exports section, you can also specify an index for the functions contained in the DLL. Later on, an application can then use this index to call these functions. However, this option is only present to ensure backwards compatibility, and it may cause problems with other programming languages, so it is not described in any further detail here.

You can also export one of the DLL's functions under another name from the actual function name. To do this, simply use the name clause. In the DLL's exports section, this is how you change the name by which you call a function. This example illustrates the procedure:

```
library MyDLL;

uses
  SysUtils,
  Classes;

{$R *.RES}

function MaxValue(x,y: integer):integer;
begin
  if x>y then
    Result := x
  else
    Result := y;
end;

function MinValue(x,y: integer):integer;
begin;
  if x<y then
    Result := x
  else
    Result := y;
```

GO AHEAD!

```
end;

exports
   MaxValue,
   MinValue name 'MyMin';

begin
end.
```

After I had jotted down this example in Delphi, I noticed that the same example is also used in the Delphi online help (with another function name, and with the `MinValue` function coming first). This wasn't deliberate; it was just the simplest function that I thought of at the time.

> **Tip** Naturally, you can also include units that you wrote yourself in the DLL. In the exports section you can also execute routines that have been declared in the integrated units. The prerequisite for this is that these functions and procedures are published.

Transferring strings

At this point, there are a few problems with strings. You must use the *ShareMem* unit if you want to transfer strings to a DLL by one method or another, or if you expect a DLL to return a string as the result of a function. This unit must be integrated both in the DLL source code and in the first unit of the project that the DLL is to use. In this case, `ShareMem` is merely an interface unit. The actual interface used to transfer the string is hidden in the *BorlndMM.dll* library. You must, of course, also provide this DLL along with your program.

> **Tip** You can also prevent the use of `ShareMem` by working with the `PChar` or `ShortString` data types instead of with strings. It is very easy to convert a `String` to a `PChar`. On the other hand, if you use `ShareMem` you don't need to worry whether you have integrated it correctly or whether you have remembered to supply the *BorlndMM.dll* file.

7.10.2 Integrating a dynamic link library

Before you can use the functions of a DLL, you must write an import unit for it. This unit regulates how the functions that are defined in a DLL are called. As the program must call something, and the DLL is only a compiled program file, you need the import unit to load the DLL and to call its functions.

You can call a DLL in two ways: statically or dynamically. The static call has the advantage that it is easier to implement. The disadvantage is that the program will not function without the statically integrated DLL because the DLL is loaded into memory immediately when the program is called. It makes no difference whether the functions present in the DLL will actually be required. If the statically integrated DLL is not present in the target system, then the program will also fail to run.

In contrast, dynamically integrated DLLs do not need to be present in the target system. However, this also means that you cannot call their functions either. A dynamically integrated DLL is not loaded until its functions are actually required. The easiest option in this case is to simply block the functions of dynamically integrated DLLs if the DLL does not exist (this is checked anyway).

Tip 32-bit DLLs differentiate between capitals and lower-case letters, so be careful how you type when you program this module or when you call its functions.

GO AHEAD!

Static integration of a dynamic link library

Although you don't really need an interface unit to statically integrate a DLL, I still recommend that you use one. It is much clearer, and keeping a program text easy to understand is the most important factor in successful programming.

The following procedure of the *MyDLL* DLL is to be integrated statically into the project:

```
function MaxValue; external 'MyDLL.dll';
```

Delphi now searches for the DLL when the program starts, because it assumes that the DLL is absolutely necessary. If the DLL is not found, then the program terminates and an error message appears.

Dynamic integration of a dynamic link library

An import unit is required to integrate a DLL dynamically. It is also a little less complicated than the static integration procedure. Once you have understood what is going on, you will see the logic behind it. Windows uses handles to access files. These handles are actually only integer values. When you load a DLL dynamically, you assign it a handle, via which access to the DLL is controlled. The handle is returned when the DLL is loaded. If the return value is 0, then a handle could not be assigned; the DLL was therefore not found, and you must block the functions defined in the DLL accordingly.

If the handle was assigned correctly, you can call the DLL's functions. To do this, you use a pointer that references the address of a particular function or procedure within the DLL. To find out a function's address, use the `GetProcAddress` function. Once again, you can also carry out a check here. If the function you are looking for does not exist in the DLL, then `GetProcAddress` returns the value `nil`.

The following code shows an import unit for the DLL you programmed above, *MyDLL*. However, this time you are integrating the DLL dynamically:

```
unit DLLImport;

interface

type
   TFuncMaxValue = function(x,y: integer): integer;
   THandle       = integer;

function GetMax(x,y:integer): integer;

implementation

function GetMax(x,y: integer): integer;
var
  Handle: THandle;
  FuncMaxValue : TFuncMaxValue;
begin;
  Handle := LoadLibrary('MyDLL.dll');
  if Handle<>0 then
  begin;
    @FuncMaxValue := GetProcAddress(Handle, MaxValue);
    if @FuncMaxValue<>nil then
      Result := FuncMaxValue(x,y);
    FreeLibrary(Handle);
  end;
end;

end.
```

The DLL is not loaded into memory until you call LoadLibrary. This reduces the amount of memory that the program requires, because as soon as the DLL's functions are no longer required, you can remove the DLL by calling FreeLibrary. In addition, the program can run without the DLL being present, because although the DLL's functions are missing, the presence of the DLL itself is not a matter of life and death for the program, as is the case when the DLL is integrated statically.

If you are wondering why you have to use a pointer, just imagine that the DLL is a closet in a room. To take something from the closet, you first need to know which room it is in (you therefore require a pointer to the closet); you then need to know which drawer the object is in (this corresponds to the pointer to the function/procedure). When you have this information, you can fetch the object from the closet. For Delphi, this means that once you know where the function you require is hidden, you can call it.

7.11 Linking and embedding objects

In this section, we are going to take a look at the technique known as object linking and embedding (OLE). You use this technique to integrate into your own application one or more documents that were originally generated in an entirely different application. With OLE, you can embed the object completely and save it within your application, or simply link the object by creating and saving a reference to the object (it must then also be possible to find the object at this location).

An application that provides the type of objects that can be embedded is called an OLE server. Applications that integrate the objects, or can save links to objects in other applications, are called OLE clients. These applications are much easier to design than OLE servers.

The special feature of OLE objects is the way in which they can be edited after they have been embedded or linked. During editing, the menu of the application that was originally used to create the object is combined with the menu of the application in which the object has been embedded. The object is then edited with the functions of the original application.

7.11.1 `TOleContainer` component

The component Delphi uses to provide OLE functionality is called `TOleContainer`. You will find it on the Component Palette System page. `TOleContainer` has many of the functions of OLE 2.0 and makes it easier for you to work with embedded objects. `TOleContainer` is therefore able to embed foreign objects and save them in a component, and also to create links to an external object and to save those links.

However, the method used by the `TOleContainer` component to save and load data uses a format that is not recognized by the external application. Therefore, if you save a object with the `TOleContainer` component, you can no longer load it into the application in which it was originally created. Nonetheless, you can still use the original application to edit the object in the `TOleContainer` component if the object has been loaded.

This is where the `GroupIndex` property in the menu entries comes into its own. Menus or menu items with a group index value of 0, 2 or 4 are not replaced by the menus of the application that generated the object. If the menus or menu items have a group index of 1, 3 or 5, they are always replaced, so these menu items disappear as soon as an OLE object is opened. They become available again only when the corresponding application is closed.

`TOleContainer` properties

`TOleContainer` has a few properties that are important for OLE objects; Table 7.6 lists the most important ones.

Property	Meaning
AllowActiveDoc	There are a number of interfaces for OLE. If you set `AllowActiveDoc` to `true`, then `TOleContainer` can use the `IOleDocumentSite` interface. If you set it to `false`, then the OLE control element must use a current interface, e.g. `IOleClientSide`. In today's systems, you can usually leave the default setting.
AllowInPlace	If `AllowInPlace` is set to `true`, then the object is activated within your application. If it is set to `false`, then a separate window is used for the OLE object.
AutoActivate	Specifies how an OLE object is activated. Activating an OLE object is the same as loading a server application so that you can edit it. The default setting is `aaDoubleClick`, which means that the user must double-click on the object before they can edit it. The other settings are `aaGetFocus` and `aaManual`. If you set the property to `aaManual`, at runtime the OLE object must be activated by calling the `DoVerb(ovShow)` method.
AutoVerbMenu	If this property is set to `true`, then Delphi automatically creates a context menu for the container component. This menu includes the functions that the OLE container provides for the object it contains. This action is called a verb. If a context menu has already been specified for the `TOleContainer` component, then the verb menu replaces it.
CopyOnSave	Shows whether a temporary copy of the container object is created when the OLE object is saved using the `SaveToFile` or `SaveToStream` methods of the OLE container. In this copy, the redundant data are compressed and then saved to use less memory. If the property is set to `false`, then the object is saved directly, without data compression.
Iconic	Specifies how the embedded object should be displayed. If you set the property to `true`, then a server application symbol appears instead of the OLE object; if the property is set to `false`, then the object is displayed.
OldStreamFormat	Specifies the format in which the object is to be saved. If you want to load data that were saved with a program created with a previous version of Delphi, then set this property to `false`, otherwise set it to `true`. The difference is that the new format also includes header information.
SizeMode	Used to specify the size of the embedded object when it is displayed in your application. Possible settings are `smClip` (normal size display), `smCenter` (display centered, normal size), `smScale` (display scaled with adjusted size ratios), `smStretch` (adjusted to fit the `TOleContainer` component) and `smAutosize` (normal size display; the container object will be adjusted automatically).

Table 7.6 **Properties of the** `TOleContainer` **component**

There are also some properties that are not usually found in the Object Inspector. Table 7.7 lists the most important unpublished properties.

Property	Meaning
CanPaste	This property is `true` if the Clipboard contains an OLE object that can be inserted into the container.
Linked	This property is `true` if the object in OleContainer was linked with the application, and `false` if this is an embedded object. To query this property, the object must be loaded into the OleContainer.
Modified	This property is `true` if the OLE object has been changed. If not, or if the OLE container does not contain an object, then the value `Modified false` is returned.
NewInserted	Specifies whether a new object was inserted using the `InsertObjectDialog` method. If `NewInserted` is true, then you can call `OleContainer1.doVerb(ovShow)` to start the server application and edit the object.
OleClassName	If an OLE object is loaded, this property returns the class name of the OLE object under which this object is stored in the Registry database.
SourceDoc	Returns the name of a linked OLE object. This only happens if one is present in the OLE container, otherwise the string is empty.
State	The status of the OLE object is stored in this property. Use a read access to find out whether the container contains an object (`osLoaded`) or not (`osEmpty`), or whether the object is being edited (`osUIActive`), or whether the server application for the object is running (`osRunning`).

Table 7.7 *Other properties of* `TOleContainer`

7.11.2 Using `TOleContainer`

As always, the best way to explain something is to use an example project. For this reason, I have written a small demonstration to illustrate the various options provided by `TOleContainer`.

Creating the program interface

The program's interface consists of a single main menu, a `TOleContainer` component that is located on `alClient`, and two dialogs (one to open the data and one to save them). The main menu consists of the `File` and `Edit` menus. For the EDIT menu, I have selected a group index of 0 so that it will not be overwritten by the OLE server application.

For the FILE menu, you require a menu item that is used to load an OLE object, a menu item to close the server application, one to close the program, one to open it, and one to save it. For the EDIT menu, you only need the CUT, COPY and PASTE menu items.

> **Tip** The simplest method here is to select the default menus for FILE and EDIT from the template and delete the menu items that are not required. To do this, simply select the menu item INSERT FROM TEMPLATE from the Menu Designer's context menu and then delete the menu items that are not required or change their names.

Figure 7.7 illustrates the complete program interface.

Figure 7.7 *The user interface of the example program*

Embedding and editing an OLE object

The first thing to do now is to add an OLE object to our application. After the object has been added, the application that is to be used to edit it should also start immediately. To do this, you require the `DoVerb` function in `TOleContainer`. This is always called with a parameter that informs the container component of the required action. In this example, this is the `ovShow` action, which loads the application that is to be used to edit the object. The object is selected via a standard Windows dialog, which is provided when you call the `InsertObjectDialog` method. The complete implementation then looks like this:

```
procedure TForm1.EmbedOLEObject1Click(Sender: TObject);
begin
  with OleContainer1 do
    if InsertObjectDialog then
      doVerb(ovShow);
end;
```

You may recognize the dialog you now see from other Windows applications. It is shown in Figure 7.8. The `InsertObjectDialog` method is a function that returns the value `true` if the user has clicked on the OK button to close the dialog, or `false` if the user has clicked on the CANCEL button.

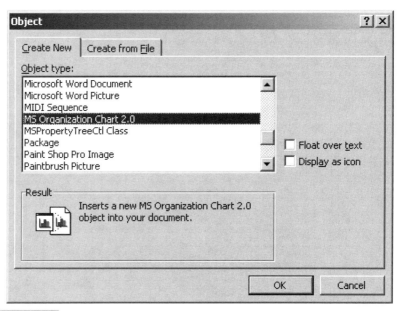

Figure 7.8 *The dialog for inserting an object*

The object has now been loaded, and the server application used to edit it has been started. You must now ensure that the user can also close the server application. To do this, call the `Close` method in `TOleContainer`. You program the functionality in a second menu item. To prevent errors, you should also check that the server application is active and then close it:

```
procedure TForm1.CloseOLEObject1Click(Sender: TObject);
begin
  if OleContainer1.State = osUIActive then
    OleContainer1.Close;
end;
```

Figure 7.9 shows the program's interface after an object has been embedded and the server application has been started. This object is a Paintbrush object, and the menus in the Paintbrush program have been combined with the menus in our application. The form's title bar shows that we are actually dealing with our own application.

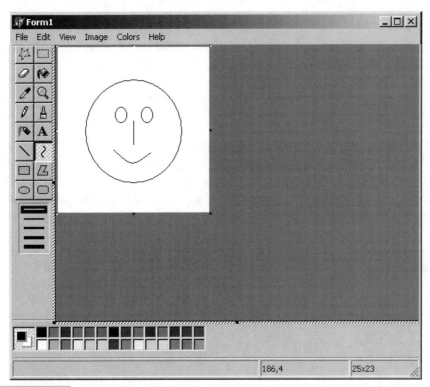

Figure 7.9 *The example project in which the server application has been started*

Loading and saving an embedded object

The next step concerns the functions used to load and save an object. In this example project, I chose the file extension *ole* as the default file extension. You can, of course, choose your own file extension if required. To load and save the files, use the `LoadFromFile` and `SaveToFile` methods of the `TOleContainer` component. As a result, it is very easy to program the corresponding functionality:

```
procedure TForm1.Open1Click(Sender: TObject);
begin
  if OpenDialog1.Execute then
    if FileExists(OpenDialog1.FileName) then
      OleContainer1.LoadFromFile(OpenDialog1.FileName);
end;
```

```
procedure TForm1.Save1Click(Sender: TObject);
begin
  if OleContainer1.State=osLoaded then
    if SaveDialog1.Execute then
      OleContainer1.SaveToFile(SaveDialog1.FileName);
end;
```

Don't worry about the procedure's name; as I have already mentioned, Delphi is responsible for name assignment and does not accept extended characters such as umlauts in descriptors.

To edit the embedded object, simply double-click on it. The last step is to program the menu items in our EDIT menu.

Cutting, copying, and inserting OLE objects

TOleContainer does not provide a specific method for cutting data. However, it does have methods for copying and inserting data. Here, we shall copy the object (if one is present) and then delete it. TOleContainer has the DestroyObject method for deleting an embedded object, and we shall use this method here:

```
procedure TForm1.Cut1Click(Sender: TObject);
begin
  if OLEContainer1.State = osLoaded then
  begin;
    with OleContainer1 do
    begin;
      copy;
      DestroyObject;
    end;
  end;
end;


procedure TForm1.Copy1Click(Sender: TObject);
begin
  if OLEContainer1.State = osLoaded then
    OleContainer1.Copy;
end;


procedure TForm1.Paste1Click(Sender: TObject);
begin
  if OleContainer1.CanPaste then
    OleContainer1.Paste;
end;
```

GO AHEAD!

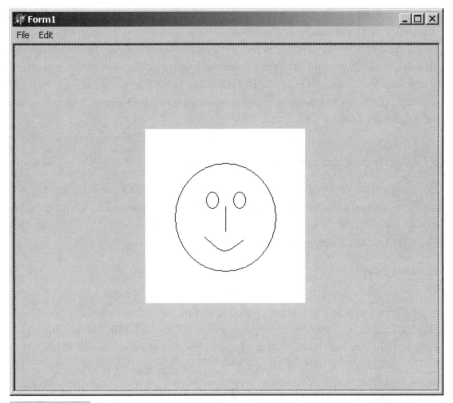

Figure 7.10 **The finished example project with an embedded object**

Our example program now has a basic range of functions that we can work with. You can now start the program. Try it out and see what happens. Figure 7.10 shows the application with an embedded object. However, the server application has not been started here.

7.12 Dynamic data exchange

Dynamic data exchange (DDE) is the term used to describe the ability of a program to transfer data to another program. In this case, one program must be a DDE client and the other a DDE server. In Delphi, you can create both types of program, or even create a program that is both a DDE server and a DDE client.

The connection between a DDE client and a DDE server is called a conversation. In this case, data are exchanged continuously between the two applications. The result is immediately visible. For example, if both programs are in a conversation and you change a character string that is exchanged during the conversation, then the result of this change can be seen in both applications.

You can also control the DDE server via the DDE client by passing commands that the server understands and then returns the result of the operations. An example of this is administering a program via a DDE client. Via a DDE client, a system administrator could call functions in a program that cannot be accessed by a regular user, and would still receive acknowledgment of this.

7.12.1 Dynamic data exchange components

The components required to use DDE are located on the Component Palette System page. To program a server, you require the TDDEServerConv and TDDEServer-Item components. To program a client, you require the TDDEClientConv and TDDEClientItem components.

TDDEServerItem

A DDE server is usually called via the client. Here, the connection is created via the name of the TDDEServerItem component. Once the connection has been established, data sent from the client can be received, and the client then be updated again. The server application therefore always supplies the data requested by the client.

The data are saved in the Lines and Text properties. Text and Lines correspond to each other. This means that the first line of Lines (which is a string list) always contains the contents of Text. If one of the properties is updated, then the other changes accordingly.

The OnChange event of the TDDEServerItem component is triggered if data are changed.

TDDEServerConv

Although the use of TDDEServerConv is optional, the component is required if the server is to run macros that are called by the client. The component is also used to specify a topic for the conversation. As Name is the only property of the TDDEServerConv, this is used to specify the topic. If this component is not present (it is optional), the TDDEServerItem component specifies the topic via the Caption in the form.

A form has only one Caption, so if you want to specify several topics, you must also use several TDDEServerConv components, each of which must have a unique name.

TDDEClientItem

TDDEClientItem enables an application to function as a DDE client. This means that the application can now create a connection to a DDE server, and send and receive data or macros to and from this server.

As in the `TDDEServerItem` component, the `Lines` and `Text` properties used here also contain the data that are to be exchanged via the DDE connection. The `OnChange` event in the `TDDEClientItem` component is triggered if the data changed.

TDDEClientConv

The `TDDEClientConv` component is the actual conversation component that the client uses to communicate with the server. `TDDEClientConv` provides several methods for carrying out a conversation. These include sending data explicitly to the server application, requesting data, and executing macros.

7.12.2 Example dynamic data exchange project

Later, you will find an example showing how to use DDE; this is more interesting than relying on a description. You will program the DDE server, which reacts to queries from the client, and then program the DDE client, which carries out the queries and executes macros or commands. In this case, we want to create a very simple program with which an administrator can change a user's password. In other words, you will write an application that can function as a server (but does not have to) and that allows only the administrator to change the password by means of a special program (which involves our DDE client). You will also implement a function to query the password so you can see if the change has actually taken place.

Programming the server

To save time and memory, and to make the procedure less complicated, the password will not be saved. For this reason, the password in our program will be entered as a global typed constant.

Server interface

First of all, we shall deal with the server's interface. The only thing you need is a way to display the password (so that you can check if it has been changed) and a button for closing the procedure. Of course, our `DDEServer` components are also required. Figure 7.11 shows the server.

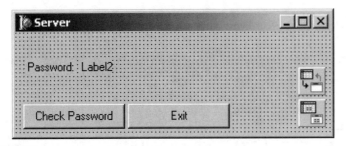

Figure 7.11   *The DDE server at designtime*

You must now make the following settings. If you do not follow the steps exactly, the example will not work. For the `TDDEServerConv` component, enter the name `DDEPassword` (spelling it exactly as shown), and for the `TDDEServerItem` component, enter the name `DDEServer1` (watch the spelling here as well). You can assign any names you like to the other components, but you will need to modify the source code later on if you use names other than those shown in the example. The project is called Server. This is also important because you will require the project name later on to call the server automatically.

The `TDDEServerItem` and `TDDEServerConv` components are required later to create the connection. This is why you must take care that the names of these components are always written correctly. You must also remember these names when you create your own projects with DDE functions.

Programming the functionality

The server has only one task; to react to commands sent from the client. In this case, we shall supply a new password along with the change password command. We must therefore transfer a macro contain several lines of code. However, this is one of the client's functions, and at this stage we are concerned only with the evaluation.

The `TDDEServerConv` component in the `OnExecuteMacro` event is used to evaluate the macros that have been sent. Therefore, we will write an event-handling routine for this event, which evaluates the command we transferred and returns a message to the client. To do this, simply set the `Text` property in the `TDDEServerItem` component. The connection already exists and the result is therefore returned immediately.

In addition to the command for changing the password, we have also implemented a way to close the server as a result of a client command. The `MyPassword` variable has been declared as a global typed constant, directly under the form declaration in the interface section of the unit:

```
var
  Form1:  TForm1;


const
  MyPassword: String = 'default';
```

Now let's look at the event-handling routine of `OnExecuteMacro`:

```
procedure TForm1.DDEPasswordExecuteMacro(Sender: TObject;
Msg: TStrings);
begin
  if msg.Count>0 then
  begin;
  if Msg.Strings[0]='ChPassword' then
  begin;
```

```
      MyPassWord := Msg.Strings[1];
      DDEServer1.Text := 'Password changed';
    end;
    if Msg.Strings[0]='Exit' then
      close;
  end;
end;
```

This code means that you have already programmed the majority of the server's functions. At this point, you must remember two of the commands that we have used. It is
also vital that you remember their spelling because I have not implemented conversion to
capital letters (although this would also be possible). Our two commands for the server
are called ChPassword and Exit. The ChPassword command is used to pass the
password itself. In other words, we must think about sending a multiline macro.

Programming the client

The client is to start the server automatically (which it will also do in the default setting) and prompt the user to change the password. To achieve this, we must create a
conversation between the client and the server, for which we require the name of the
server component and the name of the server program.

Client interface

The client requires very little coding: one TEdit component in which the user enters
the new password, buttons to change the password, close the server and close the client,
and the TDDEClientItem and TDDEClientConv components. Figure 7.12 shows
the client.

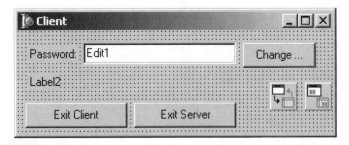

Figure 7.12   *The DDE client at designtime*

The connection will be created at runtime. So that you can start writing programs
right way, here are the component names: the TDDEClientItem component is
called DDEClient1, the TDDEClientConv component is called ClientConv1,
and the project is called Client.

Programming the functionality

First of all, you must create the connection to your DDE server. For this, you require the names of the server components and the name of the server program. The actual call (or the creation of the connection) is programmed in the event-handling routine for `OnActivate` in the client's main form:

```
procedure TForm1.FormActivate(Sender: TObject);
begin
  ClientConv1.SetLink('Server','DDEPassword');
  DDEClient1.DDEItem := 'DDEServer1';
end;
```

If you have typed everything correctly, the DDE server will now start at the same time as the DDE client. However, we have not yet implemented any commands. To pass a command to the server, you require the `ExecuteMacro` method or the `ExecuteMacroLines` method of the `TDDEClientConv` component.

The parameters that are to be passed for `ExecuteMacro` are a `PChar` (not a string) and a wait flag, which specifies whether the client is to wait until the server has processed all the macros that have already been sent to it before sending other macros to the server. In our example, where the password is being changed, you set this flag to `false`. For the command used to close the server program, set it to `true`.

The parameters to be passed for `ExecuteMacroLines` are a `String`-type object, i.e. a list of strings. For this, we shall use the `Lines` property of `TDDEClientItem`, which is a string list. In addition to this, the same wait flag is passed:

```
procedure TForm1.Button1Click(Sender: TObject);
begin
  DDEClient1.Lines.Clear;
  DDEClient1.Lines.Add('ChPassword');
  DDEClient1.Lines.Add(Edit1.Text);
  ClientConv1.ExecuteMacroLines(DDEClient1.Lines,false);
end;
```

```
procedure TForm1.Button3Click(Sender: TObject);
begin
  ClientConv1.ExecuteMacro('Exit',true);
end;
```

The only things still missing are the procedure for closing the client (a simple `close` call) and the procedure for specifying the reaction to server messages. In the server, we have generated the return messages that will be returned to the client. We can react to them in the OnChange event of the TDDEClientItem component. However, this reaction will simply be to display the message in a TLabel component:

```
procedure TForm1.DDEClient1Change(Sender: TObject);
begin
  Label2.Caption := DDEClient1.Text;
end;
```

So, our two programs are now complete. If you start the client, the server should now start automatically and appear as a button in the start bar. Try out the functions.

If Delphi displays an error message, saying that the connection could not be created, you may have typed something incorrectly somewhere. Alternatively, you may not have compiled the server. Figure 7.13 shows these two programs in use together.

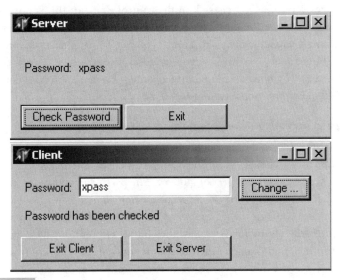

Figure 7.13 *Server and client in use together*

7.13 Drag and drop

The drag-and-drop technique is used a great deal in Windows applications. It provides the users of an application with a very user-friendly way to work; they simply drag the object they require to the place they want it by holding down the mouse button, then releasing the mouse button to execute a specific operation.

It is not difficult to implement drag-and-drop operations in Delphi. Many of the operations can be executed automatically (or manually if necessary), and the only thing you need to deal with is the implementation of the actual action when the mouse button is released.

7.13.1 Drag and drop events

Delphi 6 provides a number of events for a drag-and-drop operation for which you write an event-handling routine. However, if you have set the `DragMode` property of the component that is to be dragged to `dmAutomatic`, then the first step below (the start of the dragging operation) is no longer required.

Starting the drag-and-drop operation

To start the dragging operation, call the `BeginDrag` method. The best place to do this is in the `OnMouseDown` event of the element you want to drag. If the `DragMode` property is set to `dmAutomatic`, then you do not need to call `BeginDrag` because Delphi does this for you when you press the mouse button.

If you want to execute a drag-and-drop operation with an element that can contain the focus, you should start the drag-and-drop operation manually, otherwise the cursor would change every time you clicked on the control element; this is not a good idea because it might confuse the user. The `BeginDrag` method requires a parameter with which you specify when the drag is to start. If you pass `true`, then the dragging operation starts immediately (in this case you could also set the `DragMode` property to `dmAutomatic`). If you pass `false`, then the dragging operation does not start until the user holds down the mouse button and moves the mouse.

Checking and accepting the element that has been dragged

The target of the drag-and-drop operation can either accept an element or not accept it. The mouse arrow changes accordingly. You can check the dragged element in the `OnDragOver` event in the target component. The parameter you use to accept or not accept the dragged element is the `Accept` parameter.

This event also contains the `DragState` parameter with which you can check how the user moved the mouse in relation to the control element. `DragState` can have three states: `dsDragEnter` (the mouse is moved to the control element), `dsDragLeave` (the mouse is moved away from the control element), and `dsDragMove` (the mouse passes over the control element).

You use the `Source` parameter of the `TObject` type (just like the `Sender` parameter) to check which control element is being dragged to the target component, and then to set the `Accept` property to `true` or `false`, accordingly.

Placing the source on the target

The `OnDragDrop` event of the target component is responsible for this. In this event, you program the function that is to be executed after you drop the source object (e.g. the loading of a file). The `Source` parameter is once again available here. You use it to check the source object and, depending on the object's type, execute a particular operation. This check is carried out in the same way as for the sender object.

The drag-and-drop operation for target components is now complete. However, you can also program a final operation for the source component.

Completing the drag-and-drop operation for the source

The OnEndDrag event of the component that has been moved is responsible for this. In this event, you can evaluate the target in which the component has been stored. The Target parameter contains the target. You can evaluate Target in the same way as the Sender parameter.

7.13.2 Example project

Program interface

Here, we want to program a color change. For the program interface, we need only a few TPanel components, which have different colors. One of these TPanel components (shown as Panel1 in the example) acts as a target, and the other acts as the source of the drag-and-drop operation. To keep things simple, set the DragMode property for the source object to dmAutomatic. Figure 7.14 shows how the example application looks at designtime.

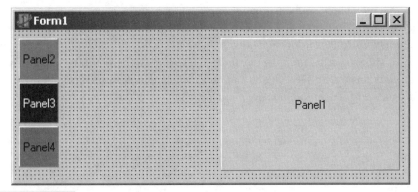

Figure 7.14 *The interface for the drag-and-drop operation*

Programming the functionality

You want to use a drag-and-drop operation to give Panel1 the same color as the element over which it is to be moved. As we have set the DragMode property of the source component to dmAutomatic, we do not need to concern ourselves with starting the operation. Therefore, all that remains to be done is to evaluate the result of the drop and then close the drag-and-drop operation.

Panel1 should then accept the dragged object if it is a TPanel component. This is what makes the implementation in the source code so easy. We shall use the is operator to check the source:

```
procedure TForm1.Panel1DragOver(Sender, Source: TObject;
X, Y: Integer; State: TDragState; var Accept: Boolean);
begin
  Accept := (Source is TPanel);
end;
```

Now all we have to do is to change the color. This functionality is programmed in the event-handling routine of the target object's OnDragDrop event:

```
procedure TForm1.Panel1DragDrop(Sender, Source: TObject;
X, Y: Integer);
begin
  if Source is TPanel then
    Panel1.Color := TPanel(Source).Color;
end;
```

As you can see, at this point we have once again checked whether the source is a TPanel component. Although our example can only include one component of this kind, other applications may be able to handle several of them. However, we only want to accept a single TPanel component.

This shows that even a drag-and-drop operation can be programmed with very simple commands. In Delphi, you can quickly create professional-looking programs that have user-friendly and intuitive interfaces.

Delphi and databases

8.1 Back to basics

The average user understands the term "database" to mean a file in which data are stored. This explanation should be sufficient for most users because they only need to work with the data. The program itself deals with the database and filters, and searches for and links data. As a programmer, you will need to do a bit of rethinking. Although Delphi's component concept takes on a great deal of the work, we still need to take note of a few things, and maybe program them ourselves, if we want to give users a clearly structured and user-friendly interface for their database evaluations.

The first question regards the kind of database to use. There are a large number of database formats, each with its advantages and disadvantages. Delphi provides the Borland Database Engine (BDE) driver, which provides direct access to some of the most commonly used formats. This chapter therefore only describes these databases. The BDE provides drivers for Paradox, dBase, and MS Access databases.

Delphi 5 also included Active DataObjects (ADO) functionality. ADO was developed by Microsoft and, according to some experts, it may be the system of the future for database systems. By using ADO components, you can create a connection to a database by means of providers. This means that you do not need to integrate the BDE in your application because this is not required for an ADO connection.

In contrast, Delphi 6 goes one step further. BDE and ADO functionality are still present, but Delphi 6 implements another way in which SQL databases such as Interbase or MS SQL server can be accessed. However, these components, which you will find in the Component Palette under DBEXPRESS are not pure SQL components.

8.1.1 Structure of a database

In Delphi, a database is always a table. The individual database records correspond to the rows in the table and the fields correspond to the columns. Therefore, you cannot enter more than one value for a field. From a technical viewpoint, these fields are known as *atomic* fields. This makes it much easier to handle databases because we always know the type of a particular field and can always access it.

Another feature of a database is its indices. There are primary and secondary indices. The primary index represents the main sorting procedure of the database. I personally always use a unique numerical value for this. Furthermore, in Paradox databases you can specify a field that automatically increases by one for every new data record. The advantage of this is that we always have an index that is unique, because the same number cannot be assigned twice. This may not be necessary for a single file, but if you link two databases together, and require a unique value, then it becomes very helpful.

The indices are used not only to sort the database but also to find data records. In this context, you should always bear in mind that indices are often not unique (e.g. the name Smith may occur several hundred times in a database that includes English-language names). For this reason, you should always combine several fields in a database into one shared index and therefore increase the search options.

Once you have finished designing your database on paper, you can start programming it. Before this, you should consider which database components are to be used.

8.1.2 BDE database components

TTable and TQuery

Delphi provides a number of components for accessing databases with BDE. These components are easy to integrate and program. BDE contains all the actual database functions, i.e. you can use the predefined methods in the components provided in it, and you do not need to program your own access routines. The two main components that we can work with are TTable and TQuery. TQuery makes it possible to use SQL, which you can't do with TTable. You do not need to know anything about SQL to program with TTable, which can also be an advantage. Whereas TQuery uses simple SQL statements for typical database functions, such as searching for, filtering, creating or deleting records, TTable has methods suitable for these functions (or events) that occur when a function is executed. Both can be defined permanently at database designtime. Another aspect they have in common is that this is not absolutely necessary; you can also define the database structure at runtime.

If the database structure is defined statically at designtime (and therefore cannot be changed), then use both the TField classes for the individual fields in the database. If the fields are created at runtime, then the instances of TField are also created at runtime. The first method, therefore, has the advantage that you can change the properties of any field in the Object Inspector. In the other case, you need to do this at runtime.

TField

The TField class represents the columns of an opened table. You then have two options for generating the descendants of TField. However, in each case, Delphi carries out the generation process itself. As the programmer, you simply enter the definition.

If you have already specified TField components in a database component such as TTable at designtime, then its descendants will be generated persistently. For the database you want to open, this means that the sequence and type of the fields in the physical database file on the hard disk must match that of the fields you have defined.

If not, then Delphi returns an error when you open the database because it cannot find one of the permanently defined fields.

On the other hand, if you simply open a file with a database component, then one single descendant of the `TField` class is created dynamically for each field in the database. This has the obvious advantage that you can always open a database without any problems. The disadvantage is that you do not know the name of the fields and therefore you must use their index value (position of the field in the table) to access them.

When you develop your own programs, it is unlikely that you will not know the structure of a particular database. In this case, if you still only want to work with your own databases, you should define persistent fields.

TDataSource

`TDataSource` creates the connection between the data-sensitive control elements and a database component such as `TTable` or `TQuery`. This component is also used to link two data sources with each other, e.g. a customer file and an invoice database. All database connections with either a display element or another database run via `TDataSource`.

This component is really easy to use; simply insert it into your application and connect it to the data source. You can also change or remove this connection at any time, even at runtime. The data-sensitive control elements will now use the `TDataSource` component to access the individual fields of the database.

However, if you want to use a function or a procedure to change a field's contents, then you do not use the `TDataSourcecomponent`. Instead, you can access the fields directly either via the `Fields` property in `TTable` or via the persistent `TField` classes.

TSession

You don't actually need this component. When you use BDE in database applications, Delphi automatically creates an instance of `TSession` called `Session` that you can use. However, we mention the component because it has two properties that are required if you use databases in a network.

Although by definition the databases created with BDE are local databases, this does not mean that you can't store the files on a network and access them with a number of programs. The term "local" refers to the way in which the database engine handles the files, not to the location. It is therefore possible to create database applications that work with BDE and that can be used both on a stand-alone computer and in a network.

For database queries, such as changing or modifying data, BDE normally uses the pessimistic locking procedure. This prevents more than one user from editing a record. All other users who access the record are not permitted to change it. Its counterpart is the optimistic locking procedure, which allows several users of the same database to make changes to a record at the same time. Nowadays, all SQL servers use this procedure.

BDE locks a record automatically. However, to do this BDE requires a protocol file, which is created automatically. Every program that accesses the database must be informed of the directory path of this protocol file. More precisely, BDE must be informed, not the program. The `TSession` component (and also the instance created automatically by Delphi) has a property that it uses for this purpose. This is the `NetFileDir` property in which you enter the directory that is to be used for the network protocol file. This can be any directory you like. The important thing is that every application uses the same directory (otherwise problems will occur) and that you enter the entire path. This isn't necessary for databases on stand-alone computers, where you can usually ignore `NetFileDir`.

8.1.3 ADO components

Borland displays all ADO components on the Component Palette page of the same name. You will notice that the component names are similar to the names of the corresponding BDE components; if you place an ADO component on a form or a data module, you will see that the properties and events are almost identical. Almost all the method names are the same, which is useful. You can, of course, also use all the data-sensitive control elements in other places.

`TAdoTable` and `TAdoQuery`

These two components correspond to `TTable` and `TQuery` and have almost identical properties and methods. However, there isn't a `CreateTable` method as there is for the `TTable` component. Instead, tables with ADO components are always created via an SQL statement.

If you are not familiar with SQL, then I can only say that it is not half as bad as it sounds. Basically, we only require an SQL statement to create the database. The `TAdoTable` component uses its own methods to open and close it. If you are familiar with SQL, you can start right away and restructure your applications.

The connection between `TAdoTable` and the data-sensitive control elements is created by the `TDataSource` component, which you will recognize from BDE.

`TAdoConnection`

As the concept of ADO implies, it must be independent of any specific kind of data source, and therefore we must first create a connection to a database. However, one database can contain more than one table. In contrast to the BDE example, we need to rethink our strategy here. Whereas a table represents a single file, a database is a collection of files, which, for example, are located in the same directory. A connection must be created to this directory. This task is carried out by the `TAdoConnection` component. If you want to use one of the other ADO components, you can specify which `TAdoConnection` component is to be used to create the connection by entering its name in the Connection property of that ADO component.

TAdoCommand

You use the `TAdoCommand` component to execute SQL commands. In the `CommandText` property, you define the SQL statement. It is then executed with the *Execute* method. However, you can only define one command here. BDE does not have any components that correspond to the `TAdoCommand` component. However, the component is very useful, as you will see in the example.

TAdoDataSet

`TAdoDataSet` is a generic dataset component. In general terms, it encapsulates a dataset. You can, for example, use this component to return a result set. However, for SQL statements such as `CreateTable` or `AlterTable`, there are other components like `TAdoCommand` that are much more suitable.

8.1.4 *The dbExpress components*

These components have another special feature. As they are SQL components, a driver is not absolutely necessary. For example, applications created with ADO components can run solely under Windows, just like applications that are based on the use of BDE. dbExpress now offers you multioperating system database functionality. These components are elements of CLX, i.e. they are also present in Kylix (Delphi for Linux). Therefore, if you want to develop an application that is to both run under Linux and under Windows, you should use this component because the porting procedure is very simple.

However, I should say a little about the differences between them because some are fairly major and could even be regarded as disadvantages.

→ Paradox and dBase databases are not supported.

→ LocalSQL is not supported. This means you cannot generate live queries, i.e. you cannot edit the returned result values directly.

→ You cannot use the `TDataSource` component to connect data-sensitive components with dbExpress components.

There is, however, one advantage. Using BDE results in a large data overhead that must be supplied along with the finished application. As you know, BDE must always be supplied in its entirety, which results in an increase in memory use of as much as 10–15 MB. If you use dbExpress, you only require a single driver DLL. Plus, of course, dbExpress runs both under Linux and under Windows, which can be seen as a further advantage.

Below, there is an overview of the dbExpress components.

TSQLConnection

`TSQLConnection` implements the connection to an SQL database. This means that the component is equivalent to TAdoConnection which you will recognize from the ADO components.

TSQLTable

As its name suggests, this component is roughly the equivalent of the `TTable` component in BDE. However, although some of the properties are the same, the dbExpress component provides less powerful performance than its BDE counterpart.

TSQLQuery

This component also has a BDE equivalent, `TQuery`. The same applies as for `TSQLTable`.

TSQLStoredProc

This component is equivalent to the BDE `TStoredProc` component. This and the previous two components should make life a little easier for BDE users. However, if you have only programmed under Windows and have already moved on to ADO, then you should not bother with dbExpress. ADO is far more powerful and consequently much better suited to big applications.

TSQLDataSet

This component works in a similar way to the `TAdoDataSet` component. It offers the same functionality.

TSQLMonitor

The `TSQLMonitor` component is used to log all the statements that have been executed.

8.1.5 Data module

In Delphi 6, the appearance of the data module has been updated, but essentially it is unchanged. The tree view on the left-hand side, familiar from Delphi 5, is no longer present. As a result, the data module looks like it did in the earliest versions of Delphi. However, this time you will find the tree view in the Object Treeview, which is usually located above the Object Inspector. Nothing has been lost in terms of functionality or user-friendliness.

8.2 Creating a database with BDE

Creating a database with the help of BDE is the easist approach because there are so few things to remember, and hardly anything can go wrong. We want to create a database that consists of two tables that are linked together. This is to be a tip database in which, later on, you can store various tips about Delphi or other programming languages.

8.2.1 Planning the database

Before we get started, we have to do a bit of thinking. We must know which type of table we want to create, which fields are to be included, and which options we want to give the user. One of the simplest variants is a Paradox database, for which BDE provides a driver. As this is a single table, we will use a `TTable` component to keep things simple.

We will allow the user to select the name of the physical file on the hard disk. The fields will be inserted statically, i.e. during development. At runtime, if the user wants to create a new table, then we only need to enter the file name and call the `CreateTable` statement in the `TTable` component.

Fields in the database

The table should contain the following fields:

- → an autoincrement counter field for the main index (a `TAutoIncField` field);
- → the tip's name (a string field);
- → the tip's text (a `DBMemo` field);
- → the date on which the tip was entered (a date field);
- → the name of the person from whom the tip originated (a string field);
- → the e-mail address of the person from whom the tip originates (a string field).

To this we will also add a Category field, which is to be a number field. We don't need this field yet, but later on we will see how to link this field to another field. Then, we will require the Category field. For safety's sake, we will create it now so that we don't need to restructure the entire table, or generate an entirely new one, later.

Database indices

Obviously, we also want to carry out database searches and sort the database. This is why we require a number of indices. The most important is the main index, which is to be a unique index. This is why we will create a counter field in the table, which increases automatically by one for each data record. We want to create the following indices:

- → the main index (contains only the counter field);
- → an index for the tip's description (contains the tip's name and the name of the person who sent it);
- → an index for the person from whom the tip originated (contains the name of the person who sent it and the tip's name);
- → an index for the date on which the tip was received (contains the date field, the tip's name, and the name of the sender);
- → an index for the category (contains the category number, the tip's name, and the name of the sender).

We can then sort the data and carry out searches using these indices. Obviously, we shall not need the category index until we want to link this database with another one in which the categories are stored.

Tip Searching, sorting and linking one database with another can be carried out only with existing indices. To create a link, the link criterion (in our case the category) must be present in the corresponding index. If you want to search for something, this search criterion must also be present in an index, which must then also be used for the search. To sort the database, simply switch to another index, which now becomes the active index.

8.2.2 Creating the database

Inserting database components

Create a new application and add a data module to it. To do this, use the FILE | NEW | DATA module menu item. Place one `TTable`-type component and one `TDataSource`-type component on the newly generated data module. Here, the `TTable` component represents our physical table, while `TDataSource` allows access to the data.

To ensure that data can be accessed correctly, we must link these two components, i.e. we must enter the name of the `TTable` component we want to access in the `TDataSource` component. Enter this name in the `DataSet` property. There, you select the `TTable` component that you have inserted. (In any case, this is the only table that you can select.)

You can, of course, decide to use the standard component names. However, I decided to use names with more precise meanings, so my components are called `TipTable` and `TipSource`. If you change the name, you will notice that the link between the two databases remains the same. This is because the name of the linked table has also changed in the `DataSet` property of the `TDataSource` component.

At this point, you must decide what kind of database you want to create. Change the value of the `TableType` property to `ttParadox`.

Adding fields

Now you want to add fields to the database. To do this, double-click on the `TTable` component. This opens the Field Designer, in which you can now add fields for the table. There are three options here: press the ⎡Ins⎤ key; select the NEW FIELD item from the Field Designer's context menu; or use the shortcut ⎡Ctrl⎤ + ⎡N⎤. Figure 8.1 shows the Field Designer together with the field data input screen.

In the input mask, you simply enter the settings you require for the fields. The `Counter` field will be our counter and should therefore be a `Autoinc` field. *Description*, *Name* and *Email* are `String` fields. *TipText* is a `Memo` field, and *Category* is an `Integer` field. The *Date* field is a `Date`-type field. Now generate the fields you require. All the fields are data fields. You must also specify the length of each string

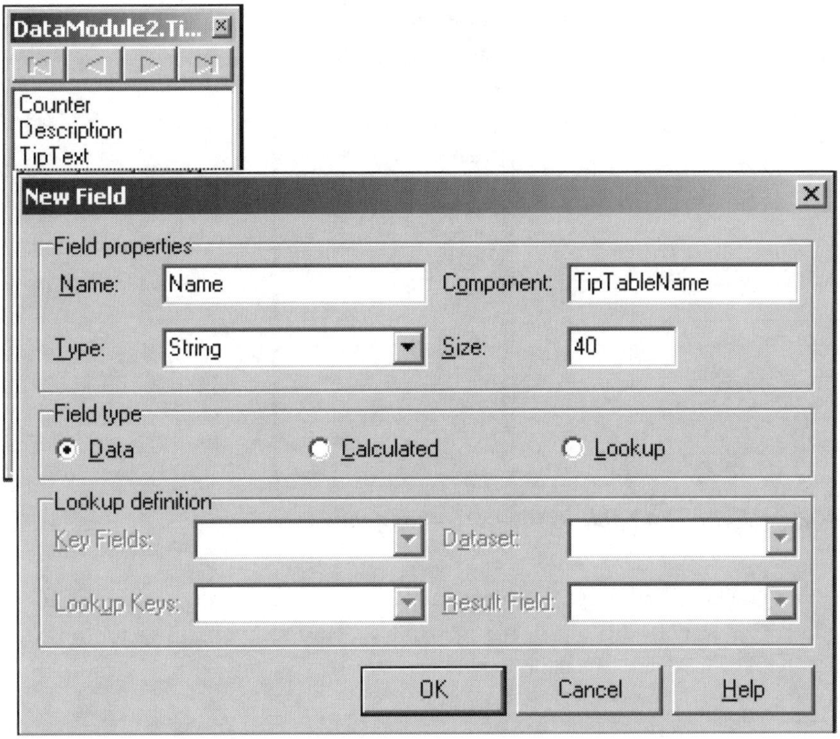

Figure 8.1 *The Field Designer with the input mask for new fields*

field in the *Size* field; 30 or 40 characters should be sufficient for the name, and we will use 50 characters for the e-mail address.

Sorting fields and setting properties

After you have created all the fields required for your database, you still need to arrange them in the correct sequence. You can move all the entries that were generated in the Field Designer. In addition, the properties of every entry appear in the Object Inspector as soon as you mark that entry. This makes it very easy to add more settings or change the ones you have already made. Now arrange the fields into the sequence shown in Figure 8.2.

As mentioned already, the properties of each marked field are displayed in the Object Inspector. You must now make a few settings here, because later on we want to display the data in a table (a `TDBGrid`-type component) in which a few things should be hidden. Therefore, the *Counter* field should not appear later on because it is required only for internal processing. The *Category* field is also not important and should not be displayed. The same applies to the *TipText* field because it is a memo. The contents of this field would not be displayed in a table anyway, therefore we can deactivate its display completely.

Figure 8.2 *The fields in the correct sequence*

The property you use to do this is called `Visible`. The default setting for this property for every field is `true`, and therefore we must set it to `false` for those fields that are to be hidden in the table.

> **Tip** You can also use the ⇧ or Ctrl keys (as in Windows) to mark several fields at the same time. The Object Inspector then displays only those properties that the marked components have in common. As `Visible` is one of these properties, you can change its value for several fields simultaneously.
>
> If, in the field properties, you set the `Visible` property to `false`, this only affects how the field is displayed later on in a `TDBGrid` component because this is always updated automatically by Delphi. In data-sensitive control elements, the data are still displayed in the same way as before.

If necessary, you can also modify the `DisplayWidth` and `DisplayLabel` properties. `DisplayWidth` is the width assigned to the field when it is displayed in a table, and `DisplayLabel` is the title in the table. After this, you can close the Field Designer. This completes the declaration of the fields in our database. We now come to the indices.

Defining indices

You can define an index either at designtime or at runtime. As we have already declared all the fields at designtime, we will declare the indices at designtime as well. Mark the `TTable` component. Use the `IndexDefs` property to access the Index Editor. This looks very much like the Field Designer. To add a new index, press the Ins key, or select NEW in the context menu, or click on the left-hand button in the toolbar. A new item then appears in the Index Editor. You must now enter the properties of this new index in the Object Inspector. The `Options` and `Fields` properties are important here. In `Fields`, you specify which fields are to be used as criteria for sorting the database. In `Options`, you can specify other options. For our main index, we only require the `ixPrimary` option; this shows that the index is a main index.

The name of the main index should be empty. The only field to be used for sorting is the `Counter` field. As mentioned above, we still require the `ixPrimary` option; because this is an automatic field, we also need the `ixUnique` option. `IxUnique` shows that this index is a unique index and therefore the same value must not appear twice in it.

For the other indices, create the fields in the same way as described above. To do this, use the field names as they appeared in the Field Designer, and separate them with semi-colons. Ensure that you follow the correct sequence and also give the index a useful name. Figure 8.3 shows the Object Inspector with the entries for the IDescription index.

Add the settings for the other indices in the same way. Once you have entered all the indices, the table is finished and we can create a new database or open an existing one.

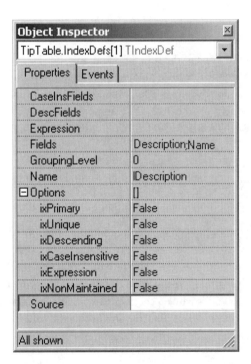

Figure 8.3 *The Object Inspector with the entries for IDescription*

Opening and creating a database

We shall deal with how to open a database and how to create a database separately. This is because databases can be overwritten. It may happen that a user has created a database using the correct name, but only for test purposes. So that they do not have to delete all the entries individually, we must make it possible for them to overwrite the database.

To open and create a database, we use functions to achieve a successful result. In addition, we require a procedure for closing the database, otherwise we could not create a new one. The result value of the functions should be a Boolean-type value. The following extract from the data module shows where the functions or the procedure are declared:

```
  TipTableCategory: TIntegerField;
  TipTableEmail: TStringField;
private
  { Private declarations }
public
  { Public declarations }
  function  OpenDB(DBName: string): boolean;
  function  CreateDB(DBName: string): boolean;
  procedure CloseDataBase;
end;
```

Now place the cursor on one of the functions and press Ctrl + ⇧ + C to use automatic completion to generate the remaining functions. Delphi jumps there immediately.

The program code for the CloseDataBase procedure is uncomplicated. Simply set the Active property in the TTable component to false. You could also call the component's Close method:

```
procedure TTipModule.CloseDataBase;
begin
  TipTable.Active := false;
end;
```

Now we come to how to create a new database. Here, I shall start from the assumption that the file path already exists and will also be passed. Nevertheless, in the main program we shall still use a dialog that returns the file name, including the path, and also allows you to create the path. This is why no checks are necessary here. The first step is to set the Result variable to false, and then check whether the database actually exists. If it does exist, then we must decide whether we should overwrite the file or not:

```
Result := false;
if FileExists(DBName) then
  if Application.MessageBox(
  'Do you want to overwrite the existing file?',
  'Overwrite',mb_Yesno+mb_IconQuestion)=IDNo then
    exit;
```

> **Tip** If the user replies NO, the the function is closed (and the value false is returned). If they reply YES, then the process continues, regardless of whether the file exists or not.
>
> You must add the `Forms` unit, in which the `Application` object is declared, manually to the `Uses` clause in the data module. If you do not do this, then you will not be able to call `Application.Messagebox`. You also need the `Windows` unit in which the constants for the dialog buttons (`mb_YesNo`) are declared.

Five more lines of program code, and our database is ready:

```
CloseDataBase;
TipTable.DatabaseName := ExtractFilePath(DBName);
TipTable.TableName   := DBName;
TipTable.CreateTable;
Result := OpenDataBase(DBName);
```

First of all, the database is closed if it is open. We do this at this point because any open database should remain open if the user chose NO at the previous prompt. Finally, you use your own function to open the database. Now assign the result value to the `Result` variable to ensure that the correct result value is supplied when we return from the function.

The way in which you open the database looks very much like the way in which you create it. The only difference is that the `CreateTable` command has been replaced by `Open`. Here are both functions in context:

```
function TTipModule.CreateDB(DBName: string): boolean;
begin
  Result := false;
  if FileExists(DBName) then
    if Application.MessageBox(
    'Do you want to overwrite the existing file?',
    'Overwrite',mb_Yesno+mb_IconQuestion)=IDNo then
      exit;
  CloseDataBase;
  TipTable.DatabaseName := ExtractFilePath(DBName);
  TipTable.TableName   := DBName;
  TipTable.CreateTable;
  Result := OpenDataBase(DBName);
end;
```

```
function TTipModule.OpenDB (DBName: string): boolean;
begin
  Result := false;
  if not FileExists(DBName) then
      exit;
  CloseDataBase;
  TipTable.DatabaseName := ExtractFilePath(DBName);
  TipTable.TableName    := DBName;
  TipTable.Open;
  Result := true;
end;
```

So, we have already created the functionality. As you can see, we first created a database, closed it, and then opened it again. However, the user is unaware of this because modern computers are so fast. Nonetheless, we can be certain that nothing went wrong when we generated the database (i.e. when we saved the table structure to the hard disk).

Specifying an index when it is opened

If we now use the procedures and functions we have to open the database, it will usually be sorted according to the index represented by the primary index. This is why this index is called the primary index. However, that you may want to sort the database according to another criterion, e.g. by the tip's description instead of the record number, from the very start. We have allowed for this option in the methods used to open the database, in which you can insert a suitable line of code. However, we can (and this is the advantage of events) also use the corresponding event in the TTable component. In this case, it is the OnAfterOpen event. A single line of code to assign the index name to the IndexName property will be sufficient for us:

```
procedure TTipModule.TipTableAfterOpen(DataSet:
TDataSet);
begin
  TipTable.Indexname := 'IDescription';
end;
```

Now our database will be sorted according to tip description as soon as it opens. As mentioned already, we could also have inserted this line in the OpenDB procedure. However, if we had done this, the database table would also be sorted automatically if we were to program another method for opening it or change the existing method.

8.2.3 Creating the interface

In addition to the main form, we still need another two forms: one in which we can enter the data later, and one in which we can display the data. You should use the following names for the forms: `FrmMain` for the main form, `FrmInput` for the input form, and `FrmDisplay` for the display form. The name you use for the unit that contains the forms is actually irrelevant. However, you should use a name that means something so that you can tell which form is located in which unit. I have called my units FormMain, FormInput and FormDisplay.

Main form

Our main form simply consists of a menu from which you call the individual functions, and a `TDBGrid`-type component linked to our `TDataSource` component. To make this available, we must first integrate our data module. In this case, simply select the FILE | USE UNIT menu item or the key combination Alt+F11.

Set the `Align` property in the `TDBGrid` component to `alClient` so that it includes the entire window. We still require a dialog for opening, the database and one for saving it. We can call these later on via the corresponding menu items.

The menu should contain menu items for creating, opening and closing a database. We also require menu items for navigation (first, last, previous (known in Delphi as "prior"), and next data record) and for creating, editing, and deleting the individual records. In our example, I divided the menu items in three categories. Figure 8.4 shows the main form.

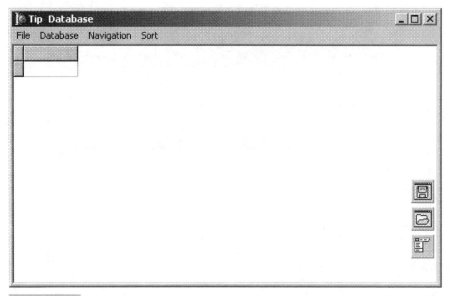

Figure 8.4 *The main form for the database application*

As we don't want to enter data directly into the database grid itself, we now use the options in `TDBGrid` to ensure that a complete row (and not just a field) of the database grid is marked at runtime. To do this, set the `dgRowSelect` option to `true`. You should not be able to edit the records in the database grid. We can use another option to ensure that this happens; in this case, set `dgEditing` to `false`.

Now we get to the dialogs. We also need to modify a few properties here. Among other things, we want the file extension .db to be the default extension if the user forgets to enter one. Therefore, set the `DefaultExt` property to `db`. You do not need to enter the period because Delphi adds it automatically We can also add a filter in the same property so that only files with the file extension .db will be displayed. You use a simple editor to enter this setting in the `Filter` property in the dialogs. This gives us enough functionality for the time being.

Input form

In this form, we must also integrate the unit that contains the data module we want to access. For the actual access, we use `TDBEdit`-type components and a `TDBMemo`-type component for the tip text. In addition, we require the CANCEL and OK buttons. However, we can use the `ModalResult` property to automate the way in which the form is closed. For the OK button, set `ModalResult` to `mrOk`, and for the CANCEL button, set it to `mrCancel`.

Once you have integrated the data module, you can attach the data-sensitive control elements to the corresponding table fields in the Object Inspector. To do this, set the `DataSource` property in the `TDataSource` component (in my case `TipSource`) and then select the field you require in the `DataField` property. Click on OK to set the data field to the current value. Figure 8.5. shows the input form at designtime.

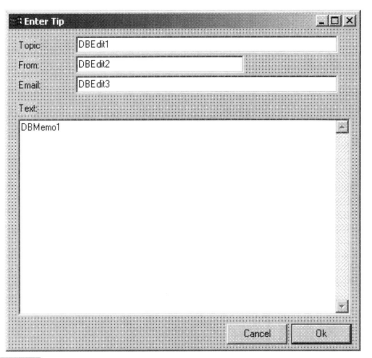

Figure 8.5 *The input form at designtime*

Display form

This is an extremely simple form. It consists of only two data-sensitive control elements and a button. The button is used to close the form and the control elements are used to display it. Once again, these are linked to the `TDataSource` component, just as in the input form. Figure 8.6 shows the display form at designtime.

Finally, you should set the following properties.

➜ For the input and display forms, set `BorderStyle` to `bsDialog`.

➜ Set all `BorderIcons` in the input and display form to `false`.

➜ Set `ScrollBars` for the `TDBMemo` components to `ssVertical`.

➜ Set `WordWrap` for the `TDBMemo` components to `true`.

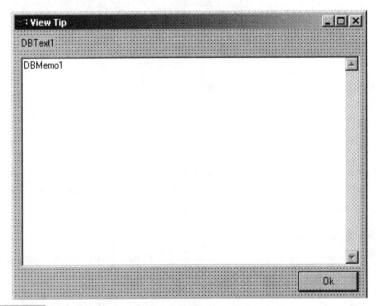

Figure 8.6   *The Display form at designtime*

8.2.4 Programing the functionality

You have already done most of the work. The only thing left is to program the individual functions. Let's start with how to create, open, and close the database.

Creating, opening, and closing the database

You get the file name for creating a database from the dialog used to save a file. In contrast, you get the file name used to open a database from the dialog for opening a file. In our example, we have left the dialog names unchanged. To close the file, you simply call the function that has already been programmed in the data module. This results in the following event-handling routines for the individual menu items:

```
procedure TForm1.New File1Click(Sender: TObject);
begin
    if SaveDialog1.Execute then
    if not TipModule.CreateDB(SaveDialog1.FileName) then
  ShowMessage('Failed to create file!');
end;

procedure TForm1.OpenFile1Click(Sender: TObject);
begin
  if OpenDialog1.Execute then
    if not TipModule.OpenDB(OpenDialog1.FileName) then
      ShowMessage('Failed to open file!');
end;

procedure TForm1.CloseFile1Click(Sender: TObject);
begin
  TipModule.CloseDataBase;
end;
```

The names of your routines might be different, depending on which names you assigned to the menu items. I am always rather lazy when I create example programs and simply allow Delphi to assign the names.

Creating and editing a record

In order to create a data record, we must first tell the TTable component what we want to do. TTable has various statuses that you can set: *browse* is a status for viewing the content, *edit* is used to change the content, and the third, which is not described here, is used to find a data record. First of all, we must set the database to a status that allows us to change data. There are three ways of doing this. Two options involve inserting or appending a new data record, and the third involves changing the current data record. The commands for these options are Insert and Append for new data records, and Edit for editing an existing data record.

Once you have called the relevant method (because these commands involve TTable methods), you then need to call the input form. You program the functionality used to save the data in the buttons in the input form. After this, the database returns to browse mode. Here, the command used to save the data is called Post, and the command used to reject the data is called Cancel. These commands are also TTable methods.

Once again, you use a TTable method to delete a data record. This is the Delete method. This deletes the data record indicated by the data record pointer when the command is called.

Here is the program code; it is a lot simpler than it appears at first glance:

```
procedure TForm1.NewDataRecord1Click(Sender: TObject);
begin
  TipModule.TipTable.Append;
  FrmInput.ShowModal;
end;


procedure TForm1.EditDataRecord1Click(
                                     Sender:TObject);
begin
  TipModule.TipTable.Edit;
  FrmInput.ShowModal;
end;


procedure TForm1.DeleteDataRecord1Click(
                                 Sender: TObject);
begin
  if Application.MessageBox('Do you want to delete
                 the data record?','Delete data
                 record',
                 mb_YesNo+mb_IconQuestion) = IDYes
                 then
     TipModule.TipTable.Delete;
end;
```

And now the two procedures from the input form: Button1 is the OK button, Button2 is the CANCEL button. As you can see, we have also added today's date. The date that appears is not the creation date but the date of the most recent change. This is because the date also changes every time a data record is edited. You can, of course, modify the program so that this no longer happens:

```
procedure TFrmInput.Button1Click(Sender: TObject);
begin
  TipModule.TipTableDate.AsDateTime := Date;
  TipModule.TipTable.Post;
end;


procedure TFrmInput.Button2Click(Sender: TObject);
begin
  TipModule.TipTable.Cancel;
end;
```

`Date` is a function that returns the current date. However, we cannot assign it directly to the `TipTableDate`; instead, we must go via the `AsDateTime` conversion method because different types are involved, so a direct assignment is not possible.

This should now mean that you can enter and edit data. If you want to, you can start the program. However, the functions for navigating in the database are still missing although everything else should already function correctly.

Navigating in the database

To navigate in the database, you use the `First`, `Last`, `Prior`, and `Next` methods in the `TTable` component. To save ourselves a bit of programming effort, and to ensure that the unit is not overloaded with procedures, we want to program navigation in just one procedure that can then be accessed by all the menu items.

A simple way of keeping the different menu items separate from each other is to use the `Tag` property, which all components, including `TMenuItem`, contain. Therefore, you assign the corresponding `Tag` values to the various menu items that are to be used for navigation.

→ The JUMP TO FIRST DATA RECORD menu item is assigned `Tag` value 1.

→ The BACK ONE DATA RECORD menu item is assigned `Tag` value 2.

→ The NEXT DATA RECORD menu item is assigned `Tag` value 3.

→ The JUMP TO LAST DATA RECORD menu item is assigned `Tag` value 4.

You program the functionality in the `OnClick` event-handling routine in one of the menu items. Here, you use the `Sender` parameter, which is passed with every event, to evaluate which menu item was selected. The sender is always the object that triggered the event, and as this is a `TObject`-type class, the `Tag` value is also passed. Here is the source code you need to program:

```
procedure TFrmMain.NextDataRecord1Click(
                                    Sender:TObject);
var
   MyTag: integer;
begin
   MyTag := (Sender as TMenuItem).Tag;
   case MyTag of
      0: Exit;
      1: TipModule.TipTable.First;
      2: TipModule.TipTable.Prior;
      3: TipModule.TipTable.Next;
      4: TipModule.TipTable.Last;
   end;
end;
```

The last thing to do is assign the event-handling routine to the other menu items. Now, when you start the program you can also navigate in the database. But only if you have actually entered any data in it. Figure 8.7 shows the current state of this program.

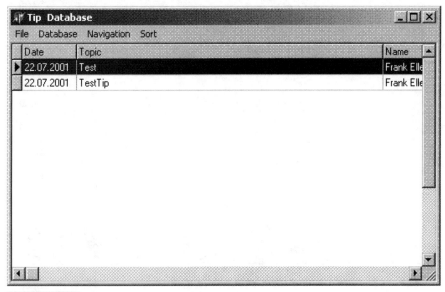

Figure 8.7   *Current state of the program*

Displaying tips

We still need to deal with display functions. You simply specify that a tip will be displayed when you double-click on it. As we have already prepared the relevant form, you only need to write an event-handling routine for the `OnDblClick` event in the `TDBGrid` component:

```
procedure TFrmMain.DBGrid1DblClick(Sender: TObject);
begin
  FrmDisplay.ShowModal;
end;
```

Figure 8.8 shows the results of this simple line of code.

Sorting the database

We have already created a number of indices that we can use to sort the data. All that remains is to respecify the index. BDE carries out the sorting automatically so we have nothing to worry about here.

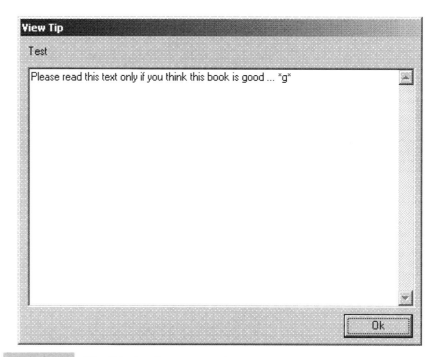

Figure 8.8 *The Display form at runtime*

Now we will insert another menu, which we will then use to sort the database. In our indices, we have already specified the following sorting options: *IDescription* (tip description), *Idate* (date on which the tip was created) and *Iname* (tip name). The *Category* remains unchanged. Correspondingly, we now create three menu items. Once again, the sorting routine is only implemented in one menu item, and therefore we proceed in the same way as for navigation. Accordingly, the program code looks like this:

```
procedure TFrmMain.Description1Click(Sender: TObject);
var
  MyTag : integer;
begin
  MyTag := (Sender as TMenuItem).Tag;
  case MyTag of
   1: TipModule.TipTable.IndexName := 'IDescription';
   2: TipModule.TipTable.IndexName := 'IName';
   3: TipModule.TipTable.IndexName := 'IDate';
  end;
end;
```

In this way, we have already implemented a certain range of functions. To complete the program, we will carry out a search.

Searching for a database record

`TTable` also provides methods that we can use for a database search. In our example, we want to look for a particular tip. To do this, you must first realise that this search can only work if the index is also set to *IDescription*. The user may have used another method to sort the database. Accordingly, we must ensure that the index setting is corrected after the search procedure has been completed.

If the tip we are looking for is not found, then the data record pointer should jump to a position that is closest to that tip. The `FindNearest` method does this for us automatically, so we will use that. Another advantage of `FindNearest` is that you do not need to enter the entire search term you are looking for because this function looks for the record (in this case, the tip) that matches most closely what you enter.

For the search procedure, I have added a menu item to the menu. To enter the search term, we will use the `InputQuery` function. This means you can evaluate the button the user clicks on and therefore decide whether the search is to take place or not. Have a close look at this routine:

```
procedure TFrmMain.Find1Click(Sender: TObject);
var
    SearchVal: String;
    OldIndex : String;
begin
    if not InputQuery('Find',
                        'Enter term:',
                        SearchVal) then
        exit
    else
    begin;
        with TipModule.TipTable do
        begin;
            OldIndex := IndexName;
            IndexName := 'IName';
            FindNearest([Searchval]);
            IndexName := OldIndex;
        end;
    end;
end;
```

When you call `FindNearest`, you will see that the parameter `SearchVal` that is passed is shown in square brackets; this is not a mistake. It is necessary because although the parameter is an array, `Searchval` is actually only a string. The square brackets mean that `Searchval` will be passed as the first value of an array, and the remaining values will stay empty.

Now that we have also implemented the search function, the example program is complete.

8.3 Master/detail databases

We now want to turn our simple database into a master/detail database. This means that we want to display the data records in another database, no matter where they are located in our first database. We will add another database in which we can store categories to the existing program; then we will make a couple of small changes so that we can sort the tips by category. This means that our category database will act as the master. Therefore, it will only display those data records in the tip database that match the category marked in the category database. This kind of master/detail database is used very frequently.

We will use an invoicing program as an example. In such a program, the customer data, including the entire address, is stored in one database. Another database contains all the invoices that have been written. Now, it would be very impractical to store all the customer data in both databases. If you wanted to change a customer's address, you would have to search through all the invoices and change the address data there as well.

Instead, you can take a criterion that is guaranteed not to change (such as the customer number) and use it to link both databases. Now, when an address changes, the correct address is used automatically because the program uses the customer number to identify it. The address is stored in only one place.

This is the kind of master/detail database we want to create (or restructure our program accordingly). We will create a 1:*n* relationship, i.e. *n* data records in the tip database will be assigned to one data record in the category database.

8.3.1 Specifying the master database

The category database will act as the master. We will create it together with the tip database, but we will give it another name. It is still a Paradox database.

The fields we require are a counter field and a field for the category's description. Once again, we require a main index and another index that will be used for sorting the categories by name. The counter field, again an *AutoInc*-type field, is called *Category*, and the field for the description is called *CatDesc*. This is another string field whose size is 20 characters (you shouldn't need any more). You can, of course, change any of these settings if you want to.

Now place a `TTable` component and a `TDataSource` component on the existing data module. Call them `CatTable` and `CatSource` and link them together. Then add the named fields and the indices. Figure 8.9 shows what this looks like.

Later on, we will hide the *Category* field because only the *CatDesc* field will be required. For this reason, set the `Visible` property in the *Category* field to `false`. This should now describe the new database completely. However, you must first ensure that this database is created together with the tip database.

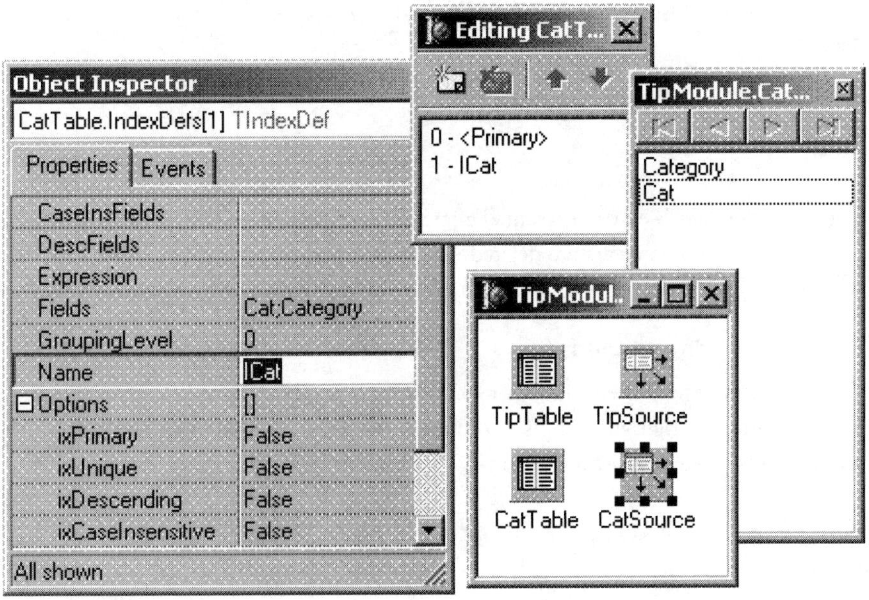

Figure 8.9 *The new data module with the CatTable fields and indices*

Tip You should take care that you use both fields in the field settings for the secondary index (`IDesc`). If you only use the description, BDE will report an error.

8.3.2 Creating a master database

First of all, you must think of a name for this new database. To keep things simple, we will use the name the user selected and extend it, e.g. by the letters "cat". The file extension remains the same. So that we maintain an overview of the whole thing, we will write a separate function for this, which is stored in the data module (because we are dealing with a database).

Assigning a name to the master database

Declare a `GetMDBName` function in the data module's header. You can also declare this function under `private`. Nevertheless, we will only access it within the data module. The name of the detail database is to act as the parameter that is passed. The return value should be a `string`-type value and should include the name of the master database. We will let Delphi create the rest of the function (⌈Ctrl⌉+⌈⇧⌉+⌈C⌉). After this, we can input the functionality:

```
function TTipModule.GetMDBName(n: string): string;
begin
  System.Delete(n,Pos('.',n),4);
  Result := n+'cat.db';
end;
```

The way this works is easy to explain. The period (full-stop) is searched for as the separator and then four characters are deleted (the period and file extension, which may also consist of three characters); cat.db is then added to the remaining string and returned.

Extending existing routines

You must now extend the functions used to open, create, and close the databases. You have one function that you can use to find out what the new database is called, so it is not difficult to extend the functions:

```
function TTipModule.CreateDB(DBName: string): boolean;
begin
  Result := false;
  if FileExists(DBName) then
    if Application.MessageBox(
    'Do you want to overwrite the existing file?',
    'Overwrite',mb_Yesno+mb_IconQuestion)=IDNo then
    exit;
  if TipTable.Active then
    CloseDataBase;
  TipTable.DatabaseName := ExtractFilePath(DBName);
  CatTable.DataBaseName  := TipTable.DataBaseName;
  TipTable.TableName     := DBName;
  CatTable.TableName     := GetMDBName(DBName);
  TipTable.CreateTable;
  CatTable.CreateTable;
  Result := OpenDB(DBName);
end;

function TTipModule.OpenDB(DBName: string): boolean;
begin
  Result := false;
  if not FileExists(DBName) then
      exit;
  CloseDataBase;
  TipTable.DatabaseName := ExtractFilePath(DBName);
```

```
CatTable.DataBaseName   := TipTable.DataBaseName;
TipTable.TableName      := DBName;
CatTable.TableName      := GetMDBName(DBName);
TipTable.Open;
CatTable.Open;
Result := true;
end;
```

If you now start the program, Delphi creates the databases. The next section describes how to link the two databases and how to define the correct indices.

8.3.3 Linking databases

Linking the two databases is not complicated; all you need to do is modify two properties in the detail database (in our case, the tip database). However, the link only works via indices, therefore the index must also be modified. We will use the *ICategory* index that has already been generated and insert it at the same time as the tip database is opened. This will also enable us to sort the database afterwards. You only need to make a few changes in the source code. First, change the index setting in the AfterOpen event-handling routine in the TipTable, then add an event-handling routine for AfterOpen to CatTable:

```
procedure TTipModule.TipTableAfterOpen(
                              DataSet: TDataSet);
begin
  TipTable.Indexname := 'ICategory';
end;


procedure TTipModule.CatTableAfterOpen(
                              DataSet:TDataSet);
begin
  CatTable.Indexname := 'IDesc';
end;
```

The properties required for linking are MasterSource and MasterFields in the detail database, which in this case is the TipTable. We then modify these properties so that they refer to the TDataSource component in the master database and to the field to which the link is to be created. In our example, these are CatSource and Category. Figure 8.10 shows the Object Inspector with the settings.

We will need to modify our program's interface so that we can see the link and actually do something with it.

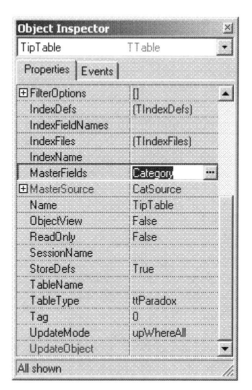

Figure 8.10 *Settings used to link tables*

8.3.4 Modifying the program interface

To display the categories, we must use another `TDBGrid` component. We also need a means of creating new categories and assigning the tips to a category.

Modifying the main form

I added the `TDBGrid` component for the categories on the left. In the options, I changed the settings so that an entire line is always marked, no titles are created, and no lines or selectors are displayed. As a result, DBGrid looks like a list box. Figure 8.11 shows the new main form.

Modifying the main menu

I have also extended the main menu so that we can add or delete categories or sort according to category. I added one menu item for sorting and three menu items for handling the categories. Obviously, the menu item for sorting is still filled with a `Tag` value, and therefore we only need to extend the existing sort routine and modify the `OnClick` event in the menu item accordingly. Figure 8.12 shows the completed main menu.

The main form has now been modified successfully, and we can start programming the functionality.

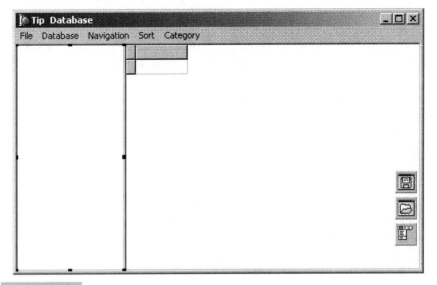

Figure 8.11 *The new main form*

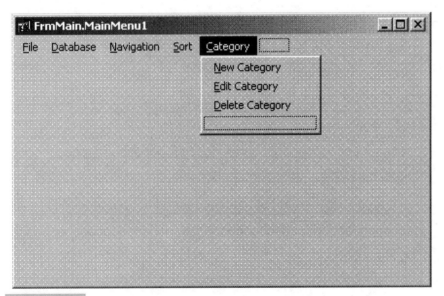

Figure 8.12 *The application's main menu in the Menu Designer*

8.3.5 Extending the functionality

The first thing to extend is the functions that concern the category table. You need functions to add a new category, and change or delete an existing category. Once again, you use the `InputQuery` function so you can enter and predefine a value. You can also use this function to check whether the user has clicked on OK or CANCEL. The way in which you delete a category is programmed in the same way as deleting a tip, i.e. with a confirmation prompt. By now, this shouldn't be a problem for you, which is why I will now list the entire source code for the three procedures without further explanation:

```pascal
procedure TFrmMain.NewCategory1Click(Sender:TObject);
var
  theResult : string;
begin
  theResult := '';
  if InputQuery('Categories',
                'New category:',the result) then
  begin;
    TipModule.CatTable.Append;
    TipModule.CatTableCat.AsString := theResult;
    TipModule.CatTable.Post;
  end;
end;


procedure TFrmMain.EditCategory1Click(
                                    Sender: TObject);
var
  theResult : string;
begin
  theResult := TipModule.CatTableCatName.AsString;
  if InputQuery('Category','Edit category:',
                theResult) then
  begin;
    TipModule.CatTable.Edit;
    TipModule.CatTableCat.AsString := theResult;
    TipModule.CatTable.Post;
  end;
end;


procedure TFrmMain.DeleteCategory1Click(
                                    Sender: TObject);
begin
  if Application.MessageBox('Delete category?',
        'Delete Category',
        mb_YesNo+mb_IconQuestion) = IDYes then
    TipModule.CatTable.Delete;
end;
```

Of course, we still can't see anything because we have only linked the two databases in the program. Now we must extend the functionality of the input form so that any new data record is assigned automatically to the current category. This is easy to do; we just use the existing event-handling routine to create a new tip:

```
procedure TFrmMain.NewDataRecord1Click(
                                Sender: TObject);
begin
  TipModule.TipTable.Append;
  TipModule.TipTableCategory.AsInteger :=
      TipModule.CatTableCategory.AsInteger;
  FrmInput.ShowModal;
end;
```

You now have a program in which you can store tips about various programming languages, sorted by category. You can, of course, extend the program. For example, you can use drag-and-drop to switch categories (simply drag the tip on to the category).

8.4 Other BDE functions

8.4.1 Splitting a database

In database applications, it is often necessary to run through all the data records in a database, e.g. to modify a value or to create statistics. However, it takes an enormous amount of time to display the data in data-sensitive control elements. This is why in Delphi you can "uncouple" the actual database from the display elements. The methods you use to do this in a TTable or TQuery component are DisableControls and EnableControls. DisableControls hides the database contents for all data-sensitive control elements. You then call EnableControls to display the database contents again.

8.4.2 Defining the start and end

You use two non-published properties to specify whether the data record pointer is placed at the start or the end of a database file. These properties are called BOF and EOF. If, for example, you want to program a complete database run, first set the pointer to the first position and then jump through each data record, carry out the function you require, and finish the run when the end of the file is reached:

```
Table1.First;
repeat
   Table1.Fields[1].AsInteger := 5;
   ...
   Table1.Next;
until Table1.EOF;
```

8.4.3 Bookmarks

You can set bookmarks in a database. A bookmark is a position that you can jump to. Bookmarks are extremely useful during a database run, e.g. when you are converting the data into another format. After the database run, you don't want the data record pointer to remain at the end of the file; instead, it should return to the position it occupied before the run. To set a bookmark, use the GetBookmark method. To jump to a bookmark, use the GotoBookmark method. However, you must remember to specify a TBookmark-type variable that is used to record the position of the data record pointer. If you no longer require the bookmark, simply call FreeBookmark to delete it from memory:

```
procedure BookmarkTest;
var
    MyBM: TBookmark;
begin;
    MyBM := Table1.GetBookmark;
    Table1.First;
    repeat

        //Database actions

        Table1.Next;
    until Table1.EOF;
    Table1.GotoBookmark(MyBM);
    Table1.FreeBookmark(MyBM);
end;
```

8.5 Database interface

When you are working with databases, the database interface is an extremely useful program. With this tool, you can open all the table types supported by BDE, look at their structures, add or delete indices, create your own tables, assign aliases, ... i.e. do anything that is possible with Delphi and a database.

8.5.1 Structure information

It is very useful to view the structure information if you do not know exactly how a database is structured but still want to access it as part of your program. The database interface shows you which fields have been defined, which field types are involved, which indices have been defined, etc. You can then either use the database just as it is (and therefore program all the fields and indices in Delphi in the same way as they appear in the database), or you can change the database's structure, e.g. by redefining the indices. Figure 8.13. shows a view of the structure information. To display it, select the Tools | Database Desktop menu item. In this, select the Tools | Utilities | Info Structure menu item.

You will find more information about the individual field types in the online help.

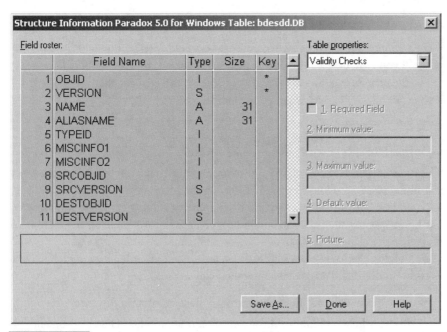

Figure 8.13 *Database structure information*

8.5.2 Restructuring the database

You use the Table | Restructure menu item to change the entire structure of a table. In this case, the dialog field view looks like the view in Figure 8.13. You can delete fields, add fields, change the field type, change the table's indices, change passwords, among other things. The most important functions are described below. The thing they all have in common is that the changes come into effect only if you click on the Save As button to save the table structure.

Changing, deleting, and inserting fields

You execute these operations in the field list. For example, to change a field's name, double-click on the field name and then enter the new name in the field list. However, you must remember that different databases have different conventions that affect the way in which field names are written.

To change the field type, mark a field type in the corresponding column and then either click Delete or right-click; this brings up a context menu, in which you can select the field type.

To add a field, mark a field in the field list and click INSERT. A new field is inserted above the field you marked. You must also enter a name and a field type for the new field.

To delete a field, mark the field in the field list and then press Ctrl+Del. The field is removed from the list.

Tip You do not get a confirmation prompt when you delete a field. Instead, the field is simply deleted from the list. If you have deleted the wrong field, just click on the CANCEL button to cancel the change to the structure. However, this also cancels all the changes that you have made up to this point. So be very careful when you delete things.

Changing table properties

The database interface also allows you to access all the table properties, such as passwords, indices, and validity checks for fields. To the right of the field list, you will see a selection box from which you can select the property you require. Here, we are interested primarily in validity checks and indices because you will probably use them more often than the other properties.

For validity checks, you can specify different rules for inputting data in each individual field. In this case, Paradox tables use the following rules.

→ INPUT REQUIRED means that a user must make an entry in this field.

→ In the MINIMUM input field you enter a minimum value. The value you enter must be greater than the value you specify as the minimum.

→ In the MAXIMUM input field, you enter a maximum value. The value you enter must be smaller than the value you specify as the maximum.

→ In the DEFAULT input field, you can specify a default value for use if the user does not make an entry.

→ In the INPUT SCREEN input field, you can display the entry format for the user to see. This is a good idea, for example, for date or time entries.

You can specify various different validity checks for each field.

If you select a secondary index in the selection box, you can change its definition, add new indices, or delete existing indices. The database interface displays a list of these indices underneath the selection box. If you mark an index, click on the CHANGE button to assign a new definition. To define a new index, click on the DEFINE button. In both cases, a dialog window appears in which you can make the appropriate entries. Figure 8.14 shows the dialog window you use to change an index.

You can also delete an existing index. To do this, click on the DELETE button located under the index list.

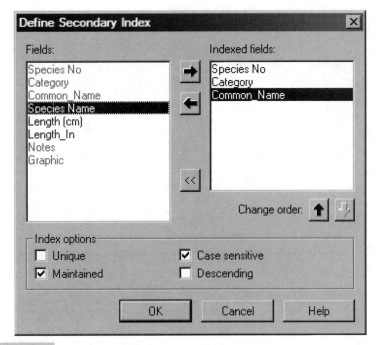

Figure 8.14 *The dialog used to change an index*

8.5.3 Defining aliases

An alias is a way of accessing a database without having to specify its position. You can use an alias to access the position of a database and all the table names. However, this alias must also be defined in the target system. The database interface also allows you to access all the aliases that are defined in the system. You can also change them and create new ones. To access aliases, first select the TOOLS | DATABASE DESKTOP menu item. In the Database Desktop window, select the TOOLS | ALIAS MANAGER menu item. Figure 8.15 shows the Alias Manager in action.

Click on the NEW button to define a new alias and click on the REMOVE button to delete an alias. PATH shows where the databases assigned to the alias are located, the DRIVER TYPE shows the database type and you can enter a name for the alias in the DATABASE ALIAS field. If you have defined an alias, you can access the corresponding databases right away, even at designtime. In other words, you can assign an alias to a BDE database component and select the name of the database you require from the list of database files that are available for that particular alias.

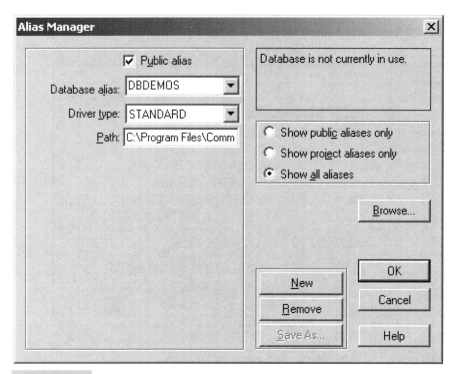

Figure 8.15 *The Alias Manager in the database interface*

8.6 ADO

Since Delphi 5, ADO components have been an element of the VCL. ADO, developed by Microsoft, is an interface to any kind of data source. ADO guarantees access to databases under Windows because Microsoft's new operating systems use this technology as well. ADO is only a programming interface that can be used with Visual Basic and other programming languages. Before you can use it, the Microsoft Data Access Components must be installed; they may not be present in Windows 95. You can do this retrospectively; the interface is available on the Microsoft website.

An enormous advantage of ADO is that you no longer require BDE. The fact that, for some applications, the use of BDE increases their size significantly for installation is a good enough reason to convert even existing projects from BDE to ADO. Since Borland carried out such excellent work during the implementation of ADO, even the conversion process is relatively easy.

8.6.1 Example ADO project

Here is an example of how to use ADO components. As the main functional differences arise when a database is created, this will be the main area I will discuss. The `TAdoTable` component is linked to the data-sensitive control elements in the usual way, using the `TDataSource` component. Navigating within the data record and changing data records involves the same commands as those used in the BDE components. However, we shall now create a database in dBase format, which we shall then work with.

Required components

At this point, I will not deal with how to design the interface. The components you need to actually access the data are more important. So, place `TAdoConnection`, `TAdoTable`, `TAdoCommand` and `TDataSource` components on the data module. Link `TDataSource` to `TAdoTable`. Set the `Connection` property in `TAdoCommand` and `TAdoTable` to `TAdoConnection`. This creates the connections. You can also specify the fields for the `TAdoTable` component. In this case, we want to create an address database, and therefore we need fields for the surname, first name, street, zip (postal) code, and town.

Creating a connection

The `TAdoConnection` component is connected to a database by means of a provider. If no provider is available, then you must retrofit the Microsoft Data Access Components on your system. You will find them on the Microsoft website.

The `ConnectionString` property creates the connection. As this string involves a tangle of statements, we will not enter them ourselves but will define them in a dialog instead. Click on the button next to the `ConnectionString` property in `TAdoConnection`. The window shown in Figure 8.16. appears. Select the USE CONNECTION STRING option and click on BUILD.

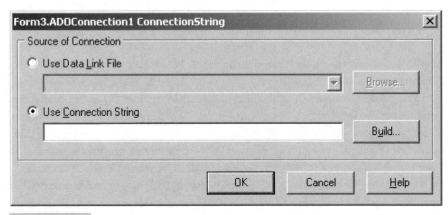

Figure 8.16 *Creating the ADO connection*

Another dialog opens, whose appearance varies depending on which option you selected. It is possible that you will not see a list of all the providers. However, the provider that we are going to use (the provider for ODBC drivers,) should be installed

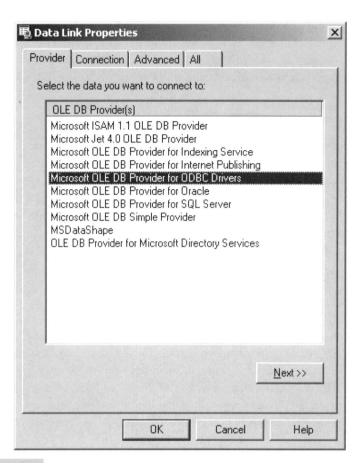

Figure 8.17   *The data connection dialog*

on your machine. Select it and then click on NEXT. Figure 8.17 shows the data connection properties dialog.

The Connection page of the dialog comes next. In it, enter the actual connection string. Select the USE DATA SOURCE NAME option. In the list, select the *dBase Files* entry. In the information for the server logon, use "Admin" as both the user name and password. You should also make it possible to store the password so that you do not need to enter it each time. Figure 8.18 shows the dialog with the activated CONNECTION page.

You can now test the connection. You have now defined the connection string. Click on OK to close all the dialogs. Before we create the connection, set the `LoginPrompt` property in `TAdoConnection` to `false`. Now, when you set the `Connected` property in `TAdoConnection` to `true`, the connection is created. You can now use ADO components to access dBase databases.

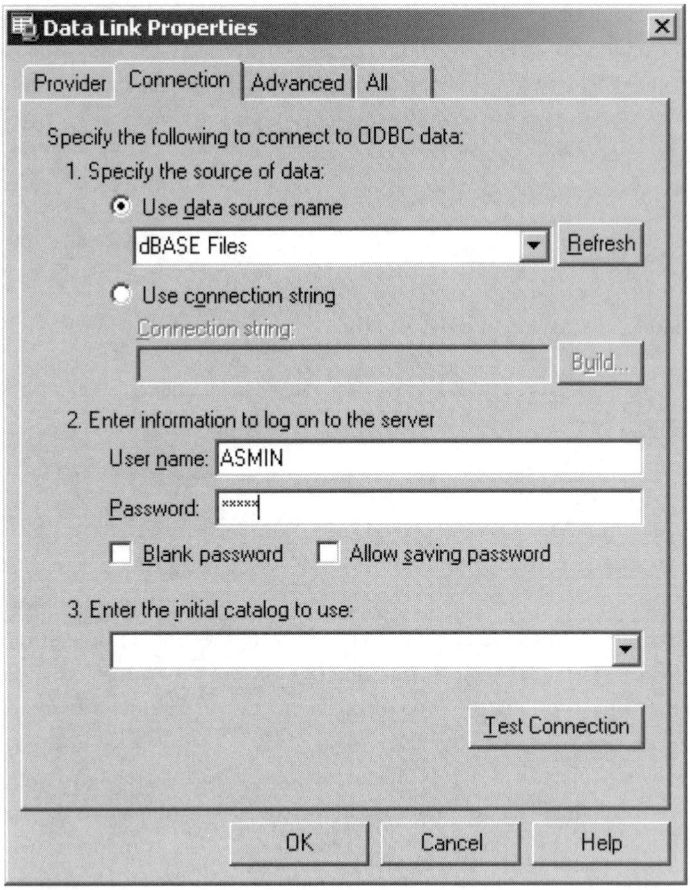

Figure 8.18 *The connection properties dialog*

Creating a database

If you are working with ADO components, you must use SQL statements to create a new database. In our example, we will use the `TAdoCommand` component for this purpose, as it is very well suited to this task. `TAdoCommand` is connected to the `TAdoConnection` component via the `Connection` property and can now be used right away.

However, before we formulate the SQL statement that is to be used to create a database, we must enter the directory in which the file is to be created in the `DefaultDataBase` property in `TAdoConnection`. This property is normally used for the default database definition, which might be a directory or an alias. From your experience with BDE you will be familiar with the way in which the `DatabaseName` property in `TTable` behaves. We can also enter the name of a directory here. After you set `DefaultDataBase`, you can create the connection. At designtime, you now set the `Connected` property to `true`. At runtime you can also call the `Open` method.

You now only need to enter the SQL statement in the `CommandText` property in `TAdoCommand`. The syntax of a statement used to open the database looks like this:

```
CREATE TABLE "<Filename>"
(<Field name> <Field type>,
 <Field name> <Field type>,
 (<Field name> <Field type>)
```

In our example, the statement looks like this:

```
CREATE TABLE "Address3.dbf"
(name char(40),
 firstname char(40),
 street char(40),
 postcode char(5),
 town char(40))
```

After you have entered the statement, you can create the table at designtime if a connection already exists. To do this, double-click on the `TAdoCommand` component (which is the same as calling the `Execute` statement). In Windows Explorer, you can check if the file really has been created.

In your own project, it is a good idea to store the SQL statement for the file you require, then insert the file name you want in the correct position and create the file. The whole process becomes a little easier if you use a `TAdoQuery` component instead of the `TAdoTable` component. This is because `TAdoQuery` can use SQL statements directly, which saves you the diversion of having to use the `TAdoCommand` component.

You use `TAdoTable` (or `TAdoQuery`) to access the database in the same way as the corresponding functions in BDE, `TTable` and `TQuery`. You use the `TDataSource` component to link the familiar data-sensitive control elements to the database, and to display and change the data they contain. The commands used to change, save, delete, or edit the database contents are also the same.

However, the best way to gain experience of ADO components is simply to try them out. Only the basic procedures can be described in this book, as there is simply not enough space to deal with the functionality of the new components. However, there is a wide range of specialist magazines and internet sites that provide more information about ADO.

Delphi and the internet

9

Delphi 6 contains a large number of useful and easy-to-use internet components. You can use them to create your own applications with the complete functionality of well-known programs for e-mail, news or FTP. You can now even use Delphi 6 to work with XML files.

9.1 TWebBrowser component

This very powerful component is located on the Component Palette Internet page. TWebBrowser encapsulates the entire functionality of a browser such as MS Internet Explorer. You use the component to access Microsoft's *Shdocvw.dll* file, which contains the web browser functionality. This component makes it possible for you to integrate Internet Explorer's functionality into your program.

The component includes a number of properties and methods that you can use to access websites. It makes no difference whether the file is present locally or on the internet, because the component creates the connection when you require it and downloads the document. If you do not want to permit access to the internet, then simply use the Offline property to instruct the component to read files only from the local cache. After you make this setting, no further connection is made to the internet.

To register the component as a top-level browser, set the RegisterAsBrowser to true. If you set the RegisterAsDropTarget property to true, then the user can move files to the browser component by dragging and dropping them. The TWebBrowser then displays these files.

The following properties are not used in TWebBrowser: AddressBar, FullScreen, StatusBar, TheaterMode and ToolBar. In other words, the component does not include a toolbar, status bar, etc., and you must implement these in your application yourself. However, with the help of the TWebBrowser events, you should have no difficulty in generating the displays you want in a status bar. You can also use the methods provided by TWebBrowser to create your own toolbar, which you can then use to access the components and their options. As Delphi provides an enormous range of useful functionality, you can set up your own browser in a very short time.

We will look at the TWebBrowser component in a short example at the end of this chapter, so I will not list the methods here.

9.2 NetMasters components

9.2.1 Common properties

As in previous versions, you will find the NetMasters components in Delphi 6 on the Component Palette FastNet page. All the NetMasters components are derived from the `TPowerSock` component, which is the basic connection component. This is why the Net-Masters components have so many properties in common. Table 9.1 lists these properties.

Property	Meaning
BeenCancelled	Used to query whether a process has been interrupted.
BeenTimedOut	Used to query whether the maximum time for a process has been exceeded. You can specify the maximum time yourself in the `TimeOut` property.
BytesRecvd	Contains the number of received bytes.
BytesSent	Contains the number of sent bytes.
BytesTotal	Contains the total number of bytes that are to be transferred.
Connected	Set to `true` if a connection to a remote server is present.
Host	Enter the address of the FTP server that you want to access.
LastErrorNo	Use the value of this property to ascertain the most recent socket error.
LocalIP	Contains the local computer's IP address.
Proxy	Only required if you are using a proxy server. In this case, enter the proxy's name or address here.
ProxyPort	Only required if you are using a proxy server. In this case, enter the proxy server's port address here.
RemoteIP	Contains the server's IP address.
TimeOut	Specifies the maximum amount of time that should be used for a procedure before an overrun happens. The value 0 means an infinite length of time.
TransactionReply	Includes the return value of the last action. The server always returns a message to say whether the action was successful.

Table 9.1 *Common properties of NetMasters components*

9.2.2 The TNmFTP component

In this component, which, like all the other components described in this chapter, is located on the Component Palette FastNet page, you can easily create a connection to a FTP server. You can then display its file structure and upload and download files. Before you can do this, you must first have a connection to an FTP server. For this connection you require the server's internet address, a user name, a password, and the FTP server's port. The default value for this is 6667. Some FTP servers also let you enter "anonymous" as the name and an e-mail address as the password, and therefore give you anonymous access. However, these accesses are usually restricted in what they can do. In other words, you may be able to display files but not download them, or you may not be able to access all the files and functions on the server.

Enter the FTP server's address as the value in the Host property. Set Port to the port address of the FTP server; the UserID property must contain the user name, and the Password must contain the password for the FTP server. In your own programs, you should ensure that the password is not visible, or you should give the user the option to decide if they want to store the password.

Once you have made all the settings, call the Connect method to generate the connection. Various events of the TNmFTP component occur depending on whether the connection is created correctly or cannot be created at all.

The Disconnect method disconnects an existing connection. Before you call Disconnect, you should make sure that a connection really is present. To do this, query the Connected property, which is set to true if you are connected to an FTP server.

Properties

Table 9.2 shows the most important properties of the TNmFTP component. Although there are quite a few, you will soon become familiar with them. Most of these properties are not located in the Object Inspector because they are used only to query a status.

Property	Meaning
FirewallType	TNmFTP can handle firewalls. Here, you specify the type of firewall involved.
FWAuthenticate	Shows whether you require a user name and a password for the firewall.
FWPassword	Enter the password for the firewall.
FWUserID	Enter the user name for the firewall.
ParseList	Indicates whether you can use the FTPDirectoryList property to evaluate the host computer's directory entries, or whether you must carry out the evaluation manually with the OnListItem event. OnListItem is triggered once for each directory entry, which makes it easy for you to create your own directory list.
Password	Enter the password that you will use to log on to the FTP server.
UserID	Enter the user name that you will use to access the FTP server.
Vendor	Enter the FTP server type. The default setting is usually sufficient here. The component then uses this setting automatically to attempt to find out the correct type. However, you can also specify an exact value if, for example, you know that the server is a UNIX computer.

Table 9.2 *The properties of* TNmFTP

Methods

Table 9.3 lists the most important methods of the TNmFTP component. It only shows the basic commands, but even these will allow you to create a working FTP program.

Method	Meaning
ChangeDir	Switches to another directory on the FTP server (but only if a connection is present).
Delete	Removes a file from the FTP server. The file name is passed to the method. You must, of course, have the appropriate authorization before you can delete a file.
DoCommand	Executes a command or a command sequence on the server. If you know which commands are supported by the FTP server, then you can send the commands directly to the server.
Download	Downloads a file from the server to your local computer. The file name on the server and a file name for saving the data on to the local computer must be passed to the method. If the file is already present on the local computer, then it will be overwritten.
List	Reads the directories on the FTP server.
MakeDirectory	Creates a new directory on the FTP server. You must have the appropriate authorization before you can create a directory.
Mode	Specifies the transfer mode between the local computer and the FTP computer. An integer value that represents the transfer mode is passed to the method. Possible modes are MODE_ASCII, MODE_IMAGE and MODE_BYTE.
RemoveDir	Deletes a directory from the FTP server. You must have the appropriate authorization before you can use this method.
Rename	Renames a file on the FTP server. You must have the appropriate authorization before you can use this method.
Upload	Uploads a file from the local computer to the FTP server. The file name on the local computer and the file name for the server must be passed to the method. If the file is already present on the server, then it will be overwritten.

Table 9.3 *The most important methods of* TNmFTP

9.2.3 *TNmNNTP component*

You use the TNmNNTP component to create a connection with a news server and to call or send messages to the various newsgroups. Despite the widespread use of websites, newsgroups are still the most popular and fastest way of getting the latest news. The news server for anyone interested in Borland (not only Delphi) is `forums.bor-land.com`. There, you will find everything there is to know about Borland's programming products. You can use the `TNmNNTP` component to construct your own news reader so that you can download the most important messages to your own computer. To connect to a news server, you require the server's address, a user name and a password. There are a few news servers that allow anonymous access, but usually your internet service provider (ISP) will supply a news server. To create a connection to a news server, assign the news server's address to the `Host` property. If you have the option of anonymous access, you then simply call the `Connect` method.

Before you can read the messages in a newsgroup, you will require a list of all the newsgroups. To get this list from the server, call the `GetGroupList` method and then use the `SetGroup` method to access the newsgroup you require. Use the `GetArticle` method to read an article from the news server, and use the `PostArticle` method to send an article to the group. Use the `Header` and `Body` properties to save the message header or the message itself.

Properties

Table 9.4 lists the most important methods of the `TNmNNTP` component. Some of these properties are not normally located in the Object Inspector because they are only used to query a status.

Property	Meaning
AttachFilePath	Enter the path in which the files attached to the messages in the newsgroup are to be stored.
Attachments	Shows the files that are attached to a message. Before you can download the files and store them in the path specified in the `AttachFilePath` property, you must set the `ParseAttachments` property to `true`.
Body	Contains the lines of the actual message.
CurrentArticle	Contains the most recently downloaded message.
GroupList	Contains a list of the newsgroups provided by the server.
Header	Contains the header of the current message.
Password	Contains the password used to log on to the news server if a logon is required.
PostBody	Contains the body text of the message that is to be sent.
PostHeader	Contains the header text of the message that is to be sent.
Posting	Used to query whether articles can be provided in the current newsgroup. If `Posting` is set to `true`, then you can do this; otherwise you cannot send messages to the newsgroup.
SelectedGroup	Shows the currently selected newsgroup.

Table 9.4 *Properties of TNmNNTP*

Methods

Table 9.5 lists the most important methods of the TNmNNTP component. You can use these methods to create your own newsreader without much time or effort.

Method	Function
GetArticle	Fetches a message from the news server. The method receives a parameter that specifies which message is to be fetched.
GetArticleBody	Fetches the text of the message you specified from the server.
GetArticleHeader	Fetches the header of the message you specified from the server.
GetArticleList	Downloads a list of available messages from the news server. You can pass two parameters to the method: the first is a Boolean parameter that indicates whether all or only some of the available messages are to be downloaded; in the second parameter you can specify the message from which this list is to begin.
GetGroupList	Calls a list of available newsgroups from the news server.
PostArticle	Sends a message to the current newsgroup.
SetGroup	Changes to another newsgroup.

Table 9.5 *The methods of the* TNmNNTP *component*

9.2.4 *TNmPop3 component*

The TNmPop3 component is half of the e-mail component provided by NetMasters; the other half is the TNmSMTP component, which is used to send e-mails to an e-mail server. TNmPop3 fetches messages from an e-mail server.

You create the connection in the same way as for the other components. You first make the relevant settings in UserID and Password and specify the e-mail server in the Host property, After this, you call the Connect method.

Once you have created the connection, you must then find out how many messages are waiting for you. The TNmPop3 component does this immediately after you create the connection. The MailCount property shows how many e-mails you have available for download. After this, you can then start fetching the messages.

The GetMailMessage method fetches a message from the e-mail server. In this method, you must specify the index number of the message you require, which means you will also need to know how many messages there are. After the message has been transferred correctly, you can call the DeleteMailMessage method to delete it from the server.

Properties

Table 9.6 lists the most important properties of the TNmPop3 component. Once again, not all the properties appear in the Object Inspector because some are only designed to call specific information.

Property	Meaning
AttachFilePath	Enter the directory in which you want to store the attachments that can be added to an e-mail.
DeleteOnRead	Specifies whether the e-mail messages are to be deleted from your local machine after they have been fetched from the server. The messages are usually not deleted there. To delete a message from the server, call the DeleteMailMessage method.
MailCount	After the connection to the server has been created, this contains the number of messages that are present on the server.
MailMessage	After you call an e-mail, this property, which has the type TMailMessage, contains the data in that e-mail.
Password	Enter the password for the connection to the POP3 server.
Summary	Contains the summary of an e-mail message.
UserID	Enter the user name for the connection to the POP3 server.

Table 9.6 *The properties of* TNmPop3

Methods

Table 9.7 lists the methods of TNmPop3 that enable you to fetch e-mails from a server.

Method	Function
UniqueID	Returns the ID of an e-mail message. Enter a number to specify which message this is.
DeleteMailMessage	Deletes the message whose number you passed to the method from the server.
GetMailMessage	Fetches an entire e-mail message from the server. The parameter that GetMailMessage expects is the index number of the message you want to fetch.
GetSummary	Functions like the GetMailMessage method, except it only calls a message's summary. The parameter that GetSummary expects is the index number of the message whose summary you want to download.
List	Used to fetch a list of all available messages. This list also contains the size and number of the messages.
Reset	Recreates deleted e-mail messages on the server. However, it only does so during the same session in which the messages were deleted.

Table 9.7 *Methods of* TNmPop3

9.2.5 *TNmSMTP component*

The *TNmSMTP* component represents the second half of an e-mail program; it is used to send e-mails. The only reason that these two components are separate is because some programs only require functions for sending an e-mail. This component also requires a connection to an e-mail server, which you create in the usual way (I won't describe it again here).

After you have created the connection, you are ready to send e-mail. In the PostMessage property, you can specify which parts of the e-mail message you want to send. This is a TPostMessage-type property and contains the properties listed in Table 9.8.

Property	Meaning
Attachments	TStringlist-type property that contains the names of the files to be attached to the e-mail.
Body	Assign the text of the message you want to send.
Date	You assign a date here. Note that this is a String-type property. If you do not assign a value here, the current date is used automatically.
FromAddress	Assign the e-mail address of the person sending the message.
FromName	Assign the real name of the person sending the message.
LocalProgram	Enter the name of the program used to send the e-mail.
ReplyTo	Enter the e-mail address to which the reply is to be sent. This is usually the same as the sender address.
Subject	Enter the subject of the e-mail message.
ToAddress	Enter the e-mail address of the person who is to receive the message.
ToBlindCarbonCopy	Specifies who is to receive a copy of the message without their name being visible to other recipients of the message.
ToCarbonCopy	Enter the e-mail address of anyone who is to receive a copy of the message.

Table 9.8   *Properties of* TPostMessage

After you have specified all the values, call the SendMail method to send the message.

Properties

Table 9.9 lists the properties of the TNmSMPT component.

Property	Meaning
ClearParams	Specifies whether the PostMessage fields that contain the data of the message to be sent are to be stored or deleted after the message has been sent.
EncodeType	Enter which coding type is to be used to send the message; you can select either UUEncode (generally used on UNIX systems) or Mime (generally used on Windows systems).
FinalHeader	Contains the actual message header of the e-mail you want to send. You can still change this before you send the message.
PostMessage	The sub properties of this property contain the e-mail message that is to be sent.
SubType	Specifies the format in which a message is to be sent (ASCII or HTML).
UserID	Enter a user name. Some servers require this for sending an e-mail.

Table 9.9 *Properties of TNmSMTP*

In this context, only the SendMail method really needs to be described. You will generally not require the other methods.

9.3 Your own browser

Now we will program a small, but fully functional, browser. We will use the TWebBrowser component from the Internet Component Palette.

9.3.1 *Program interface*

The interface of our browser consists of a main menu, a toolbar with a TEdit component, and the TWebBrowser component that includes the remainder of the form. In the example, we have also used the TActionList and TImageList components. These components make it easier to implement the same functions in the toolbar's buttons and in the menu.

As the TWebBrowser uses Internet Explorer's cache, we only need functions for calling the previous and the next website, and for canceling and updating a website. We also need a function to close the program. We will program these functions in the TActionList. We will store the corresponding icons in the TImageList and then assign them to both the menu components and the TActionList component.

Figure 9.1 shows what the program interface looks like at designtime.

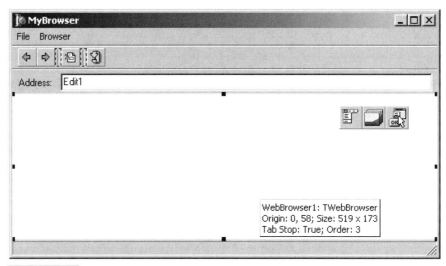

Figure 9.1 *The browser at designtime*

9.3.2 Programing the functionality

Navigating to the target

As you know, the main function of a browser is to display websites. The `TWebBrowser` component provides the `Navigate` method for this purpose. We must pass the internet address to this method as its parameter. To enter the address, you use the `TEdit` component. The user indicates that they have finished entering it by pressing Enter. To intercept a keystroke we use the `OnKeyPress` event in the `TEdit` component. In this event, we check if the user has pressed Enter. If yes, we can transfer the contents of Edit1 to the `TWebBrowser` component for navigation:

```
procedure TForm1.Edit1KeyPress(Sender: TObject;
                              var Key: Char);
begin
  if Key = #13 then
    WebBrowser1.Navigate(Edit1.Text);
end;
```

`TWebBrowser` carries out the navigation itself and even, if necessary, creates the connection to the internet. All we need now are ways to navigate between the websites, to stop a page from being displayed, and to update the page that is currently being displayed. As already mentioned, we have included a `TActionList` in the program for this purpose and set up the corresponding actions there. The functionality can be programmed very quickly.

Back and forward

GoBack goes to the previous website and GoForward goes to the next one. You can create each of these actions:

```
procedure TForm1.ActBackExecute(Sender: TObject);
begin
  WebBrowser1.GoBack;
end;


procedure TForm1.ActForwardExecute(Sender: TObject);
begin
  WebBrowser1.GoForward;
end;
```

In addition to these methods, there is also the GoHome method, which takes you to the page that you specified as the start page in Internet Explorer, and the GoSearch method, which takes you to the page you specified as the search page.

Cancel and update

The buttons you use to cancel navigation or update the contents of TWebBrowser are as quick and easy to program as the navigation buttons. TWebBrowser also provides methods for these functions, which will do some of the work for us. The Stop method stops an operation:

```
procedure TForm1.ActStopExecute(Sender: TObject);
begin
  WebBrowser1.Stop;
end;
```

One of the Navigate or Navigate2 methods updates the page. Here, the Navigate method sends a command to the web server, requesting it to send the updated page. However, some servers may not recognize this type of call, so we have used the Navigate2 method because it can be called in a number of different ways.

For our call, we require an OleVariant-type variable, which we must pass to the method. We must use a variable because this is a variable parameter. You will find the values that you can pass in Delphi's online help, using the keyword Navigate2:

```
procedure TForm1.ActRefreshExecute(Sender: TObject);
var
  MyLevel: OleVariant;
begin
  MyLevel := 1;
  WebBrowser1.Refresh2(MyLevel);
end;
```

Despite the fact that we haven't done much programming, our program is a functioning browser that you can now test. We are still missing a few displays in the program's status bar, but we will add them now. To do this, we must evaluate the events in `TWebBrowser`.

Programming the status bar

You are no doubt familiar with the displays in the status bar in your standard browser, e.g. when you find a new page or when you finish downloading a page. We want to program these as well, and also display the title of the page being displayed in our program's title bar. `TWebBrowser` provides us with all the events and variables we need. If you are looking for a URL, this should appear in the status bar. To do this, we will use the `BeforeNavigate2` event, which has an amazing number of parameters. Don't be put off by this; the only one we want to use is the `URL` parameter:

```
procedure TForm1.WebBrowser1BeforeNavigate2(
                             Sender: TObject;
                     const pDisp: IDispatch;
                     var   URL, Flags,
                           TargetFrameName,
                           PostData,
                           Headers: OleVariant;
                     var   Cancel: WordBool);
begin
  Statusbar1.SimpleText := 'Loading Page: '+URL;
end;
```

As you can see, this function is really easy to implement. Now for the display when a download is finished. We will not only write the word "Finished." in the status bar but also update the URL in the input field so that this always refers to the current URL. This is important, because otherwise the input field would always show the page that you entered in it, even if you have clicked on another page to switch to that page. The event we will use is `OnNavigateComplete2`:

```
procedure TForm1.WebBrowser1NavigateComplete2(
                              Sender: TObject;
                     const pDisp: IDispatch;
                         var URL: OleVariant);
begin
  Edit1.Text := URL;
  Statusbar1.SimpleText := 'Finished!';
end;
```

The only thing left is the form's title bar. This should show the title of the website you found and also the time at which it was downloaded. This takes place in the `OnTitleChange` event in `TWebBrowser`, which we will also use for this function:

```
procedure TForm1.WebBrowser1TitleChange(
                                    Sender: TObject;
                          const Text: WideString);
begin
  Form1.Caption := 'MyBrowser - '+Text;
end;
```

The document's title appears in the parameter text as soon as the browser downloads it. Before this, the parameter contains the address of the website to which we want to navigate. This completes the web browser (although you can still add a lot more functionality if you want). Even if the browser does not have much functionality, you can still start surfing the web with the basic functions you have implemented. Figure 9.2 shows the finished browser at runtime.

Figure 9.2 *The finished browser with the current Borland website*

9.4 Creating a cgi counter with Delphi

This is not one of my examples but comes instead from Anders Ohlsson, a developer who works for Borland, who was kind enough to let me use his source code in this book. I haven't changed the code at all. You will find it all on Anders Ohlsson's own website, http://homepages.borland. com/aohlsson/

The first thing we need is the basic functionality, i.e. a new webserver application. Select FILE | NEW | OTHER and then click on the WEB SERVER APPLICATION icon at the bottom of the Object Repository New page. Another dialog appears in which you can select CGI STAND-ALONE EXECUTABLE.

You now see a web module. In the Object Inspector, click on the `Actions` property and add a new web action object. Later on, this object, or rather its event-handling routine for `Action`, will form the core of the cgi script.

9.4.1 Basic requirements

First of all, we must add a couple of units. These are necessary because we want to create a .jpg file. Apart from that, we require a `TPanel` component and a `TMemo` component. Add the following units to the implementation section of the unit:

```
uses
    ExtCtrls, StdCtrls, Controls, Forms, Graphics, JPEG;
```

Now we require another two procedures so that the script can be ported (i.e. able to run on any server) later on. First, we need a procedure that discovers two important paths: the path in which our script is stored on the server relative to the web server, and the local path. The `GetPaths` procedure does this for us:

```
procedure GetPaths(Request: TWebRequest;
                var ScriptPath, LocalPath : String);
var
    ScriptFileName : String;
begin
    ScriptPath := Request.ScriptName;
    ScriptFileName := ExtractFileName(ParamStr(0));

  // Chop off the EXE/DLL name so that we get the path
    Delete(ScriptPath,Pos(ScriptFileName,ScriptPath)-1,
        Length(ScriptFileName)+1);

  // Chop off leading '/'
    Delete(ScriptPath,1,1);
    LocalPath := ExtractFilePath(ParamStr(0));
```

```
// Chopping off the ScriptPath gives us the root path
Delete(LocalPath,Pos(ScriptPath,LocalPath)-1,
        Length(ScriptPath)+1);
end;
```

The second procedure we require is used to set variables:

```
procedure SetVariable(var S : String;
                       const Value, Default : String);
begin
  S := Value;
  if S = '' then
    S := Default;
end;
```

9.4.2 *OnAction* event

This event is the core of the script. We will go through it step by step.

Declaring the variables

First, a few important variables:

```
procedure TWebModule1.WebModule1WebActionItem1Action(
        Sender: TObject;
        Request: TWebRequest;
        Response: TWebResponse;
    var Handled: Boolean);
var
  ScriptPath,
  LocalPath,
  FileName,
  Txt, FontColor,
  BackgroundColor,
  FontName,
  FontSize          : String;
  Today, LastEver,
  Ever, LastToday   : Integer;
  LastDate          : TDate;
  MS                : TMemoryStream;
  Panel             : TPanel;
  Memo              : TMemo;
  Bitmap            : TBitmap;
  Form              : TForm;
  fp                : TextFile;
```

Specifing the paths and parameters

The first step is to specify the paths. To do this, we use our `GetPaths` procedure:

```
begin
  GetPaths(Request,ScriptPath,LocalPath);
  LocalPath := LocalPath+'counters\';
```

Now we will determine all the parameters that have been passed to the script. In this case, a default value is used if an appropriate parameter has not been passed. We use the `Request.QueryFields` property to determine the parameters:

```
with Request.QueryFields do begin
  FileName := LocalPath+Values['FileName']+'.txt';
  SetVariable(Txt,Values['Txt'],
           'You are visitor %d today, and visitor %d
           ever.');
  SetVariable(FontName,
             Values['FontName'],'Arial');
  SetVariable(FontSize,
             Values['FontSize'],'10');
  SetVariable(FontColor,
             Values['FontColor'],'clWhite');
  SetVariable(BackgroundColor,
             Values['BackgroundColor'],'clBlack');
end;
```

Creating and reading the counter file

Now, we must ensure that there is a file present in which we can store the current counter status. If this file does not exist, then we create a new one and set all counter statuses to 0. The file name is shown in the `FileName` parameter.

```
try
  //Write a new empty counter file if it doesn't exist
  if not FileExists(FileName) then begin
    AssignFile(fp,FileName);
    Rewrite(fp);
    WriteLn(fp,0);
    WriteLn(fp,Date);
    WriteLn(fp,0);
    CloseFile(fp);
  end;
```

This ensures that the file exists, and we can now open it. This file contains both the total number of hits and the number of hits on the current day:

```
// Read the old counter values
AssignFile(fp,FileName);
Reset(fp);
ReadLn(fp,LastEver);
Ever := LastEver+1;
ReadLn(fp,LastDate);
ReadLn(fp,LastToday);
if Date = LastDate then
  Today := LastToday+1
else
  Today := 1;
CloseFile(fp);
```

After the current data have been fetched, we return them:

```
// Write the new counter values
AssignFile(fp,FileName);
Rewrite(fp);
WriteLn(fp,Ever);
WriteLn(fp,Date);
WriteLn(fp,Today);
CloseFile(fp);
```

Generating the graphic

So far, so good. Now we can generate our .jpg file. First, we need a form to hold our `TPanel` and `TMemo` components. We can use this to generate a three-dimensional appearance (to some extent). We therefore simply create an invisible form that will act as the parent. To this, we add our `TPanel` and `TMemo` components and then check that the memo also contains the correct data:

```
Form := TForm.Create(nil);
with Form.Font do begin
  Name := FontName;
  Size := StrToInt(FontSize);
end;
Txt := Format(Txt,[Today,Ever]);
Panel := TPanel.Create(nil);
with Panel do begin
  BevelInner := bvRaised;
```

```
  BevelOuter := bvLowered;
  Parent := Form;
  Width := Form.Canvas.TextWidth(Txt)+9;
  Height := Form.Canvas.TextHeight(Txt)+9;
end;
Memo := TMemo.Create(nil);
with Memo do begin
  Top := 2;
  Left := 2;
  Width := Panel.Width-5;
  Height := Panel.Height-5;
  Alignment := taCenter;
  Color := StringToColor(BackgroundColor);
  BorderStyle := bsNone;
  Parent := Panel;
end;
```

Now to the actual bitmap which we will save or display later on. We start off by generating a bitmap that we then convert into .jpg format:

```
Bitmap := TBitmap.Create;
with Bitmap do begin
  Width := Panel.Width-1;
  Height := Panel.Height-1;
  Canvas.Lock;
  Panel.PaintTo(Canvas.Handle,0,0);
  Canvas.Unlock;
  Canvas.Brush.Style := bsClear;
  with Canvas.Font do begin
    Name := FontName;
    Size := StrToInt(FontSize);
    Color := StringToColor(FontColor);
  end;
  Canvas.TextOut(4,3,Txt);
end;
```

Now carry out the conversion into a .jpg file and send the file as the result of the cgi script:

```
with Response do begin
  MS := TMemoryStream.Create;
  with TJPEGImage.Create do begin
```

```
      CompressionQuality := 75;
      Assign(Bitmap);
      SaveToStream(MS);
      Free;
   end;
   ContentType := 'image/jpeg';
   MS.Position := 0;
   SendResponse;
   SendStream(MS);
end;
```

The only things still missing are the tidying-up tasks and error checks. Nevertheless, we have programmed the functions into a `try` block and therefore only need to program the `except` block:

```
      Panel.Free;
      Bitmap.Free;
      Form.Free;
   except
      on E: Exception do
         Response.Content := E.Message;
   end;
   Handled := True;
end;
```

You can call the counter from an HTML file, for example, with the following command:

```
<img src="/cgi-bin/counterCGI.exe?FileName=count">
```

The counter parameters are optional. You can set these parameters (as usual on the internet, you must remember where you use capital and lower-case letters):

→ `Txt` for the text that is to be displayed. The string must include two placeholders that use %d format: the first is used for the date counter and the second for the total counter.

→ `FontName`, if you want to use a particular font.

→ `FontColor`, if you want to assign a particular color to the font.

→ `BackgroundColor` for the background color.

By the way, this example also works with Delphi 5.

Developing components

One of Delphi's greatest advantages is that it gives you a way to develop your own components or to extend the functionality of existing ones. You can also modify an existing component to meet specific requirements. In addition, you can even use components from other manufacturers in Delphi by adding them to the Component Palette.

There isn't really enough space to go into detail here, but I will discuss the main issues as thoroughly as possible. This chapter contains a description of some basic elements and then an example to show you how to derive a new component from an existing one.

10.1 Back to basics

Component development is very different from application development. Application developers can always resort to the advantages of visual programming, or use component properties and events, but component developers cannot do this. Instead, they are responsible for deciding which events and properties the component has, and how they behave within a program.

Basically, components are classes. When you develop a new component, you can either derive a new component from an existing one, and then modify it, or you can use one of the abstract classes provided by Delphi. Although a number of properties, events and methods are already defined in these abstract classes, they do not have any functions. Many of Delphi's control elements are derived from the same abstract class but have different functionality.

Table 10.1 shows some components and the base classes from which they are usually derived.

Base class	Use
TComponent	To create a non-visual component.
TWinControl TCustomControl	To create a window-oriented component. This is not a window, but Windows treats these components as if they were, and therefore they require the corresponding resources. This control element can be given the input focus. Input fields such as TEdit are window-oriented elements.
TGraphicControl	To create a graphic component that cannot be given the input focus. As this is not a window-oriented component, it also requires correspondingly fewer resources. An example of this kind of component is TLabel.
Any kind of component	To derive a new component from an existing one. If you only want to change a part of an existing component's functionality, then you can derive your new component from any other component. Delphi VCL also contains a number of abstract component classes that you can use to generate a completely different range of functionality. These classes have the word "custom" in their name, e.g. TCustomGrid and TCustomEdit.

Table 10.1 *Base component classes*

10.2 Conventions

When you develop a component, you must take note of a few things that are not relevant for application developers but are nonetheless required by them. A component must function in each program in which it is used; it cannot depend on anything else. As a component developer, you must make sure that your component will always function, no matter how or where it is used.

You are also responsible for ensuring that the user can always use properties to change the component or its appearance, or even how it behaves. You must provide the programmer with these properties and make sure that they are useful. The assignment of values to a property must also be triggered in a logical way, i.e. via property editors such as the FileName property. Another issue that you must deal with are the events to which the component can react. These should also be logical and, most importantly, easy to use.

The last aspect you must be aware of are the component's methods. You should have realized already that Delphi's components have not only events and properties but also methods that are used to execute various different functions. For example, in list boxes, these are the Add or Insert methods that you use to add new items to the list. You must also specify these methods yourself.

Finally, we must emphasise the naming conventions used in component development. Some conventions have been used in components since Delphi 1. The same applies to the names of functions and procedures, and to the variable descriptors in the component classes. You must follow these naming conventions; they are tried and trusted, they will make your source code clear, and all other programmers use them too.

10.3 Structure of a component class

A component class has several visibility levels. Table 10.2 lists the available visibility levels.

Visibility	Meaning
Private	Methods or variables defined in this section can be accessed only by source code programmed in the same unit. In this section, you should program the implementation that users cannot access.
Protected	Methods or variables defined in this section can be accessed only from the source code present in the unit in which the class or its descendents are defined. You usually program your own component interface (rather than the programmer's) in this section. However, although derived components can access this section, anyone who uses the component later on cannot do so (directly).
Public	Methods or variables defined in this section can be accessed from any source code.
Automated	Methods defined in this section can be accessed from any source code. However, this section is only used for OLE automation, which is why this is the only place it is mentioned in this book.
Published	This is the publication section. The published properties and events can be accessed from any source code. In addition, published properties and events are also displayed in the Object Inspector.

Table 10.2 *Visibility levels of a component*

When you create a new component, Delphi can provide you with a basic framework that has been created by the Component wizard. However, this is only a basic framework. The only procedure it contains is the `Register` method, which is used to register the component in the Component Palette. To access the Component wizard, click on the COMPONENT | NEW COMPONENT menu. Figure 10.1. shows the Component wizard.

The first thing you specify is an ancestor for the new component. This can be either one of the standard ancestors listed in Table 10.1 or a component that you want to

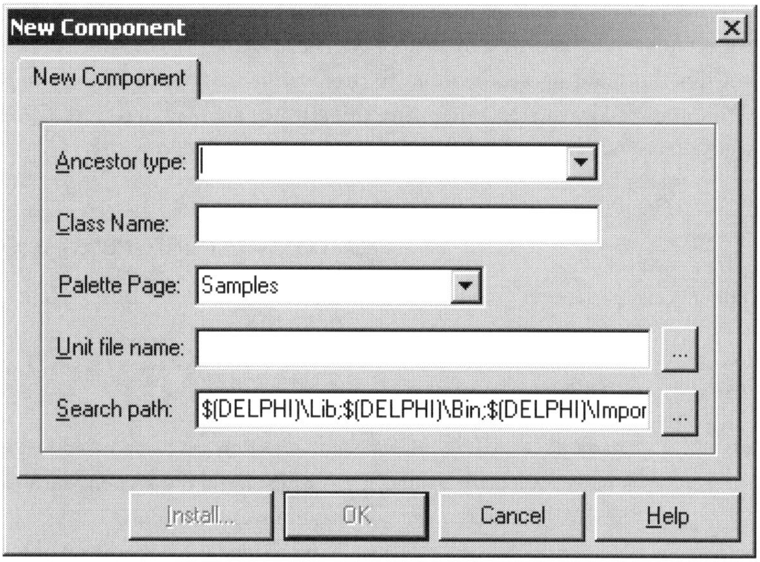

Figure 10.1 *Delphi's Component wizard*

extend. The next thing you enter is the name of your new component. It has become traditional (and you should do this too) to start all new class names with a capital "T". Borland's Delphi class names start with "T", and even developers from other countries and companies follow this convention.

The next piece of data you have to specify is the Component Palette page on which the new component is to be stored. Here, you can either select an existing page or specify a new Component Palette page, which Delphi then creates automatically as soon as you register the component.

Finally, you enter the name of the unit in which the component is to be defined. Delphi creates the unit, complete with the basic framework for a new component. The next extract of program code shows the basic framework of a new component called TMyEdit, which is derived from a standard TEdit component:

```
unit MyEdit;

interface

uses
  Windows, Messages, SysUtils, Classes, Graphics,
Controls, Forms, Dialogs, StdCtrls;

type
  TMyEdit = class(TEdit)
```

```
private
  { Private declarations }
protected
  { Protected declarations }
public
  { Public declarations }
published
    { Published declarations }
end;

procedure Register;

Implementation

procedure Register;
begin
  RegisterComponents('Examples', [TMyEdit]);
end;

end.
```

This component already has all the properties of the original component, so we do not need to make many changes here. If you register the component in this form, then it will have the same functions and properties as a TEdit component.

10.4 Properties

10.4.1 Property variables and properties

The properties of a component are simply variables that are declared within that component and, where useful, released so that they can be displayed in the Object Inspector. However, there are also properties that should not be displayed in the Object Inspector, either because it doesn't make sense to do so or because they are read-only.

Users can access some properties directly, i.e. these values are assigned immediately without being checked. The Caption property is an example of this. Here, a variable is declared in the private section of the component, which is used to control access to the property. Another tradition has established itself here. The variables responsible for a property start with a capital "F" and otherwise have the name of the property, whose value they buffer. Anyone who uses your component later on can therefore never access properties directly. If you use methods only to access a property value, then you do not need to use this kind of variable.

10.4.2 Accessing a property

You can access properties in two ways, either directly (or rather sort of directly, because later users of the component cannot access variables that are declared in the `private` section), or by using methods. In this case, the `Set` method is combined with the property name and used to set the property value, and the `Get` method is combined with the property name and used to read it. As an example, let us assume that you specified a variable called `FLength`. The property's name would then be `Length`, and the methods used to set and read the value would be `GetLength` and `SetLength` respectively

In this case, the `Get` method is always a function and the `Set` method is always a procedure. Both of these are also declared in the `private` section of the component, because later users of the component should not be able to access them either.

If you want to assign a value directly, without having to process it first, you do not need to use a method to read it or describe the property variables. You can specify them when you publish the value instead.

10.4.3 Publishing properties

All the properties (and events) that are visible in the Object Inspector are published in the `published` section. Properties and events that should not appear in the Object Inspector, but which the programmer should still be able to access (at runtime), are published in the `public` section. If you want to provide properties or events that are to be published by derived components, then you must declare them in the `protected` section.

The keyword for publication is `property`. When the value is published, the following information is also shown: how the value is accessed, if it is to be stored, and if the property has a default value. A typical declaration is structured like this (the declaration of our property `Length` is used as an example):

```
property Length: integer read GetLength write SetLength
default 0;
```

Here, the keyword `Default` refers to a default value for the property, which is specified during initialization. If we didn't use the methods to describe the property, we could also write:

```
property Length: integer read FLength write FLength
default 0;
```

and, as a result, access the variable directly. However, there is usually no point in doing this. In this context, do you remember the tag property, which every component has? This is declared in exactly the same way:

```
property Tag: Longint read FTag write FTag default 0;
```

You are probably wondering why we don't allow the people who use the component to access variables directly. As you know, encapsulating a variable as a property provides a uniform interface for accessing values. To this is added the user's entries, which must be checked before they are actually assigned (also by a method). This prevents errors (if the component is programmed correctly), and the assignment of a value to the property at designtime will highlight any changes to the component's appearance.

> **Tip** You may also wonder how it is possible that these changes are visible immediately. This is because, even at designtime, source code that has already been complied is displayed transparently for the application developer, i.e. the source code for the components. The Compiler runs in the background, without the programmer being aware of it, to make any changes to the properties visible immediately.

10.4.4 loading and saving property values

The properties of components are stored together with the form data of the form on which they are located. Delphi uses its form files (files with the extension .dfm) to do this. Up to Delphi 4, these were binary files, but since Delphi 5, they have usually been text files. You can change the format used for form files by using environment options if required (select TOOLS | ENVIRONMENT OPTIONS, then on the Designer page select NEW FORMS AS TEXT in "Module creation options").

When you create a component, Delphi loads and stores the property values. This usually looks as though all the property values of the properties declared in the `public` or `published` sections are stored in the sequence in which they occurred. If you create a form, the components are also generated and filled with default values; then the individual values are loaded from the form file. Usually, you do not need to change this standard procedure, but you can if you want to.

Defining default values

As you have already seen, you can define default values for properties. However, these are not the default values that Delphi assigns automatically to the property but a change to the way in which the component is stored. In fact, the properties for which a default value exists are not actually saved until the current property value differs from the default value. You are still responsible for assigning the default value.

To assign a default value, use the reserved word `default`. You then carry out initialization with the default value in the component's constructor. Simply add the reserved word `default` to the end of the property declaration and write the default value after it.

To save or not to save?

You use the reserved word `stored` in the property's declaration to specify whether the value is to be saved or not. Here, `True` means that the value of this property is always saved, and `False` means that it is never saved. You can also use a function with a Boolean return value. In this case, the value is stored depending on this function.

Although you can call this function anything you want, it has become traditional to use names like `IsLengthStored` or `IsStyleStored`, names that are similar to property names to make it easier for you to see the structure. As only the component itself needs to access these functions, you declare them in the `private` section. Obviously enough, the return value must be Boolean, because this is what `Stored` expects.

10.5 Windows messages

Before we start defining events, here is some basic information about Windows messages and how to handle them. Events merely encapsulate the corresponding Windows messages. As these messages come from the (Windows) operating system, we need a way of identifying and intercepting them.

10.5.1 Basic principles of messages

Generally speaking, you do not need to worry about intercepting messages if you have derived your component from an existing one. However, you must change the relevant handling routine, so that your component can react to a message in the way you want it to. To do this, you must know a bit about Windows messages.

Structure of a message

Fundamentally, a message is a record. A message is identified by a particular field in this record that contains an integer value. These values are specified in the `Messages` unit. The other fields in the record are the parameters that Windows transfers along with the message. In the past, there were only these parameters, so programmers had to remember what each parameter contained and how that was stored. You could, of course, also look in the help for the Windows API, but ws annoying if you had to do it every time.

In the meantime, Microsoft has realized that this is not the best solution and has recently provided names for the individual parameters. These are much more meaningful than the original parameters (which were always called `wParam` and `lParam`). Delphi itself also defines records whose parameters have names that actually mean something, and each message type has one.

Path taken by a message

All Delphi components have a system for distributing messages. There are four methods responsible for the path a message takes within the component. If you have derived a component from an existing one or from a base class, then these methods are already implemented, but you can overwrite them if you want to change something about the way a message is handled.

`MainWndProc` is the method of the component that first receives the message. `MainWndProc` receives the message and passes it on. You cannot overwrite these methods, although they don't actually do anything apart from passing the message on to the virtual `WndProc` method, which you can overwrite. Exceptions are passed by `MainWndProc` to the application's exception handler, not to `WndProc`.

`WndProc` is a procedure in which you can intercept and react to messages before the component does. This is a good idea, for example, if you want to intercept a message that is not to be passed on. `WndProc` itself calls another method, and the distribution process really gets started there.

The `Dispatch` method distributes the messages. The Message ID shows which of the component's methods is responsible for editing the message. The message is then passed on to this method. If no method is responsible for the message that has been received, then `Dispatch` calls the default message-handling routine. You cannot overwrite the `Dispatch` method.

The `DefaultHandler` method is the default handling routine for messages. It is called if no handling routine is present for a message that has been processed by the `Dispatch` method.

10.5.2 Defining message-handling routines

Usually, all the useful message-handling routines have already been declared in the base classes. To change this kind of routine, you must overwrite it. Here, a message-handling routine always has the same name as the message itself. When you overwrite it, you must make sure that the message can be passed on to the message-handling routine. Once again, here is an example from `TCustomEdit`:

```
procedure WMSetFont(var Message: TWMSetFont); message
WM_SETFONT;
```

The message-handling routine is called `WmSetFont`, the message is `WM_SETFONT` (note the underscore), and the message type is `TWmSetFont`. This is, of course, passed on to the message-handling routine.

When you overwrite a message-handling routine, you do not require the reserved word `override`; you simply use the same message index (in this case `WM_SETFONT`).

10.5.3 Declaring your own messages

Before you can declare your message, you must define a message record. You will find a few records in the Messages unit in the Delphi subdirectory *Source\RTL*. You also need an ID for the message. Here, you must use an ID that is greater than 1024 because Windows fills all the IDs up to this value. Delphi provides you with a constant called WM_APP for this, from which you can define your own messages.

The basic structure of the record for the message is predefined. The first field is always the message ID, which is a Cardinal-type ID. The manual shows this as the TMsgParam type; however, all message records with a Cardinal-type Msg field are also declared in the Messages unit. You should therefore use this type here. This is followed by a Word-type parameter and a Longint-type parameter. The Word data type fills 2 bytes, and the Longint data type fills 4 bytes. This gives you 6 bytes that you can use.

Finally, you must add a field called Result. This is the record's result field; it is a Longint-type field.

The following declaration comes from the Messages unit:

```
TWMMouse = packed record
   Msg: Cardinal;
   Keys: Longint;
   case Integer of
     0: (
       XPos: Smallint;
       YPos: Smallint);
     1: (
       Pos: TSmallPoint;
       Result: Longint);
   end;
```

After you have declared your own message you can use it within your components in the way described above.

10.6 Events

10.6.1 Declaring events

A large number of Windows messages are processed in events. When something happens, the user does something (even if they are only moving the mouse around), and Windows sends messages that can be intercepted by Delphi (or the components). The events are the result of this. Therefore, an event is nothing more than the interception of a Windows message, which presents you with the opportunity of writing a procedure for it. As an application developer, you have nothing to do with intercepting messages because the components take care of this for you. When you write an event-handling routine, you can be certain that the relevant message will be intercepted.

However, as a component developer, you must grit your teeth and intercept the Windows messages that you require for your component and make them available as an event. In this case, you declare an event-handling routine in the same way as you would a `TNotifyEvent`-type variable. The naming conventions remain the same, i.e. an event is handled in basically the same way as a variable, whose name therefore also starts with "F".

As I have already mentioned, this is an event-handling routine. The actual event is declared as a method that reacts to the corresponding Windows message and calls the event-handling routine (if you have programmed one). The declaration of the `OnChange` event in a `TEdit` component looks like this:

```
...
  private
...
  FOnChange: TNotifyEvent;
...
protected
...
  property OnChange: TNotifyEvent read FOnChange write
FOnChange;
```

In this example, the event has only been declared and is not yet published because the declaration originates from a base class.

10.6.2 Intercepting messages

Up to this point, however, the event still can not be called automatically (i.e. by a Windows message). We still require a method for intercepting the message that causes the event and for calling the event-handling routine (if you have programmed one). For the `OnChange` event, the Windows message is `CM_TEXTCHANGED`. This is intercepted in the `CmTextChanged` method (basically, the method therefore has the same name as the message, but without the underscore). The method is declared in the `private` section of the component like this:

```
procedure CMTextChanged(var Message: TMessage); message
CM_TEXTCHANGED;
```

To complete the picture, here is how you implement the method:

```
procedure TCustomEdit.CMTextChanged(var Message:
TMessage);
begin
  inherited;
  if not HandleAllocated or
```

```
      (GetWindowLong(Handle, GWL_STYLE) and
        ES_MULTILINE <> 0) then
    Change;
end;
```

The event is then called in the Change method:

```
procedure TCustomEdit.Change;
begin
  inherited Changed;
  if Assigned(FOnChange) then FOnChange(Self);
end;
```

In this case, the reserved word inherited calls the previous method. Inherited on its own calls the method with the same name from the previous method, and inherited together with a method descriptor calls the corresponding method from the parent component.

Assigned checks whether the transferred pointer indicates a value or nothing at all. In this case, the check also shows if the appropriate event-handling routine has been programmed. The routine is only called if it has been programmed. This is very important because it must never happen that a event-handling routine that has not been programmed causes an error. Nonetheless, it is up to the programmer whether they write one or not.

10.6.3 Publishing events

As mentioned already, events are usually of the TNotifyEvent-type or of another declared type (such as TMouseEvent or TMouseMoveEvent – there are several). As there is no interim method, you can access an event's value directly. You publish events in the same way as properties:

```
property OnChange: TNotifyEvent read FOnChange write
FOnChange;
```

When you publish the event, it also appears in the Object Inspector. The rule that you must declare the event for components that are to be the basis for other components in the protected section instead of the published section also applies here. In this case, the event is not published until it reaches the derived component.

10.7 Methods

10.7.1 Published methods

Component methods that a programmer must be able to access later on are declared in the `public` section of the component and programmed in the same way as for procedures or functions. As methods do not appear in the Object Inspector, you do not need to publish them or follow any kind of conventions. However, different method names have also become established for different procedures, e.g. the `Add` method, which is used to insert a list item into a list. If possible, you should also use the standard names for these different methods because this will make things easier for the programmer later on.

Obviously, methods that should not be available to the application developer, because they are used only internally, should not be declared as `public`. You must declare these methods as `protected`.

10.7.2 Constructors and destructors

There are two particular methods that you should always declare as `public`. One is the method used to create components (the constructor) and the other is the method used to remove components from memory (the destructor). Application developers do not need to concern themselves with such things, unless they really want to. Therefore, you must give the programmer the option of generating or releasing a component at runtime. You must declare both the *constructor* and the *destructor* as public, so that the programmer can also use these methods. As a component developer, you are still responsible for generating and initializing a component, because it is your job to be aware of, and deal with, everything that a programmer takes for granted.

You must generate and initialize a component's constructor; the name of a constructor is always `Create`. The destructor removes the component from memory; the name of a destructor is usually `Destroy`.

The constructor for visual components usually has a parameter that is passed. This parameter tells the constructor which component is the higher-level component. This parameter is a `TComponent`-type parameter and is usually called `AOwner`. A destructor does not have a parameter that is passed.

The way in which you declare a `constructor` and a `destructor` looks like this:

```
public
  constructor Create(AOwner: TComponent); override;
  destructor Destroy; override;
```

When you implement a constructor or a destructor, you must first call the constructor of the previous component so that you can check that all parameters have been set correctly before you make your own modifications. Here is the constructor from `TCustomEdit`, the base class for input fields:

```
constructor TCustomEdit.Create(AOwner: TComponent);
const
  EditStyle = [csClickEvents, csSetCaption,
               sDoubleClicks, csFixedHeight];
begin
  inherited Create(AOwner);
  if NewStyleControls then
    ControlStyle := EditStyle
  else
    ControlStyle := EditStyle + [csFramed];
  Width := 121;
  Height := 25;
  TabStop := True;
  ParentColor := False;
  FBorderStyle := bsSingle;
  FAutoSize := True;
  FAutoSelect := True;
  FHideSelection := True;
  AdjustHeight;
end;
```

In the constructor, you first use the reserved word `inherited` to call the constructor of the component from which it is derived. You can then set the various properties to the default values.

10.8 Property editors

Some properties have an editor in which you can easily change a property's value. Examples of this are the Font and Glyph properties. You can provide your properties with a property editor that you design yourself, or you can use one of the standard property editors. Property editors are derived from the `TPropertyEditor` class. There are a few predefined types for property editors, e.g. `TFontNameProperty` for font names, and `TFontProperty` for the entire font (the standard Windows font dialogs are used here).

10.8.1 Programming a property editor

To program a property editor, simply derive the new class from the standard class for property editors. The standard class for property editors already provides a number of methods, which you can overwrite to create your own property editor.

Converting values

All properties are displayed as strings in the Object Inspector. You can check this because even Boolean values are shown as strings. This is why each property editor needs a method for preparing a string so that it can be displayed in the Object Inspector. Even if the person using your component can change the property directly in the Object Inspector, you still need a method that handles the value they enter. The methods for this conversion are called `SetValue` and `GetValue`. `GetValue` is a function and `SetValue` is a procedure where the parameter that is passed is a string-type `Value`.

The `SetValue` method receives a string from the Object Inspector and converts it into the correct format for your property. If the value is not the one it expects, then `SetValue` generates an exception. You should be familiar with this already, e.g. from the error message "is not a valid integer value".

`GetValue` converts the property's value into a string that can be displayed in the Object Inspector.

Editor attributes

Property editors have a number of different attributes that you can set as required. These are sets of values that influence the editor's behavior. The values are `TPropertyAttributes`-type values. To change the attributes you overwrite the `GetAttributes` method in the property editor type. Table 10.3 shows a list of possible values and their meaning.

Attribute	Meaning
paValuesList	The editor displays a list of property values from which the programmer can make their selection.
paSubProperties	The property has subproperties. You can open the list of subproperties and enter a value for each one.
paDialog	The editor can provide a dialog to make it easier for users to enter a value.
paMultiSelect	Displayed if more than one component has been selected.
paAutoUpdate	Usually, the component is not updated until the property's value has been declared as valid. If you add this attribute to the attribute list, then the component is updated immediately.
paReadOnly	You cannot change the value of this property.
paRevertable	The property can be reset to its original value.

Table 10.3 *Attributes of a property editor*

GetAttributes is a function whose return value is a TPropertyAttributes-type value. If you overwrite this method, the only thing you need to do is combine the attributes you require into a list and then return it:

```
function TMyPropertyEditor.GetAttributes:
TPropertyAttributes;
begin;
  Result := [paDialog,paRevertable];
end;
```

10.8.2 Registering a property editor

Before you can use your own property editor, you must register it. There is a method called RegisterPropertyEditor for property editors (as there is for components). You call this editor with the relevant parameters for your property editor. The first parameter is the type information pointer. For this, you must always call the TypeInfo function, e.g. TypeInfo(TMyComponent). The second parameter shows the component type that is to be valid for the editor. Here, you can also pass nil, which means that the editor can then be used for all the predefined components of this type (the type you transferred in TypeInfo). The third parameter specifies the name of the property for which the editor is to be used. This parameter is only taken into consideration if you did not pass nil in the second parameter. The last parameter specifies the type of editor you want to use.

You call the RegisterPropertyEditor method in the Register procedure. The call might look like this:

```
RegisterPropertyEditor(TypeInfo(string), TDBEdit,
'EditMask', TMaskProperty);
```

10.9 Numerical components

10.9.1 Framework for the new component

You use the Component wizard to create a framework for a new component. Our component will be derived from TCustomEdit, which is the base class for all input fields. In theory, you could also derive a new component from TEdit. However, if you check back in the VCL source code, you will see that TEdit only publishes TCustomEdit properties that are already present. As we want to leave a couple of properties out of our component, we will use TCustomEdit as the basis. Figure 10.2 shows the settings for the new component.

Here, the unit's name may be different, depending on your path settings. However, in every case this is the *Lib* subdirectory of your Delphi directory. Click on OK, and the Component wizard creates the basic framework for the new component.

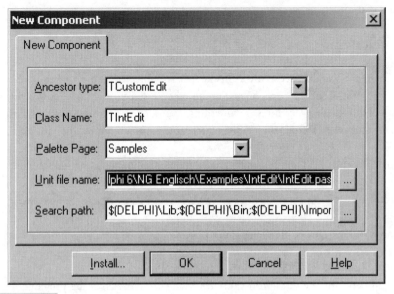

Figure 10.2 *The Component wizard with the settings*

10.9.2 Features of the new component

Our new input field should allow the user to enter an integer value. You could also implement this with a normal TEdit component. However, we want our component to have a few properties that are missing from the normal input field. First of all, the user should not need to think too much about their entry. In other words, we must make it impossible for them to enter anything other than a number. In addition, the component is to make this number available immediately in a property called IntValue. Finally, if the user changes the value of IntValue, then this change should also be shown in the Text property.

To make things even more user-friendly, we also want to include the option of signaling an incorrect entry. This means that the user hears an alarm tone if they attempt to enter a letter or another character that is not supported. It should also be possible to deactivate this alarm so we require the appropriate property, which the programmer can set as required.

10.9.3 Component properties

Property for the signal

We need a variable that will allow us to activate and deactivate the audible signal. By convention, component variables always start with "F". Of course, you do not have to follow this convention, but it does make things easier. Our new variable should be a Boolean-type variable; I have decided to call it DoBeep. The variable is declared in the private section of our new component:

```
private
    { Private declarations }
    FDoBeep    : Boolean;
```

So, that's the variable declaration finished. It is published as a property in the `published` section of the component. It can be accessed directly, without having to go through any other procedures or functions. We therefore create a DoBeep property, whose value is taken from the FDoBeep variable (or is written to this variable):

```
published
    { Published declarations }
    property DoBeep: Boolean read FDoBeep write FDoBeep;
```

So now we have created the first property.

Property for the numerical value

The property for the numerical value with which the user is to be provided does not need a special kind of variable that we need to declare (a property is, of course, already a variable). We only need to access two methods: one to load the value and one to read it. This means we can declare the new property directly in the `published` part of the component framework:

```
published
    { Published declarations }
    property DoBeep: Boolean read FDoBeep write FDoBeep;
    property IntValue : integer read GetIntValue write
SetIntValue;
```

The last things we need to do are implement the access methods and restrict the user to inputting numbers. Let's first deal with how to access the IntValue property.

10.9.4 Access methods for IntValue

Declaring the methods

To assign the value to our property, we need one routine for setting the value (SetIntValue) and one routine for reading the value (GetIntValue). In this case, SetIntValue is a procedure and GetIntValue is a function that has an Integer-type return value. We declare both procedures in the private part of the component:

```
private
    { Private declarations }
    FDoBeep    : Boolean;
```

```
function GetIntValue: integer;
procedure SetIntValue(const Value: integer);
```

You do not need to declare the methods. It is sufficient to specify then as access methods for the property and use code completion. Delphi then adds the methods to the component declaration and creates the framework. The only thing you need to do is to fill in the framework.

Implementing the methods

The GetIntValue method is not complicated. We read the value of the Text property from it and then convert this value into an Integer value. However, we must make sure that an invalid value cannot be entered. As you know, we want to restrict users to entering numbers here to ensure that problems don't arise later on. However, if the Text property is deleted completely, then Delphi also handles this as an invalid value. This is why we must intercept invalid entries. To do this, we use a try...except block; otherwise, Delphi would generate an exception. The source code for GetIntValue looks like this:

```
function TIntEdit.GetIntValue: integer;
begin
  try
    Result := StrToInt(Text);
  except
    Result := 0;
    Text := '0';
  end;
end;
```

The SetIntValue is even easier to implement because it is only a single line of source code:

```
procedure TIntEdit.SetIntValue(const Value: integer);
begin
  Text := IntToStr(Value);
end;
```

Our new property should now be implemented. At runtime, the Text and IntValue properties are synchronous, i.e. when the Text property contains the input value as a text value, IntValue contains the corresponding numerical value. The Text property's value changes when a value is assigned to the IntValue property, and vice versa. So, we have already programmed part of the functionality; there are just two things missing. First, we must restrict the input accepted by the input field, because it should only be possible to enter numbers; second, we must publish all the relevant properties that have already been declared in TCustomEdit.

10.9.5 Restricting the input field

TCustomEdit has a method that you can use to restrict the input field. This is the KeyPress method. Usually, this method checks only if the user (in this case, the programmer who uses this component later on) has written an event-handling routine for the OnKeyPress event. If they have, then this event is called here.

We can easily overwrite this method in our derived component and add our own functionality to it. At the end of the procedure, we simply call the method of the original component so that we don't forget the original functionality. To do this, we use the reserved word inherited.

Now, simply declare the KeyPress method in the protected section of our new component. When you do this, don't forget the reserved word override, which tells Delphi that this is a method that has been overwritten:

```
procedure KeyPress(var Key: Char); override;
```

Use class completion to generate the framework for the method. Now add the following source code to the method to restrict the user input to numbers and the delete key:

```
procedure TIntEdit.KeyPress(var Key: Char);
begin
  //Only numerical values allowed
  if not (Key IN [#8,#13,#48..#57]) then
  begin;
    Key := #0;
    if FDoBeep then
      Beep;
  end;
  inherited KeyPress(Key);
end;
```

This method also includes the FDoBeep variable. We will use this variable to specify whether an audible alarm signal is emitted if an incorrect key is pressed.

The component's functionality is now complete. Only the properties of TCustomEdit are still missing, so we must publish them. We won't include all of them because they are not all relevant here, e.g. we don't require properties such as CharCase, OEMConvert, and PasswordChar in our component. You will find the complete list in the next section, where the entire source code of our component is shown.

10.9.6 Finished framework

Our component is now complete. Here, once again, is an overview of the entire unit. Although we haven't done that much, nevertheless we have created a useful component that can be extended as required:

```
unit IntEdit;

interface

uses
  Windows, Messages, SysUtils, Classes, Graphics,
Controls, Forms, Dialogs, StdCtrls;

type
  TIntEdit = class(TCustomEdit)
  private
        { Private declarations }
    FDoBeep    : Boolean;
    function GetIntValue: integer;
    procedure SetIntValue(const Value: integer);
  protected
    { Protected declarations }
    procedure KeyPress(var Key:Char); override;
  public
    { Public declarations }
  published
    { Published declarations }
    property DoBeep: Boolean read FDoBeep write FDoBeep;
    property IntValue : integer read GetIntValue write
    SetIntValue;
    //From TCustomEdit
    property Anchors;
    property AutoSelect;
    property AutoSize;
    property BiDiMode;
    property BorderStyle;
    property Color;
    property Constraints;
    property Ctl3D;
    property DragCursor;
    property DragKind;
```

```
        property DragMode;
        property Enabled;
        property Font;
        property HideSelection;
        property ImeMode;
        property ImeName;
        property MaxLength;
        property ParentBiDiMode;
        property ParentColor;
        property ParentCtl3D;
        property ParentFont;
        property ParentShowHint;
        property PopupMenu;
        property ReadOnly;
        property ShowHint;
        property TabOrder;
        property TabStop;
        property Text;
        property Visible;
        property OnChange;
        property OnClick;
        property OnContextPopup;
        property OnDblClick;
        property OnDragDrop;
        property OnDragOver;
        property OnEndDock;
        property OnEndDrag;
        property OnEnter;
        property OnExit;
        property OnKeyDown;
        property OnKeyPress;
        property OnKeyUp;
        property OnMouseDown;
        property OnMouseMove;
        property OnMouseUp;
        property OnStartDock;
        property OnStartDrag;
      end;

  procedure Register;

  implementation
```

```
procedure Register;
begin
  RegisterComponents('NittyGritty', [TIntEdit]);
end;


{ TIntEdit }

function TIntEdit.GetIntValue: integer;
begin
  try
    Result := StrToInt(Text);
  except
    Result := 0;
    Text := '0';
  end;
end;


procedure TIntEdit.KeyPress(var Key: Char);
begin
  //Only numerical values allowed
if not (Key IN [#8,#13,#48..#57]) then
  begin;
        Key := #0;
    if FDoBeep then
      Beep;
  end;
  inherited KeyPress(Key);
end;


procedure TIntEdit.SetIntValue(const Value: integer);
begin
  Text := IntToStr(Value);
end;

end.
```

10.9.7 Installing the component

Installing the new component is also quite easy. Simply select COMPONENT | INSTALL COMPONENT in Delphi. All the fields in the next dialog have already been filled correctly, so all you need to do is to click on OK. Figure 10.3 shows the dialog used to install the new component.

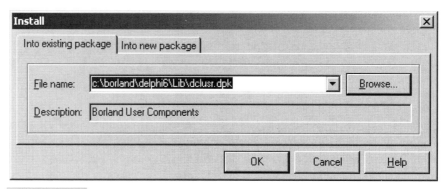

Figure 10.3 *Installing the component*

You will see the new component on the added NittyGritty Component Palette page. Now you can test the component. You will see that the `Text` property in the Object Inspector does not change immediately when you change the value in the `IntValue` property. However, at runtime you will not notice any delay because both values will be synchronized with each other.

You will see another special feature with our new `DoBeep` property. As this is a Boolean property, we can also select the value we require from a selection field, as we can with other Boolean properties. More importantly, we do not need to have programmed a property editor to do this. The reason for this is that a number of different standard property editors are already present and these are used automatically.

This chapter cannot describe all aspects of component development, but it is a start. Component development is a very interesting subject, even if the actual programming is not quite as user-friendly as visual programming.

Error-handling and debugging

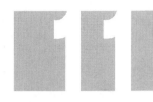

You are probably familiar with some of the exception errors in Windows, such as when the operating system displays a message to say that an error has occurred and therefore the program had to be terminated. In other cases, Windows crashes completely and presents you with a blue screen, saying that the system is either unstable or busy. In both cases, the only solution is to restart the system. It is usually no good to simply wait for the system to become available again.

Delphi provides a number of exceptions that help you to intercept these program errors in your own programs without losing your data or crashing the operating system.

11.1.1 What is an exception?

The Exception class (not TException) encapsulates the runtime errors that can occur in a program running under Windows. If this kind of error occurs, Delphi generates an instance of the relevant error class and then displays it. You can also use Delphi's class concept to create and display your own exceptions. The advantage of this is that the standard error-handling routine automatically displays the exception along with a descriptive text, so you do not need to concern yourself with it. All you need to do is to generate the exception when you intercept an error, and leave the rest to Delphi.

It has become traditional to start derived exceptions with "E", in the same way that derived classes always start with "T".

At runtime, you can use exception blocks to intercept any exceptions, and write routines that are executed if an exception occurs. You can also overwrite the standard handling routine for exceptions and provide your own routine, which may have a different display format from that predefined in Delphi. This chapter describes the various exception-handling options.

11.1.2 Protecting source code

In every program, situations occur that might trigger a runtime error (an exception). Examples are if the system attempts to open a file that is not present, or if the system attempts division by zero. In Delphi, you can protect parts of the source code in those places in a program where an exception may occur. The statements you use to do this are `try...except` and `try...finally`.

Try...except

In the `try...except` block, you encapsulate the critical statements that may trigger an error. In this case, the program code after the keyword `try` is executed . If an error occurs, the program continues after `except`, and then the routine in which the error occurred is closed. The source code may look like this:

```
try
   Memo1.Lines.LoadFromFile(AFilename);
except
   on EFOpenError do
      HandleFileOpenError;
end;
```

The statements after `try` (in this case, there is only one single statement) are executed. If the execution runs correctly, nothing happens. However, if an error occurs, e.g. if the file from which the text is to be loaded does not exist, then the program jumps to the exception routine and executes it. In our example, the routine checks whether this is a `EFileOpenError`-type exception. If it is, then the `HandleFileOpenError` routine is called.

The important thing here is that the rest of the program code in the routine in which the error occurred is not processed any further. Instead, the routine is closed.

You can also check several exceptions in one exception block. To do this, simply program more `on <exception> do` statements and call the corresponding routines to handle the exceptions.

You can, of course, do the opposite and not program any statements in the exception block. In this case, although the exception occurs, the procedure in which it occurs is simply quitted. No message appears and the user remains unaware that anything has happened. However, this procedure is not recommended.

If the routine contains statements that must be executed, regardless of whether an exception occurs, you must program a `try...finally` block instead of `try...except`.

Try...finally

This exception block allows you to execute program text that must be executed no matter what else happens. The statements after `try` are executed. If this execution is successful, then the statements after `finally` and the remaining statements are also executed. If an exception occurs, then the statements after `finally` are also handled. However, the exception block is closed after this and the exception is triggered again.

If you execute one of the standard `Exit` or `Break` procedures within the `try` section to quit the program block, the statements after `finally` will also run before you can quit the procedure. This code extract shows how `try...finally` is used:

```
try
    Memo1.Lines.LoadFromFile(AFilename);
finally
    //This block is always executed
end;
```

Retriggering exceptions

Once an exception has been intercepted by an exception block, it can no longer be used by the program. In some situations, however, it might be useful for the exception to still be present. There are even scenarios in which a totally different exception would be a good idea, or where you need to trigger your own exception. Delphi has a solution for this. You can use the reserved word `raise` to retrigger an exception or to call an entirely different exception. Within the exception block, you simply call `raise` to retrigger the exception that has just been dealt with:

```
try
    Memo1.Lines.LoadFromFile(AFilename);
except
    on EFOpenError do
        HandleFileOpenError;
    raise;    //Raise exception again
end;
```

Alternatively, you can trigger a completely different exception, or even none at all:

```
try
    Memo1.Lines.LoadFromFile(AFilename);
except
    on EFOpenError do
        HandleFileOpenError;
    raise EFCreateError.Create;
end;
```

In this example, after `EFOpenError` had been processed, `EFCreateError` was triggered in place of `EFOpenError`. `EFCreateError` represents an exception that occurs when a file is created. However, this is only an example. It doesn't make any sense to display the error message "Error when creating file xyz" when the user simply wants to open a file.

Nesting exception blocks

You can also nest several exception blocks within each other. However, take care that you do not get carried away with this, otherwise no one will know where anything is. Generally speaking, you should not use more than three or four nesting levels. This kind of construction looks something like this:

```
try
    Memo1.Lines.LoadFromFile(AFilename);
    try
        y := StrToInt(Memo1.Lines[2]);
    except
        //Inner exception block
    end;
except
    //Outer exception block
end;
```

This loads the file's contents into `Memo1`. If an error occurs here, then the outer exception block becomes active. If no error occurs, the conversion process continues after the second `try` statement. However, if an exception occurs now, it is handled in the inner exception block.

You can use both `try...except` and `try...finally` together and also nest them in each other.

11.1.3 Exception-handling

General and standard exceptions

As explained already, in exception-handling procedures you can deal with several exceptions in one exception block. However, if you want to concentrate on a particular exception, then you must know its class name. In Delphi, the class names for exceptions always start with "E":

```
try
    Memo1.Lines.LoadFromFile(AFilename);
except
    on EFOpenError do
        //Error-handling for EFOpenError
    else
        //Error-handling for other exceptions
end;
```

You use this kind of construction to differentiate between the special exceptions that are important in this program block and general exceptions that may otherwise occur. In this scenario, you can also use more than one `on <exception> do` construction:

```
try
......
except
    on EInvalidOp do HandleInvalidOp;
    on EOverFlow do HandleEOverFlow;
    on EUnderFlow do HandleEUnderFlow
    else
        HandleOtherErrors;
end;
```

Application.HandleException

`HandleException` is the method that is called when an exception occurs without being intercepted. This is, therefore, a default handling routine for exceptions.

The `TApplication` class has an `OnException` event that you can use for general error-handling, even if you have intercepted the exception. This is very easy in Delphi 6. You simply use the `TApplicationEvents` component on the Component Palette Standard page. This provides all the important events in `TApplication`, including the `OnException` event. You can now write a handling routine write for this event and call it within an exception block as shown below:

```
try
    Memo1.Lines.LoadFromFile(AFilename);
except
    on EFOpenError do
        Application.HandleException(self);
end;
```

`HandleException` automatically calls the `OnException` event-handling routine if it is present. This gives you the option of writing your own global routine with which you can handle any exceptions that occur. If an exception occurs, then it is passed on to the event-handling routine. You can, therefore, write your own handler in the event-handling routine to deal with any exceptions that may occur.

Generating your own exceptions

In Delphi, exceptions are nothing more than `Exception`-type (not `TException`) classes, and therefore they are basically just objects. There is no reason why you shouldn't create your own exceptions; in some cases it is actually quite a good idea. The only thing you must do is to derive your own exceptions from the base class used for all exceptions

As I have already mentioned, the tradition here is that all exception names start with "E":

```
type
    EMyException = class(Exception);
```

There are two ways in which you can trigger your newly created exception. The first is to generate the exception with Create. The second is to use the CreateFmt constructor to output a formatted message string.

Obviously, you do not need an exception block to trigger your own exception; after all, you want to trigger the exception, not prevent it from happening. You therefore define an exception as shown above and trigger it, for example, if you enter an incorrect password:

```
if YourPassword<>RightPassword then
    raise EMyException.Create('Wrong password');
```

11.1.4 Silent exceptions

Silent exceptions are errors that do not trigger a screen message even though they interrupt the current procedure. The standard exception for this kind of construction is EAbort. The default setting for EAbort exceptions is that the dialog fields are not displayed unless you have written a console application in which even EAbort exceptions are accompanied by an error message.

In this situation, you do not need to wait until an EAbort exception occurs. The default setting for the Abort procedure is that it generates an EAbort exception so that you can also trigger this yourself.

11.2 Debugging

Delphi's integrated debugger makes it easy for you to fix bugs in your programs. The integrated debugger starts up as soon as you start your program in the IDE. You use this tool to carry out detailed evaluations, check variables, compare and evaluate the contents of variables, set breakpoints, and control the program flow; among other things. This section will describe the most important functionality.

You will need to use the debug functionality a lot (for bugfixing in a program that is running). No program ever runs without errors from the very start, and I am convinced that there is no such thing as a program that is entirely error-free. Moreover, these errors are usually not obvious and you must do more than simply scrutinize the program code. In most cases, it is inevitable that you will have to work with Delphi's debugger tools.

11.2.1 Breakpoints)

Setting breakpoints

You use breakpoints to interrupt a program run at a specific point, e.g. so that you can then proceed step by step or evaluate variable contents. To set a breakpoint, click on the left-hand side of the source code window next to the statement you want to stop at. A red dot appears, which indicates a breakpoint. The program stops as soon as it reaches this point.

Before you can set a breakpoint, the debug information must also be compiled when you compile the program code. This is what usually happens, and you can make the corresponding settings in the Project Options. Figure 11.1 shows the source code editor with a valid breakpoint.

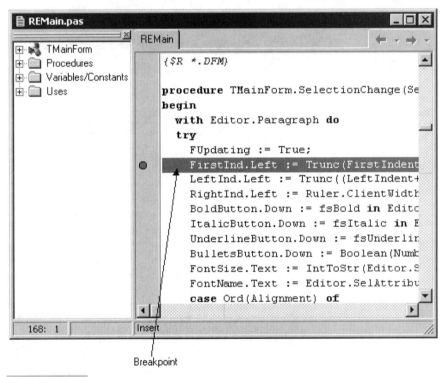

Breakpoint

Figure 11.1 *A valid breakpoint in the source code*

Invalid breakpoints

There are also invalid breakpoints that are identified by a cross in the red dot on the left margin, and a green background behind the line next to it. There are a variety of reasons for breakpoints being invalid:

→ The breakpoint stands next to a reserved word, such as Begin or Type. These words merely show where a section starts and are not statements that can be executed. You can only set breakpoints on executable statements.

➜ The breakpoint stands on a statement but is still not valid. This happens if the compiler simply removed this statement during compilation to optimize the code. You can switch off this optimization, which then makes the breakpoint valid, but you should switch it on again after you locate the error.

➜ No breakpoints are valid, no matter where you set them. In this case you must set the Project Options to instruct the compiler to insert the debug information into the project. Then restart the compiling procedure so Delphi recognizes that all the information required for debugging is now present. To do this, select the Project | Compile Project menu item, which is the only way to compile all the files in the project. It is not enough to simply restart the program.

Figure 11.2 shows an example of an invalid breakpoint.

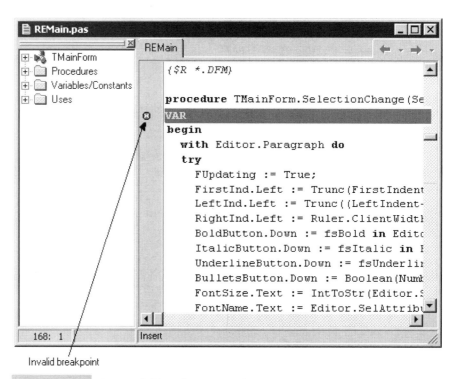

Invalid breakpoint

Figure 11.2 *An invalid breakpoint in the source code*

Executing programs step by step

You can instruct Delphi to execute a program step by step or block by block. The buttons you require are shown in the toolbar. Alternatively, you can select the appropriate menu items from the START menu. These functions also have keyboard shortcuts, but I will not list them here because they may vary according to the environment options used in keyboard mapping.

The step-by-step execution (menu item RUN I STEP OVER) executes the marked statement and stops the program again. If this statement is a function or procedure call, then Delphi jumps to the first statement in the called function or procedure. This only happens, of course, if the unit concerned is actually available.

If you select block-by-block program execution (menu item RUN I TRACE INTO), then the entire procedure or function that is called is executed as shown above. The program is stopped again at the next statement.

You use this functionality to execute the program bit by bit and check the data after every step. This procedure is often successful, especially where logical or programming errors are concerned.

The toolbar usually includes a button for each of these options. The default settings for hotkeys are (F8) to execute the entire routine, and (F7) to execute program code step by step.

11.2.2 Evaluating variables

You can evaluate variables at any time when the program is running because it expects to react to users' actions. Simply toggle to Delphi and select the DEBUG I EVALUATE/MODIFY menu item in the source code editor's context menu. A dialog appears in which you see the variable's current value if it is valid at this specific point in the program. Figure 11.3 shows the variable evaluation window.

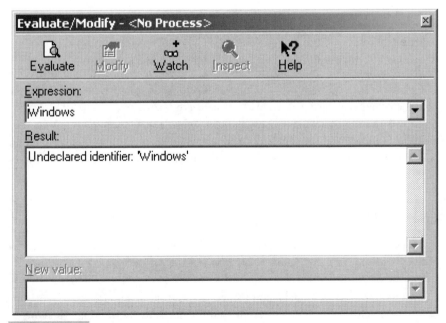

Figure 11.3   *The variable evaluation window*

If the variable is valid (the one in the figure is not!), then you can also assign a new value to it, e.g. to make loop operations shorter. Variable evaluation is one of the most commonly used tools in bugfixing because careless mistakes happen so often.

Click on the WATCH button to add the selected variable to a list of monitored expressions, so that the updated value is always available. This makes it easier for you to check more than one variable at once.

11.2.3 Watched expressions

You can also add various different variables whose values you want to watch (monitor) to the list of monitored expressions. This list remains in the foreground and always shows the current values of the different variables. Figure 11.4 shows the list of monitored expressions.

Figure 11.4 *List of monitored expressions*

This window is always visible and gives you a clear overview of the variable values you want to check. However, you cannot change this list in any way. To do this, you need the window in which you evaluate or change the values.

To call the list of monitored expressions, select the DEBUG | ADD WATCH AT CURSOR menu item in the source code editor's context menu. If the cursor does not point to an expression that can be monitored, you will be prompted to enter an expression (usually a variable name).

11.2.4 CPU window

The CPU window is designed for advanced programmers who want to get an overview of the procedures in the CPU or in memory and the registers. Figure 11.5 shows the CPU window.

This window is only available at runtime. This is logical because there is no point in observing CPU procedures if the program is not actually running. To show the CPU window, select the DEBUG | VIEW CPU menu item in the source code editor's context menu.

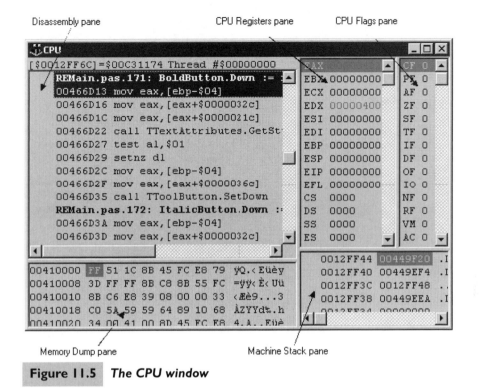

Disassembly pane   CPU Registers pane   CPU Flags pane

Memory Dump pane   Machine Stack pane

Figure 11.5   *The CPU window*

The CPU window gives you exact information about the memory, the currently running statement, the CPU registers, flags, and the stack. This information is less interesting for beginners, but more advanced programmers will find it useful, especially if they are familiar with Assembler programming.

GO AHEAD!

Appendix: ASCII table

0		31		62	>	93	]
1		32	Space	63	?	94	^
2		33	!	64	@	95	_
3		34	,,	65	A	96	`
4		35	#	66	B	97	a
5		36	$	67	C	98	b
6		37	%	68	D	99	c
7		38	&	69	E	100	d
8	Backspace	39	'	70	F	101	e
9	Tab	40	(	71	G	102	f
10	LF	41	)	72	H	103	g
11		42	*	73	I	104	h
12		43	+	74	J	105	i
13	Return	44	,	75	K	106	j
14		45	-	76	L	107	k
15		46	.	77	M	108	l
16		47	/	78	N	109	m
17		48	0	79	O	110	n
18		49	1	80	P	111	o
19		50	2	81	Q	112	p
20		51	3	82	R	113	q
21		52	4	83	S	114	r
22		53	5	84	T	115	s
23		54	6	85	U	116	t
24		55	7	86	V	117	u
25		56	8	87	W	118	v
26		57	9	88	X	119	w
27		58	:	89	Y	120	x
28		59	;	90	Z	121	y
29		60	<	91	[	122	z
30		61	=	92	\	123	{

124			157		190	3/4	223	ß
125	}	158		191	¿	224	à
126	~	159		192	À	225	á
127		160	Space	193	Á	226	â
128		161	¡	194	Â	227	ã
129		162	¢	195	Ã	228	ä
130		163	£	196	Ä	229	å
131		164		197	Å	230	æ
132		165	¥	198	Æ	231	ç
133		166	¦	199	Ç	232	è
134		167	§	200	È	233	é
135		168	¨	201	É	234	ê
136		169	©	202	Ê	235	ë
137		170	ª	203	Ë	236	ì
138		171	«	204	Ì	237	í
139		172	¬	205	Í	238	î
140		173		206	Î	239	ï
141		174	®	207	Ï	240	
142		175	¯	208		241	Ñ
143		176	°	209	Ñ	242	ò
144		177	±	210	Ò	243	ó
145		178	²	211	Ó	244	ô
146		179	³	212	Ô	245	õ
147		180	´	213	Õ	246	ö
148		181	µ	214	Ö	247	÷
149		182	¶	215		248	ø
150		183	·	216	Ø	249	ù
151		184	¸	217	ß	250	ú
152		185	¹	218	Ú	251	û
153		186	º	219	Û	252	ü
154		187	»	220	Ü	253	
155		188	1/4	221		254	
156		189	1/2	222		255	ÿ

Appendix: Virtual key codes

Constant	Hex	Dec	Key
VK_Cancel	03	3	Ctrl + Pause
VK_Back	08	8	⇦
VK_Tab	09	9	⇆
VK_Return	0D	13	↵
VK_Shift	10	16	⇧
VK_Control	11	17	Ctrl
VK_Menu	12	18	Alt
VK_Pause	13	19	Pause
VK_Capital	14	20	Caps lock
VK_Escape	1B	27	Esc
VK_Space	20	32	
VK_Prior	21	33	Pg↑
VK_Next	22	34	Pg↓
VK_End	23	35	End
VK_Home	24	36	Home
VK_Left	25	37	←
VK_Up	26	38	↑
VK_Right	27	39	→
VK_Down	28	40	↓
VK_SnapShot	2C	44	Print
VK_Insert	2D	45	Ins
VK_Delete	2E	46	Del
VK_0	30	48	0
VK_1	31	49	1
VK_2	32	50	2
VK_3	33	51	3
VK_4	34	52	4
VK_5	35	53	5

VK_6	36	54	6
VK_7	37	55	7
VK_8	38	56	8
VK_9	39	57	9
VK_A	41	65	A
VK_B	42	66	B
VK_C	43	67	C
VK_D	44	68	D
VK_E	45	69	E
VK_F	46	70	F
VK_G	47	71	G
VK_H	48	72	H
VK_I	49	73	I
VK_J	4A	74	J
VK_K	4B	75	K
VK_L	4C	76	L
VK_M	4D	77	M
VK_N	4E	78	N
VK_O	4F	79	O
VK_P	50	80	P
VK_Q	51	81	Q
VK_R	52	82	R
VK_S	53	83	S
VK_T	54	84	T
VK_U	55	85	U
VK_V	56	86	V
VK_W	57	87	W
VK_X	58	88	X
VK_Y	59	89	Y
VK_Z	5A	90	Z
VK_Numpad0	60	96	0 (number pad)
VK_Numpad1	61	97	1 (number pad)
VK_Numpad2	62	98	2 (number pad)
VK_Numpad3	63	99	3 (number pad)
VK_Numpad4	64	100	4 (number pad)
VK_Numpad5	65	101	5 (number pad)
VK_Numpad6	66	102	6 (number pad)
VK_Numpad7	67	103	7 (number pad)
VK_Numpad8	68	104	8 (number pad)
VK_Numpad9	69	105	9 (number pad)
VK_Multiply	6A	106	* (number pad)
VK_Add	6B	107	+ (number pad)

VK_Subtract	6D	109	☐ (number pad)
VK_Divide	6F	111	☐ (number pad)
VK_F1	70	112	Key F1
VK_F2	71	113	Key F2
VK_F3	72	114	Key F3
VK_F4	73	115	Key F4
VK_F5	74	116	Key F5
VK_F6	75	117	Key F6
VK_F7	76	118	Key F7
VK_F8	77	119	Key F8
VK_F9	78	120	Key F9
VK_F10	79	121	Key F10
VK_F11	7A	122	Key F11
VK_F12	7B	123	Key F12
VK_Numlock	90	144	Num
VK_Scroll	91	145	Scroll

Index